Bringing the Left Back Home

Bringing the Left Back Home

A CRITIQUE OF AMERICAN SOCIAL CRITICISM

Gary Thom

NEW HAVEN AND LONDON, YALE UNIVERSITY PRESS, 1979

Published with assistance from the foundation
established in memory of James Wesley Cooper
of the Class of 1865, Yale College.

Designed by Sally Harris
and set in IBM Press Roman type.
Printed in the United States of America by
The Murray Printing Co., Westford, Mass.

Published in Great Britain, Europe, Africa, and
Asia (except Japan) by Yale University Press,
Ltd., London. Distributed in Australia and
New Zealand by Book & Film Services, Artarmon,
N.S.W., Australia; and in Japan by Harper & Row,
Publishers, Tokyo Office.

Library of Congress Cataloging in Publication Data:

Thom, Gary, 1941–
  Bringing the Left back home.

  Includes bibliographical references and index.
  1. Political science–United States. 2. Sociology
–United States. 3. Democracy. I. Title.
JA84.U5T47   301.5'92'0973   79–14712
ISBN 0-300-02332-4

To my parents
—who probably had something like this
in mind

Contents

Acknowledgments

I wish to thank Robert Lane for his unwavering support, dating from that tender time during which it would have been easy and natural to confuse my project with one of his, and to steer me accordingly. This he refused to do, and not merely because he suspected that the attempt would prove futile. I do hold him responsible for much of whatever coherence, depth of insight, and breadth of sympathy are achieved here—and also for some of the book's more eccentric qualities, which he encouraged more than he knows.

Several friends and colleagues read all or portions of the manuscript, responding in most kind and constructive ways. These include: Robert Dahl, Douglas Rae, Isaac Kramnick, Charles Lindblom, Chris Webster, Bill Johnston, Gabriel Motzkin, Graham Little, and Willie Schonfeld. I especially benefited from Robert Dahl's sterling personal as well as professional example, and from his gentle but pointed suggestion that if the idea of a liberal democratic community was worthwhile, then it deserved better treatment than it had yet received at my hands. Graham Little deserves special thanks for his trenchant psychoanalytic insights and his help in arranging a summer's teaching stint in Melbourne, Australia—from which distant vantage point the contours and contradictions of American culture were far easier to make out. Charles Miller kept me on my toes and supplied with blintzes. And Bernt Hagtvet provided reminders that when depression does strike, Marx as well as Nietzsche is good for the soul.

Special thanks are also due Marian Neal Ash and Laurie Borchert at Yale University Press. Laurie Borchert did an extraordinarily conscientious and competent job of taming and then fine-tuning a prose style which frequently threatened to get out of hand. The vast majority of her thousands of astute suggestions I sheepishly incorporated in the text, and when there were disputes my wife usually joined her in outvoting me, almost always for my own good.

The lapses that remain are exclusively my own, stemming from innate stubbornness and a penchant for the colloquial. And I am keenly grateful for the encouragement and enthusiasm of Marian Ash, without whose support the project might well have been abandoned, or broken like Humpty Dumpty into irretrievable pieces. There are three others without whose timely and vital contributions I could not have seen the project through in any fashion whatsoever. The first is Will Jones, my philosopher friend, who took both manuscript and author in hand when both were in an advanced state of shambles. Not only did he offer hundreds of cogent suggestions, most of which I gladly followed, he also provided the necessary guidance and impetus for a thoroughgoing and much need reorganization. If there were absolutely no other evidence, his example would nevertheless suffice to show that neither utilitarian nor neo-utilitarian premises can adequately explain why the world continues to go round.

But my wife Martha provides further evidence. She believed in the book long before I did, and by the time she had read and criticized several drafts she often knew better than I what I was trying to accomplish, and how and where my prose was interfering. It is distressingly routine for authors to credit their wives with absolutely crucial contributions as well as the standard wifely virtues. Suffice to say there is nothing conventional nor commonplace about her contribution, intellectual or conjugal, nor the virtues it reflects.

Finally, also a bit unconventionally, I wish to thank our dog Moby, the great white dog, who stuck with his dogly pursuits and demands in the midst of this crisis and that, and thereby helped restore a saving sense of proportion to it all.

Introduction

In this book I attempt to rethink certain crucial aspects of the leftist and left-liberal critique of American society. In particular, I seek a better account of a somewhat neglected aspect of human nature—human ambivalence, or "humanly general ambivalence"— and its relationship to the alienation which Marxists, American intellectuals influenced by Marxism, and most moderns find so serious, so pervasive, and ultimately so difficult to explain. Then I suggest what this implies 'or democratic theory. I proceed in this fashion not because I consider analysis of the institutional sources of our alleged alienation noncontroversial or unimportant, but because that story is better told elsewhere, and is not the whole story. And because liberals and leftists alike have too often implied that it is, that society, described in various familiar pejorative ways, is more or less the sole source of what ails us. "Thus," Nietzsche suggested in reference to the like practice in his own day, "standing truth happily on her head."

My argument emerges from an extended period of dwelling in the perspectives of numerous recent American theorists and critics, leftists and left-liberals whose intellectual plights and projects, despite many obvious differences, came eventually to seem fundamentally akin. All are self-consciously engaged in picking up the pieces of the Marxist image of man and in refurbishing the argument for collective concerns. All seem to assume that this is neither the time nor place to adopt a strictly Marxist vocabulary and viewpoint, and that leftist and left-liberal views must be argued and justified to an audience for whom the arguments, the vocabulary, and many of the root assumptions of Marxism are neither familiar nor congenial. Seen in one light, such attempts strike us as examples of fabled American naiveté and provincialism, especially when we highlight their sometimes promiscuous eclecticism or the frequent faddish shifts in perspective and prescription. Viewed more sympathetically and sociologically, however, they can be seen as

modern, honest, and in some ways sophisticated responses to a pluralistic society and to a chaotic and fragmented intellectual universe.
That fragmentation is reflected in the variety of their approaches,
which tend to array themselves, not surprisingly, along disciplinary
lines.

Indeed, the three groups of left-liberal theorists I initially considered can be loosely but significantly associated with the disciplines of political science, psychology, and sociology. The first of
these, the "democratic critics of democratic pluralism," are the
non-Marxist successors to C. Wright Mills. They rely heavily on
the vocabulary of political science and democratic theory to carry
the burden of their critique, and they argue in various complementary ways that our society should be further democratized. The
second group consists of those theorists who, whatever their home
discipline, are turning to various psychologies in their attempt to
give social and democratic theory fresh human underpinnings. The
third group consists of those whose vocabulary and perspective,
irrespective of their discipline, is sociological in important respects.
Mulling over and sorting through their various arguments, I became
convinced that their projects are fundamentally similar; that each
perspective and discipline has something distinct and important to
say to each of the others; but that all of them cannot be all right all
of the time.

It may be that in fashioning an argument which attempts to take
seriously all of these apparently disparate critics and concerns I
inevitably juxtapose and combine points of view better left at
loggerheads, or segregated. But if fragmentation itself is a good part
of the problem, then a certain disciplined promiscuity may be a
good part of the solution. No doubt to puritanical Marxists, or even
to some latter-day hard-shell "methodists" hell-bent on sharpening
their specialized tools, such an approach will probably seem hopelessly eclectic, even heretical. To them I can only suggest, with
Russell Lowell, that we should not treat ideas, even great ideas of
great thinkers like Marx, the way ignorant people reportedly treat
cherries, thinking them unwholesome unless swallowed whole.

Because the eventual destination of my argument, shared with
many of the critics I encounter along the way, is the reorientation
of democratic theory, I begin with democratic pluralism, the still

dominant theoretical persuasion in American political science. After briefly discussing the competing concerns and ideals that pluralism addresses, I consider several straightforward democratic critiques of pluralism, and the light such criticisms shed on the gap between what is expected of pluralism and what is delivered by it. While I find these criticisms compelling, I find their account and appreciation of that gap wanting. I argue this in connection with recent developments in the axiomatic or economic approach to democratic theory, an approach which takes a tough-minded instrumentalist view of democratic institutions. Its basic assumptions are shared by most pluralists and their democratic critics alike, but this literature is much more persistent and systematic in pursuing the question of just how much conflicting individuals and groups can expect of democratic procedures and institutions. The net result is to add significantly to our confusion concerning what democracy is and what can be expected of it.

Accordingly, in Part Two I turn from straightforward democratic theorists to more radical critics, radical in the sense that they concern themselves with the wants impinging on the political system and seek to explain the difference between what we want and what we really need. Generally influenced by the Marxist literature on alienation, specifically influenced by the various psychologies to which they turn, these theorists do social criticism by explicit reliance on their conception of what it means to be more fully human. After considering a small but representative sample of this "left literature of freedom," I suggest that their conception of what is involved in being human suffers from a neglect of human ambivalence—that tendency for our most important emotions and thoughts to come in apparently opposite pairs—and their critical project suffers as well. In particular, I suggest that this underlies their overemphasis on alienation, to the virtual exclusion of concern with anomie; and that alienation is often a protection against anomie. I further argue that the notion of humanly general ambivalence can be derived or made plausible from an analysis of our most "primitive" thought-act, the making of distinctions, which may well be our distinguishing human characteristic.

I do not offer the notion of humanly general ambivalence as an exhaustive account of the nature of human nature, but merely as a neglected aspect, one whose implications for social criticism and democratic theory have not been adequately explored. Neither do I offer it as the sole basis of a social ethic or critique. Indeed, my other principal criticism of the "left literature of freedom" is that the contribution of their views of human nature to their critical task seems to be overestimated, or in any event poorly articulated. In particular, it is not always clear whether society is being criticized because it is "sick" or violating basic human needs, or merely because it is unreasonable or unworkable in some sense, irrespective of whether the goals it encourages are humanly satisfying or frustrating. With this shortcoming in mind—and because of a strong hunch that human ambivalence and the social accommodation and "self-overcoming" of personal polarities lie near the heart of their concern with psychological development and basic needs, properly interpreted and reconstructed—I consider the possible connections with another view of psychological development. This view derives from cognitive developmental psychology, specifically Kohlberg's work on the stages of moral reasoning, which suggests that moral reasoning akin to the Kantian imperative may well be part of most people's psychological-developmental capacities. On the basis of such speculations I suggest that social criticism should simultaneously concern itself with what is satisfying, in the sense suggested by the notion of human ambivalence, and with what is socially shareable or mutually satisfiable.

The purpose of Part Three is to sketch the outlines of such a critique, one based on individual ambivalence and related cultural contradictions, the relationship of anomie and alienation, and the interaction between what is individually satisfying and what is mutually shareable or satisfiable. On the negative side, this involves the reinterpretation of anomie, or rulelessness, as a disjunction, not only between what the culture encourages us to want and what social institutions allow us to achieve (as in Merton's interpretation), but also between what we want and what else we want, between dominant "success" goals and "communal" needs. I suggest that the frustration of such needs underlies our malaise and animates much of our protest, and not merely that of critics on the left. This conception of anomie is then applied to the questions of distributive justice and the control of spillovers of economic activity, questions not usually treated in this context. On the positive side, the argument implies the need for a relatively explicit communal ethic informed by each of these distinct concerns.

I then return, in Part Four, to the "quiet crisis of democratic theory" with which I began. I first look at the implicit justification of democracy found in the axiomatic or economic approach to democratic theory, an approach which, again, is so helpful in revealing the gap between expectations of democracy and its ability to meet those expectations. Secondly, I look briefly at more explicit and philosophical attempts, essentially utilitarian or neoutilitarian, to justify and defend democracy. In both cases, given their apparent failure to reconcile the conflicting demands impinging on democratic institutions, it would appear that they have exposed the inadequacy or impossibility of democracy. I contend, however, that they have really exposed their own faulty conception of democracy—and with it their escapist attempts to effect such a reconciliation in the abstract, without critical consideration of the nature of the wants impinging on the political system, of the cultural context, of the anomie and alienation which hound that culture. This is not intended as a denigration of their analyses, especially when these are focused on and limited to strategic behavior and institutional reform within given institutional arenas. Nor do I mean to suggest that democratic theorists should be nothing more than cultural critics. Nor, finally, is it to suggest that a concern with the role of democratic institutions in furthering or thwarting private ends is altogether ignoble and wrongheaded. Rather, I mean to suggest that once explanations and defenses of liberal democratic systems as a whole are sought, we must explicitly concern ourselves to a much greater degree than we have yet realized with the liberal democratic *community*. In this direction lies their elusive reconciliation, or at least a better accommodation, of competing demands and ideals.

That direction, as well as the mood, the basic assumptions, the leading concepts, and many particulars of my argument, is "sociological," in the sense of that sociological tradition of which Robert Nisbet has written—in its concern with the social bases of personality, with socially generated wants and ideals, with anomie, with community. But if sociologists of that tradition have served, as Philip Reiff has asserted, as a group of would-be priests and professional mourners at the wake of a shared Christian community, then I must protest that my stance is neither so professional nor my attitude so mournful. Nor are my politics so conservative, at least not in the ordinary, perverted sense of the term.

Indeed, I will argue that the knee-jerk equation of communal concerns with conservative or even reactionary concerns is itself anomic, and a major symptom of what ails us. Moreover, the failure to see the intimate connection between alienation, which we rightly deplore, and that species of subjection which is chaos and confusion, which we typically ignore or misinterpret, is itself a reflection of our anomie, an important piece of the evidence that we suffer from it.

While that anomie is pervasive and its manifestations are many, my particular concern here is with the confusion, the disarray, the nagging sense of loss on the left and the liberal left, and with what remains viable in that tradition despite the hammer-blows it has received. In our casting about for new ways of making the old arguments, in our willingness to jettison burdensome baggage, there is much hope. But if in multiplying fresh perspectives and in pushing out the frontiers we neglect those communal concerns and needs which underlie the quest, if we thereby misinterpret our difficulties only to push the frontiers farther and farther from home, both intellectually and emotionally, then I fear our escapist theoretical wanderings, however ingenious and brilliant, will continue to resemble symptons more than solutions.

PART 1
Social Criticism, Political Science, and Democracy

Whenever any term becomes universally honorific, no doubt it is time for sensitive and sophisticated souls to stop using it or to make finer distinctions. Perhaps we have reached this point with democracy. John Schaar has suggested that "democracy is the most prostituted word of our age, and any man who employs it in reference to any modern state should be suspect either of ignorance or bad motives."[1] Actually our situation may be worse still. For it is not solely nor even primarily a matter of the practice of modern states falling short of some intelligible democratic ideal. Nietzsche was convinced that the general welfare is "no ideal, no goal, no remotely intelligible concept," but only an "emetic." And the ever-probing lynx-eyes of modern scholars seem to reveal that the advocacy of democracy amounts to meaningless exhortation or serves as a front for special interests—and at very best is remotely intelligible.

Yet the use of the term has not really died out, not even among the sensitive and the sophisticated, much less the suspect. More realistic and operational substitutes are suggested from time to time—Dahl's "polyarchy," for example—but never seem to catch on. To render the new terms interesting and meaningful they must be discussed in the very terms they were supposed to improve upon and replace. No doubt this says a great deal about the nature of democratic theorizing and the limitations on possibilities of radical new departures. So if indeed the concept of democracy has been prostituted, its continued use must say something about the attractions of the pristine idea that so many continue to compliment in this way.

By democratic critics I mean those who use the concept of democracy in one form or another to carry the burden of their criticisms.[2] They do not pillory this society because it is "inactive" or "inauthentic" or "sick," scornful of "man's potentiality for development," "lonely," or "constrictive of the political present"—

9

but because it is not democratic enough. The differences in emphasis and vocabulary from other forms of social criticism may be quite pronounced or partially obscured by the mixing of different approaches and vocabularies, but they are real and significant.[3]

The democratic critique of American society is virtually synonymous with the critique of the theory and practice of democratic pluralism, that model and image of society and polity so applauded as our genius or reviled as our nemesis. The critique begins by berating democratic pluralism for not living up to its own ideals. These critics appear to accept interests and wants as defined and expressed by the American people, arguing that in too many cases when the wants of some conflict with the wants of others the relevant majority is frustrated and defeated. There are few overt attempts to distinguish what we want from what we need, or should want, neither by reference to some external normative standard nor to laws of psychological development. This modest refusal contrasts significantly with the attitude of those critics who are willing to tell us, for example, that we are not really free, but manipulated so as to think so; or that only sick persons could make the political demands the American people do.

Yet having made this distinction among critics, I must hasten to add that the question of whether it is more apparent than real is high on my agenda here. Indeed, I will argue that the basic impetus behind much of this criticism, even that expressed in the most narrow, straightforward democratic terms, is toward a conception of an overarching political community which values certain results as well as democratic participation, procedures, and institutions. It is a community not obviously nor necessarily consistent with the pluralist conception, which is at best a community of communities. However, explicit concern with desired communal ends is rare among these critics. The same is true for their consideration of the possibility that their underlying concerns run counter to the consensus or a majority of the American people. There is little doubt that the two omissions are related. But rather than broaching such issues directly, their tendency is to exploit, or perhaps to create, ambiguities in the concept of democracy.

Foremost among these concerns is inequality. In many contexts the critics' interests in democracy and equality—both economic and political, both of results and opportunities—are closely linked and practically indistinguishable. If this is confusion, perhaps it is natural enough, and I shall take great pains to point out that democracy resonates with equality in the minds and hearts of many pluralists as well as their critics. Thus the critics contribute in an important way by indirectly encouraging us to question the extent to which we equate or confuse more democratization with greater equality.

But this does not exhaust their concerns, nor the question of what democracy delivers, nor our possible confusion on such matters. Stretching matters somewhat, I suggest that in the final analysis this literature appeals to a conception of democracy as a political community which seeks to incorporate not only liberal principles and egalitarian goals, but also "conservative" sociological concerns. With this in mind, I will begin with a loose sketch of pluralist democratic theory as if pluralism did purport to concern itself with liberty, equality, and fraternity alike. Granted, it is not altogether conventional nor entirely accurate to think of pluralist democracy in this way; but perhaps this is a necessary first step in reaching a better understanding of what these and other criticisms of American society are all about.

1 The Democratic Critique of Democratic Pluralism

Pluralism as a Reconciliation of Liberal Principles, Egalitarian Goals, and Conservative Sociology

To imagine any political system addressing itself to liberty, equality, and fraternity may seem vaguely ridiculous and clearly utopian, the kind of quest Keynes once referred to as a circle-squaring expedition. Rarely have all three themes been simultaneously pursued with equal vigor, even in political theory, much less political practice. Yet at various times in various contexts democratic pluralism has been conceived of, defended, and criticized on all three grounds.

Let us begin with a lesser-known variety of pluralism or pluralist theory which can be labeled sociologically-minded pluralism, that takes seriously the threat of anomie—the sociological state of rulelessness—and the related theory of mass society (the crude expression of which is that industrialization leads to mass society which leads to totalitarianism).[1] As Rogin observes, this variety of pluralism is heavily influenced by studies of the authoritarian personality, by scores of small-group and brainwashing studies and experiments which indicate how very tenuous our precious individuality is when stripped of its social supports, and by the alleged importance of "deep" psychological variables. Such factors are seen at work in various mass phenomena, movements which speak to the desperation, rootlessness, and irrational longings of isolated and unattached individuals.

For these reasons sociological pluralists applaud the existence and the sheer quantity of groups both within and outside the political process. As Rogin points out, groups are never clearly distinguished from mass or anomic phenomena. The principal distinctions they have in mind are that groups are more specialized; involve more "proximate" concerns, often economic in nature;

are less "ideological," and generally less radical. With such distinctions in mind, sociological pluralists can in good conscience applaud groups for helping provide that otherwise missing sense of belonging, thus contributing to integration, social order and harmony. In this view, groups tend to impose or encourage rationality, not irrationality, by providing the individual with multiple ties to the social order; from these ties he supposedly derives a self-image which is distinctive yet firm and stable. Thus, Rogin contends there is a kind of "pluralist psychology," though it is rarely made explicit. The connections between pluralist psychology and pluralist politics, moreover, are direct and clear. Group memberships and crosscutting group memberships tend to result in pragmatic, piecemeal, low-key, low-passion politics: the politics of civility, as Shils puts it.

But despite this sociological emphasis on the integrative, order-and-harmony-promoting functions of pluralism, sociological pluralism is potentially compatible with authentically liberal concerns, with individual freedom and immunity from or control of power. The sociological and the liberal conceptions and defenses of pluralism are not altogether different and incompatible; indeed, some sociologically-minded pluralists are thoroughgoing liberals. They do not reject a concern with the individual but emphasize the necessary group supports of individuality. They are interested in individuals as participants in groups: as Rogin points out, the right of the individual to differ tends to be transformed into the right of groups to differ. Individual freedom, they feel, can be found in the interstices, in the individual's choice among groups, perhaps in the moment of choice itself. Group power offers at least partial immunity from other group power, and the constellation of groups can serve as a counterbalance to state power. Expecially important in the latter case, it is often argued, are powerful private economic institutions: corporations, unions, trade associations. Moreover, the multiplicity of groups and group-memberships supposedly affords the individual some immunity from the power and control of the groups to which he does belong. Finally, groups are no longer inclusive of his whole being: they control or prescribe for small slices of his life. He can afford to do without any particular one, both psychologically and economically.

A liberal community of communities, perhaps. Yet such a persuasion can be converted into a theory of the exercise of power as well as its control. It is even compatible, some have argued, with democratic power and the exercise of democratic authority. The demonstration begins by recognizing that while the individual may remain the ethically primary unit of society, to maintain his individuality on the personality level and to express himself and press his demands on a sociopolitical level requires the recognition that groups, not individuals, are the basic building blocks of society and polity. In their absence, control by the people is a hopeless abstraction: isolated unorganized individuals are generally powerless to press their demands. Moreover, if groups are free to organize, if their strength and influence is proportionate to their size, weighted by the intensity of their interests, then in a crude majoritarian sense the system of competing groups might be viewed as democratic.

Such influence might involve the circumvention of elected representatives, but not necessarily. If not, it still might involve the circumvention of the people. But again, not necessarily, and no doubt many representatives appreciate the help of organized groups with specific demands or interests in bringing to life the faceless abstraction which is the people. (Let us leave aside, for the moment, the fact that they may be well compensated for their appreciation.) And even if we are so brash as to associate democracy with ameliorating inequalities, with the pursuit of social and economic justice, group competition may well be the best or only practical way to achieve a more satisfactory distribution of rights and rewards than that which would result from strict laissez-faire or from abstract speculation on the subject of justice. A more allegiant citizenry may be the result. If everyone is accommodated and everyone compromised, then an overall shared conception of the goals of the society and the just distribution of rewards may be unnecessary. Finally, if group and institutional policies and activities are responsive to and directly involve the relevant individuals, then democracy in an additional sense, what Dahl calls the third wave of democratization, may be served. An alert, informed, participant citizenry may be nurtured—even in a large nation-state.[2]

Most pluralists would part company with the above amalgam at some point or another. But the general orientation which is pluralism seems to partake of all three concerns; certainly it has been criticized from all three standpoints.[3] All three varieties tend to merge into and inform that loose general orientation in American political theory labeled *democratic pluralism*, or simply *pluralism*. The primary difference from earlier versions of pluralist theory is the widespread acceptance of a larger role of the modern welfare state and a larger federal role in economic growth, stabilization, and regulatory policies as a result of the Great Depression and the Keynesian revolution. Most of us, pluralists included, are Keynesians now and liberals in the twentieth-century sense. The added proviso is that there should be fair competition among different groups for the favors increasingly at the disposal of the state.

Thus it is possible and helpful to think of pluralism as incorporating concern with liberty, equality, and fraternity as well. In subsequent chapters I will discuss these competing claims largely apart from the political process, the vocabulary of democratic theory and the close analysis of political institutions. I will argue that a conception of democracy predicated on self-interested individuals and groups using liberal democratic institutions to maximize the gratification of wants—a conception which is utilitarian, instrumentalist in its essentials—does not achieve the purported reconciliation, not even in theory. The argument amounts to an extended if modest elaboration of the sociologist's profound guiding intuition that social order, in this case the democratic social order, cannot be achieved or sustained on the basis of individual or mutual self-interest, however enlightened. Central to this approach, as I interpret it, is the notion that the self- and other-defeating nature of the wants with which the political process must deal are of crucial importance in explaining the survival and success of liberal democratic regimes. To speak of liberal democracy and its survival, then, is already and inevitably to speak of liberal democratic people and a liberal democratic community. Approaching the subject of democracy in this way may appear to be a species of debunking; but among the real enemies of democracy are those who innocently place impossible burdens on democratic institutions. Our concern with liberal democratic institutions, procedures, and ideals should lead us to a more inclusive conception of democracy, the liberal democratic community.

But first let us look at the democratic critique of pluralist-democratic America, for the moment taking that critique at face value and in its own terms. These critics forcefully and cogently argue that pluralism does not live up to some of its own ideals. In the process, however, they help raise and make urgent the larger question of what democracy is, can deliver, and should promise.

Pluralism: Poor Description or Inherently Conservative?

The democratic critics differ with each other along a number of dimensions, beginning with the way they label and conceive of their target.[4] It is doubly difficult to do justice to the differences among these critics while adequately criticizing their tendency to take too little note of the variety found in American political science (even among self-acknowledged pluralists). Yet all these critics might agree that Dahl's "fundamental axiom" of pluralism ("there must be multiple centers of power, none of which is wholly sovereign") serves to characterize their target. They seem to agree that pluralist theory remains a pervasive orientation in American political theory despite its having lost many of its explicit apologists. Despite differences in terminology ("pluralism," "democratic elitism," "interest-group liberalism," and so on) all are criticizing roughly the same phenomenon. And their criticisms have significant complementarities as well as common implications.

At the outset, many do not seem to fault the pluralist ideal of shared power, or the pluralist system of group competition. Instead, they typically begin by questioning its applicability to American reality. They argue that power, both private and political, is more concentrated than meets the pluralist's eye. With its private enclaves of power, pressure groups competing for governmental largess, and the capture of regulatory agencies by the regulated, the system is not representative of actual interests but of already established powers, that often have a distinctly capitalist look. As such, pluralism can amount to an attempt to avoid majority control. Established groups, the critics argue, are among the most conservative institutions in society, both in the sense of not reflecting emergent, unorganized interests and in not being internally democratic. To the extent that pluralist theory fosters a reliance on such groups, it is conservative, a kind of "conservative liberalism."

It is important to distinguish their argument—that such pluralistic power-sharing as we enjoy is severely flawed—from arguments associated with C. Wright Mills, or more Marxist conceptions of the state as a reflection of economic interests and class structure. Most recognize more readily than Mills that some decisions are necessarily the task of small elites, however democratically they may have been chosen. Some freely voice the suspicion that conjuring up a power elite is often the radical's way of obscuring the unresponsiveness of the average American citizen to radical candidates and causes. Others, Bachrach for example, recognize that the sociologist's assumption that a structure of power exists, added to his sociograms and reputational methods, could scarcely fail to identify men and groups in positions of apparent power, and thus to overstate its degree of concentration.

Instead, they admit that power is shared but point to the existence of some groups and some interests which are shortchanged or systematically excluded. And on some issues they suggest that this involves thwarting the will of the relevant majority. This complaint that Schattschneider makes about the remarkably narrow spectrum of organized lobbies is typical: "When lists of these organizations are examined, the fact that strikes the student most forcibly is that *the system is very small*. The range of organized, identifiable, known groups is amazingly narrow; there is nothing remotely universal about it . . . the business character of the pressure system is shown by almost every list available."[5] While the business of most of us is bound up in one way or another with business, mostly big business, the interests of many others, and other kinds of interests, are neglected. Wolff writes of the "tens of millions of Americans—businessmen and workers alike—whose interests are ignored by the genial give and take between big business and unions."[6] There is also the apparent underrepresentation of the interests of such groups as consumers and white-collar workers, a phenomenon pointed to by Olson and others. The crucial point is that aside from whether different group interests receive token representation, the obvious exclusion of blacks, women, Chicanos, American Indians, migrant laborers, and others from a larger share of the fruits of this affluent industrial society glares at us and bespeaks the flawed, uneven character of pluralistic power-sharing.

Thus democratic critics argue that in several important respects pluralism is an inaccurate or misleading description of the real state of affairs. But they go on to try to answer the question of why some interests do not or cannot organize effectively. And what they contend is that there may be something inherently conservative about the concrete application of pluralist theory, particularly insofar as it encourages a reliance on organized groups and a circumvention of elected representatives.

First they argue that the group in existence simply has an inherent advantage over the group that is trying to form and to press its demands, irrespective of any artificial entry barriers or discriminatory biases with which the new group may have to contend. Several suggest this is because it is often the group which needs most to organize that has least in the way of organizational skills and experience, or funds, or sheer confidence. It is precisely these prerequisites for success in the competition among groups for which disadvantaged groups must try to compete. Thus the rich tend to get richer in both politics and economics, and for similar reasons. Furthermore, as Wolff and others have pointed out, any conception of the government as the mere overseer or neutral referee among competing groups in practice tends to favor the stronger party. If the smaller party has no gloves, no previous boxing experience, and little confidence, it becomes difficult to regard the fight as fair, and the referee who enforces rules which do not take account of these disparities as neutral.

These same concerns can be articulated from a somewhat different perspective, that provided by Bachrach and Baratz's concept of "nondecisions." Their argument puts teeth into the contention that pluralism is inherently conservative. Following Schattschneider, they argue that nondecision-making shores up the existing "mobilization of bias":

a non-decision . . . is a decision that results in suppressing or thwarting of a latent or manifest challenge to the values or interests of the decision-maker . . . . non-decision-making is a means by which demands for change in the existing allocation of benefits and privileges in the community can be suffocated before they are even voiced; or kept covert; or killed before they gain access to the relevant decision-making arena; or, failing all these things, maimed or destroyed in the decision-implementing stage of the policy process.[7]

In this way they analyze the failure of the poverty program to achieve redistribution, and argue that the concentration on decision-making in pluralist theory and community power studies has produced a distorted, rosy impression of how equally power is shared.

Another line of argument complementary to these is offered by Theodore Lowi in *The End of Liberalism*. The distinctive virtue of Lowi's argument is to show that the unrepresentative results of a reliance on groups are quite compatible with an extension in the scope and size of government. Lowi argues vigorously that we should seek and find the source of the present "crisis" of democratic authority in our implicit public philosophy, which he calls interest-group liberalism. He labels its more sophisticated academic counterpart democratic pluralism. Both perspectives amount to ways of avoiding majority control, he argues. Both lead to the subversion of the notion of the state as a separate entity, one important reflection of which is the domination of regulatory agencies by those ostensibly being regulated. The ends of government; the justification of one policy as opposed to another; indeed, justice itself—these crucial matters are rarely discussed. The price of one group's acceptance of a governmental favor or subsidy is their reduction of concern, their loss of the moral right to concern themselves, with what other groups are doing. In this "atmosphere of universalized ticket-fixing," society-wide problems are neglected because they require society-wide solutions. Accordingly, government expands as its impotence increases, and as the respect of the populace for democratic forms decreases.

As Lowi sees it, a better public philosophy would be one which calls for explicit, highly visible, and more centralized policy. He calls his alternative "procedural democracy." Revolution by stealth is impossible, he contends, as those who sought to use the poverty program for radical purposes quickly discovered. Excessive administrative discretion, excessive local control, and generally vague objectives—mere sentiments more often than specific goals—doomed that program. The same is and will be true, he argues, of all programs concerned with social welfare and social justice which are similarly misconceived. As a nation we should be more honest and explicit about what it is we are up to, what we are willing and not willing to do and try.

One final approach serves to round out and to deepen the significance of this general line of argument. It is deceptively simple. Mancur Olson, in *The Logic of Collective Action*, suggested that latent groups with common interests will not organize to press their demands for change, or their demands that change be blocked. Starting from the premise of self-interested rationality, he develops the thesis that groups simply will not pursue their interests. Not if the individuals who compose the group are rational, membership is voluntary, the size of the group is large, the costs of organizing are substantial—not unless they can offer selective benefits to individual members as well as the collective or group "good."[8] And so many groups remain latent groups. It is the rational, self-interested man, whose interests place him squarely in a latent group, who will not help the group organize and pursue its collective goals. Assuming that the group is reasonably large, he knows that his nonparticipation will have a negligible effect on whether it secures its collective objectives. And he also knows that not helping the group will not affect his opportunity to enjoy the collective good, should it be obtained without his help. For by definition the collective good accrues to all members of the group: they cannot be excluded from its benefits.

Olson applies these considerations to the political process, to the theory of groups, and to the theoretical and practical consequences of viewing politics as a mere equilibrium among pressure groups. As a rule the smaller group has the advantage that each of its members has a significant and visible effect on the outcome of efforts to obtain collective goods for the group. This advantage is independent of those stressed earlier of already having money and resources, though both are often found together. Any member's nonparticipation would jeopardize that effort, both because his contribution is a significant part of the whole and because his nonparticipation would be more likely to provoke retaliatory nonparticipation from other members of the group. Large groups, latent groups, on the other hand, are at a distinct disadvantage.

Although in relatively small groups . . . individuals may voluntarily organize to achieve their common objectives, this is not true in large or latent groups. It follows that the "group theorists" have built their theory around an inconsistency. They have assumed that, if the group had some reason or incentive to organize to further its interests, the rational individuals in that group would also have a reason or incentive to support an organization working in their mutual interest. But this is logically fallacious, at least for large, latent groups.[9]

This argument has important implications for pluralist theory. Olson suggests that pluralists are just as guilty of the "anarchistic fallacy"—that natural, voluntary groups will form whenever there are common needs—as the anarchists themselves. And he ends his study on this note: "The existence of large unorganized groups with common interests is therefore quite consistent with the basic argument of this study: they also suffer if it is true."[10]

Let us pause to take stock. I suggest that, however varied in approach, the arguments outlined here are largely of a piece in their implications for pluralist theory. While seemingly remaining consistent with pluralist perspectives, they suggest certain amendments and changes in emphasis. Above all they point to the rationality of developing a commitment to what might be called, if only for convenience, the public interest. They are alike in suggesting a more exalted view of politics than the view that politics is or should be the mere sum of organized group activity, interaction, compromise, and conflict. They point to the fallacies involved in assuming that group politics will be democratic in the sense of groups having influence roughly proportional to size. They remind us that social movements and political philosophies which seek to reduce the influence of interests whose activities are considered detrimental to larger sectors of the population are not necessarily undemocratic. They inject the point of view of those generally excluded from the system of group competition, for whom the supposedly pluralistic system often appears a monistic disaster. They therefore call for the presence of a stronger, more positive, independent state, not merely a referee, if only to keep the competition fair, the opportunities equal, and to make sure the interests of all receive proper consideration. Finally, they suggest that any pluralist theory which is complacent in these matters will tend to negate its own ideals.

Criticizing the Critics: Problems in Defining the Problems

It is quite possible to interpret the above criticisms as little more than an affirmation of the pluralist ideals of power sharing, conflict settling, and securing the consent of all. A radical affirmation, perhaps, but an affirmation. In most cases, however, their quarrel with pluralism runs considerably deeper. This is primarily due to their pervasive if not explicit concern with systemic results as well as democratic forms and personal and political liberties. These results are not necessarily nor obviously compatible with some of the accepted promises, the culturally dominant goals of American private and political life. Nor are they obviously compatible with the increased participation these critics advocate. Moreover, there is a concern with the quality or certain qualities of American life, a concern whose relationship to democratization is by no means clear.

The problem is that these critics are often less than candid and consistent in discussing the sense in which the whole rightness of the system—the wants it fosters and frustrates, the results it produces—are matters of dispute. In large part this is due to their excessive reliance on the idea of democracy to convey their criticisms, their tendency to substitute "undemocratic" for more precise explanations of what agitates them. We will encounter this tendency again in considering other modes of criticism, involving other honorific and pejorative terms.

Lists of problems they hope democratization will combat are surprisingly infrequent, but there are a few. Ponder the following "well known and much recited" problems:

urban decay, rural overrepresentation, maldistributed medical care, chaotic public transportation, unequal employment opportunities, inequitable taxation, wasted natural resources, insipid recreation, meretricious entertainment, indefensible penal policies, scandalous mental hospitals and homes for the aged, collusive trade and employment practices, mindless communications media, unfulfilled educational promises, technological unemployment . . ."[11]

There are other such lists and they typically exhibit the same tendency to lump disparate problems together, to assume that all are equally urgent, totally interrelated, inevitable results of common systemic causes, and amenable only to "the most precedent-shattering and radical measures."[12] But these are questionable assumptions. Surely the problem of "meretricious entertainment" has a highbrow ring to it, and it is common knowledge that more Americans are agitated by supposedly leftist news commentators than by "mindless communications media." Furthermore, it is difficult to share their apparent confidence that these various desirable results would be obtained by applying a simple formula: neither the problems nor their solutions are so simple. And even if this were the case, it is possible that the critics do not see eye to eye with the people whose society they seek to democratize.

Yet in most cases it is fair to say that the formula proposed *is* simple. Basically they advocate two things, as I have indicated: a more extensive government and (often implied, though less often stated) a system of decision-making considerably more centralized, in which single decisions affect larger numbers of citizens. Tussman, for example, speaks of "creative leadership" and bringing more issues before the public tribunal. Wolff suggests that we should increase the number of "objects of collective decision," thus increasing "society's" power and "rationality." Bachrach and Baratz argue for making more decisions of "non-decisions." Kariel speaks of using collective power to secure increases of freedom, of rejecting the "impotent state" and entering "enclaves private in name only." Similarly with Lowi and McConnell, who vigorously argue that state and local governments tend to be more reactionary and corrupt than the federal government. There are numerous references to society-wide problems which require society-wide solutions. Thus they take an expansive view of Dahl's "Principle of Affected Interests": "Everyone who is affected by the decisions of government should have a right to participate in that government."[13]

Yet ambiguities lurk here, and their loose use of the language of democratic theory does not help to expose or resolve them. Therefore it will be helpful to proceed by asking what in fact would result from the implementation of these critics' suggestions and principles. Are their suggested means really instrumental to their desired ends? And in what sense are they advocating democratization?

First consider problems in the case for participatory, self-developmental democracy. This emphasis can often conflict with an emphasis on goals, with tackling the society-wide problems that likewise concern them. (Set aside, for the moment, the question of what developmental models they have in mind, and whether politics is the place to pursue such development.) The inevitable trade-off between the individual's share of influence over the decision-making process (presumably related to his self-development, the inculcation of responsible attitudes, citizenship-building) and the scope of the decision (how many are affected by the decision) is neglected.[14]

From the individual's standpoint there are at least three relevant dimensions. In addition to his share of decisions and their scope, there is the question of their salience for him. If problems the individual considers important must increasingly be solved on a large or even society-wide scale, if scope and salience are positively correlated for him, then any too-general exhortations to participate, any uncompromising advocacy of participatory ideals may amount to suggesting that the individual expend his efforts to gain a significant share of some insignificant action. At least this may be so in the absence of detailed discussion of the different forms of participation and democratic authority, and the different levels on which democratic authority may be exercised.

Participation, one gathers, generally connotes something more and different to these critics than merely voting and keeping informed. Yet just what else it is supposed to entail is typically unclear. In many passages voting, for example, seems to be more of an object of derision than the exercise of a fundamental democratic right and obligation. If we listen closely we hear the echoes of Rousseau's laughter at the English, who used their free votes, he claimed, to enslave themselves to their representatives. But the familiar problem is that their attitude seems to assume too much interest in participation (beyond voting) on the part of the average citizen and too little interest in desirable policy outcomes, however obtained.

Given a choice in the matter and assuming little interest in political participation per se, the average citizen might rationally opt for an insignificant share of significant action, especially if he saw better chances for a favorable outcome in the larger political unit. Yet in discussing participation these critics tend to overlook this possibility, and often lapse into the assumption that there is but one proper form of democratic participation and democratic authority, a form particularly and demonstrably ill-suited to the solution of large-scale problems. Their related tendency is to speak as if each of us finds himself, or perhaps should find himself, situated in but one polity. Surely this is neither accurate, nor feasible, nor even desirable.[15]

Thus they are vulnerable to the charge that Lane has directed to those who speak of community: that they forget and obscure the important distinction between the city-state and the nation-state. Perhaps for this reason, once these critics do get around to specific examples and suggestions, these are often surprisingly modest. For example, Bachrach ends a throughgoing indictment of "the theory of democratic elitism" and a resounding call to overcome "social alienation" with the frank admission that the only realistic hope for expanded participation these days is at the individual's place of work.[16] However important the advocacy of this aspect of democratization, it does seem to be a small bang from such a large gun.

There is yet another important neglected ambiguity: what affects a person's interests is sometimes far from evident to the outside, objective observer. This ambiguity is but partly due to the impoverished state of our knowledge of what the social consequences of alternative courses of private behavior and public policy actually are. I will subsequently argue that in many cases our interdependencies and spillovers are physical, visible, sometimes smellable, and indisputable, and that they seem to be growing. In many cases our need for collective decisions and the appropriate polity to make those decisions are more or less obvious. A solution to the problem of downstream pollution, as Schelling points out, must involve or at least affect those who are upstream doing the polluting. But in many other cases, some of crucial importance, these supposed needs for collective decisions, these conceptions of what is a problem and who is affected, depend on ideas and ideals we carry around in our heads and hearts. Even in the case of the demonstrably polluted stream, it is possible to deny that pollution is a high priority problem. Where you stand on this issue no doubt depends on how far up the river you happen to sit—or whether your plant is doing the polluting.

So by no means do all such ideas and ideals point us in the direction of making decisions public and centralized. This is true, I must emphasize, even of the notions entertained by these theorist-critics. Interestingly, the very pluralism they sometimes deplore as undemocratic can be defended, as Dahl points out, because it helps provide a rough but workable method for "insuring that the specialized knowledge of the groups most deeply involved in some activity will be brought to bear on the solution."[17] This certainly involves participation of a sort, and comes perilously close to an argument for the regulation of the regulatory agencies by those industries which are themselves being regulated. After all, who has more firsthand knowledge of their industry? Nor does it take a great flight of imagination to interpret the principle of state's rights in the same manner.

Without additional guidance, then, the Principle of Affected Interests becomes yet another conveniently ambiguous cover for whatever interests we may have in mind, especially when it is applied selectively. No viable conception of what should be public (and what is the relevant public) and what should be private emerges to challenge that division of public and private which presently exists. For example, Kariel speaks of moving into enclaves "private in name only." Presumably this has something to do with private industry. Yet he provides no clear criteria by which to name or rename what is public and private: certainly the criteria are not clearly nor consistently Marxist. Similarly, Tussman observes that:

Of course there are private decisions. Of course there are economic and social and religious institutions making decisions in which

public authority does not intervene. But *should* it intervene
is itself a public question, properly posed, if nowhere else, before
the amending power. There we may argue wisdon or folly, but to
do so is to concede jurisdiction.[18]

While finding pluralist theory to be no more than a "reiteration of
the arrangements" by which "within our system many decisions
are declared to be beyond the jurisdiction of the subordinate public
tribunals," he provides no principles by which to guide a rearrangement. He scorns the conception of politics derived from economics—
that is, the marketplace of interests—along with the companion
conception of the marketplace of ideas. But it is never clear what
alternative idea of politics and leadership he is advocating, nor
what better, nonmarket ideas democratic leadership should entertain, nor in what sense leadership would still be democratic should
such ideas be found.

With this in mind, we must consider the possibility that their
quarrel is not so much with the pluralist ideal as with the pluralistic
demos. We have seen that one important aspect of this apparent
conflict relates to the definition of what should be made public
and what should be left private. If there is such a thing as majority
tyranny, then one form it may take is the tacit agreement to keep
some decisions out of the reach of democratic authority. Insuffi-
cient attention is given to the possibility that present arrangements,
divisions among public and private and among different levels of
public jurisdiction, reflect a loose consensus on who should decide
what, where, and for whom. Admittedly such a consensus is both
rough and constantly changing, both because of the lack of agreement on what are the problems affecting this or that segment of
the community and because of the presence of high-intensity
concerns which must be kept inviolate in order to keep the peace.
These result in a shifting series of mutual guarantees by which each
group avoids interfering with the high-intensity concerns of the
other. From time to time the guarantees may break down, to be
replaced by others.

Instead of facing this possibility, Lowi for example seems to regard
our implicit public philosophy ("interest-group liberalism") as an
alien and diseased import grafted onto an otherwise healthy polity.

That is, instead of viewing its chaos, its proliferation of authorities, its excessive local and administrative discretion, and its private preserves of power as being firmly rooted in the cultural emphases and the sheer heterogeneity and complexity of this society. More-over, pluralist theory may reflect the "atmosphere of universalized ticket-fixing," but surely pluralist theorists did not invent the practice. Furthermore, both Lowi and Tussman give too little weight to the fact that action on some matters must often be secured by leaving other matters open to special influence by specially affected or interested groups. From their point of view, such mutual guaran-tees can be crucial in determining whether the system appears democratic (perhaps far more important than Lowi's democratic forms), however much such arrangements appear to these theorists as negations of democratic ideals or impediments to getting anything accomplished. Tussman scorns the notion of compromise because it "leaves unsolved the external problem." Indeed, compromise often creates the external problem for those groups not party to the compromise. But often a great part of that external problem consists of keeping different groups in this society from each other's throats. Forestalling this ever-present possibility is no mean achieve-ment. Similar objections apply to Bachrach and Baratz's concept of the "mobilized bias" which renders potential decisions "non-decisions." It may well be that the mobilized bias is identical to the bias that was there all along, and that the implicit decision is to keep decisions on many matters nondecisions.

Finally, in reference to Wolff's notion of situations which are not "objects of collective decision" (as for example, traffic jams), but which could and should be made so: we should be open-minded to the possibility that Americans may have chosen to have traffic jams. Later I will suggest reasons why this is not necessarily so, why there is this disparity between rational individual adaptations and collective results no one wants. But Wolff offers little argument, even in the most general terms, explaining what desired collective results are not being obtained and why our individual adaptations do not produce them. Thus the question of which situations should be "objects of social decision" is left unanswered. It is a serious and significant omission, for with no more guidance than Wolff gives us the possibilities are literally infinite. And improvements in technology, including techniques of propaganda and human engineering, increase their number daily.

In this way, apparent or possible disagreements with the American citizen are obscured, together with the possibility that at best the critics' proposed enlargement and implied centralization of the public sphere might produce no change and at worst might produce change in the wrong direction. They are thereby enabled to argue as follows:

> There is a fundamental sense of the term "rational" in which "to be rational" means to be the author of one's actions, to act rather than be acted upon . . . . a man becomes more rational just insofar as he brings within the scope of his will some datum of experience which previously confronted him as independent of his will . . . . liberals, by and large, employ only the more superficial notion of rationality as the fitting of means to ends.[19]

This is a definition of rationality which certainly reflects some willfulness on Wolff's part. Moreover, leaping immediately to the social level, he argues for a more rational, more powerful society: "Society requires an increase in power, a transforming into objects of decisions of important matters which are now the consequences of uncoordinated acts."[20]

It is quite possible that the notion of increasing social rationality by increasing collective power lacks all intelligibility—that is, if we use Wolff's definition of rationality and offer no further explanation. By comparison, otherwise vague Marxist references to the possibility of constructing a more rational society seem crystal clear. Much of the data of my experience consist of other people and situations and institutions which involve other people. If I increase my rationality by bringing these people, as Wolff puts is, "within the scope of my will," their rationality apparently decreases. Has *society's* rationality (or power) increased or decreased? Here again, it might depend on whether you asked me, or them. What is clear is that in the process of indiscriminately applying the principle of increased collective power, Wolff would probably rediscover the important liberal emphasis on the distributive or zero-sum aspect of power, especially if his freely admitted lack of faith in the American electorate proves justified. His book might even be banned, were such matters left to popular prejudice. Ironically, to the extent that the populace shared his ideas about the "poverty of liberalism" and took seriously his attack on the pluralistic virtue of tolerance, this would be more likely.

I suggest that what Wolff reveals is representative of a general ambivalence the critics have about democracy as process and procedure versus democracy as results, and that this in turn is part of their ambivalence concerning whether democracy should be thought of as enabling as many as possible to get as much as possible of whatever they want. Granted, in some contexts the critics do see the dilemma more clearly. For example, Bachrach roundly criticizes Popper's notion of an "open society" (open to whom? for what purposes?). He likewise criticizes Thorson's "first commandment" of democracy: "Do not block the possibility of change with respect to social goals" (*any* change? in *any* direction?). Nevertheless, we are generally offered open-ended exhortations to participate. Kariel suggests at one point that we should become even *less* goal-oriented ("there is no effort here to fill in what the citizen is to be free *for*"), despite his obvious concern with results and his criticisms of pluralism's focus on procedures. Data on majorities hostile to their desired goals are usually confronted obliquely or not at all. Or the easy assumption is made that in the process of participating more fully in public affairs the citizenry will gain the enlightenment and maturity requisite to seeing things the critics' way.

By such means as these, the full range, depth, and exact nature of their dispute with pluralism are rendered obscure. They seem to wish to affirm the value of liberal democratic institutions and at the same time to argue for results, particularly egalitarian results, not obviously nor necessarily compatible with those institutions. Behind this ambivalence is an ill-defined critique of American society which bears an obscure relationship to their ostensibly democratic critique and egalitarian concerns. This subterranean critique is suggested by their vague rhetoric concerning participation, what it consists of, and, precisely what ailments it is supposed to cure. Yet by relying so heavily on the notion of democratization, they forcibly raise the question of how democracy is to be conceived and defended. Now let us ask the question in a more straightforward manner, with the help of the deductive rigor of recent democratic theory.

2 Democracy, Demands, and Deliveries

It is not at all clear whether the democratic critics are criticizing pluralist practice, pluralist-democratic ideals, democracy itself, or the American citizenry. Here their critique will be placed in the context of recent American democratic theory, particularly the axiomatic or economic approach to defining, explaining, and implicity defending and justifying democracy.[1] At first glance these recent theoretical developments seem to encourage us to take a more modest view of democracy and what it can deliver. At the same time we are encouraged to focus consistently and resolutely on the deliveries, the payoffs, of democratic institutions. As might be expected of an approach heavily influenced by economics, it takes a decidedly unsentimental, instrumental view of our institutions, as means to individual and group ends. The same view informs much of pluralist theory, as John Plamenatz has recently and persuasively argued.[2]

Or perhaps the word is infected. Eventually I will argue that this approach serves to spell out in splendid detail why its own implicit conception of democracy—a conception shared by most pluralists and by many democratic critics—is radically deficient, and that we must look in a different and more sociological direction to reduce the gap between what is demanded of and what is delivered by democracy. For the moment, however, the axiomatic rigor of this approach to democratic theory, coupled with its consistently instrumental view of democratic institutions, will serve us well in underlining the dilemmas of liberal democracy and the supposed crisis in democratic theory.

Democracy Debunked?

Someone has suggested that while there is indeed a serious crisis in democratic theory, it certainly is a quiet one. Apparently many eminent theorists have not even heard the news, and not just those few sociologists who have donned earmuffs because of their passion for social order and stability, democratic or no. Nor has the ordinary man gotten the word. He continues to cast his demonstrably inconsequential vote; to pay his taxes with little cheating; to keep himself informed; to write letters to editors and congressmen and participate in political discussions and campaigns—all to an utterly irrational extent. At least it looks this way when we view him from the standpoint of self-interest. So it is disturbing. To make our betting on democracy dependent on the common man's ignorance of the implications of economic theory for democratic politics is an unpleasant state of affairs, especially if you were brought up to believe that democracy amounts to a long-run bet on his common sense and intelligence. Nevertheless, this may well be the turn things have taken:

> There the matter stands among the sophisticated. The most benighted savage of yesterday's anthropology, sacrificing to his totemic ancestor and groveling before his sacred king, is no worse off for a theory of legitimacy that will pass the tests of reason than is the most advanced "democratic" theorist among us today.[3]

But before jumping to such a dramatic conclusion, let us take a look at some of the less esoteric wonders (or crises) that the economic approach has wrought in its application to democratic theory. Then we will consider what it portends for both the savage and the sophisticated.

Begin by returning to the point where we left off with Olson—the criticism he levels at the pluralist's reliance on organized groups in the political process. There I suggested that his argument is a most significant attempt to explain why pluralist practice falls short of pluralist ideals. Yet if we reflect on the full range of its possible applications and implications, Olson's simple argument seems to call democracy itself into question. At least it does if we are prone to think of democracy as a set of institutions instrumental to the purpose of self-interested individuals and to view political participation accordingly.

As Plamenatz points out, Olson's book can be thought of as a generalization of another pioneering application of economic analysis to the discussion of democratic theory: Anthony Downs's *An Economic Theory of Democracy*. Downs's model pictures political parties competing for votes in order to acquire power, and "self-regarding" citizens trying to use their votes to put in power the party that will benefit them most. This conception clearly owes a great deal to Schumpeter, who characterizes democracy as a competitive struggle for the people's vote.[4] The difference between the two is that Downs confronts the obvious question left unanswered by Schumpeter's tough-minded definition: just what, after all, do the citizens get out of this competitive struggle? The answer seems to be: quite possibly a great deal. But then another question suggests itself: if we view the individual through the Downsian spectacles of self-interested rationality, why should *he* bother to vote and keep informed?

Downs is aware of the "paradox":

(1) rational citizens want democracy to work well so as to gain its benefits, and it works best when the citizenry is well-informed; and (2) it is individually irrational to be well-informed. Here individual rationality apparently conflicts with social rationality . . . . This paradox exists because the benefits men derive from efficient social organization are indivisible . . . . let us assume that everyone benefits in the long run if government is truly run "by the consent of the governed"; i.e., if every voter expresses his true views in voting. By his "true" views, we mean the views he would have if he thought that his vote decided the outcome.

But in fact his vote is not decisive: it is lost in a sea of other votes. Hence whether he himself is well-informed has no perceptible impact on the benefits he gets . . . therefore, as in all cases of indivisible benefits, the individual is motivated to shirk his share of the costs.[5]

To be more precise: the expected value of the voting game to the Downsian participant is the probability that the outcome will hinge on his vote, times the personal benefit he will receive if his party wins, minus the costs connected with informed voting. That probability is typically miniscule, so the benefits would have to be virtually infinite to make the expected value of voting anything but negligible. The costs, on the other hand, are not negligible, not to the person whose time is of value. Thus the sum is negative, the rational individual "shirks his share," and we are left to wonder why the game has any players—or players who are not being duped by a meaningless ritual.[6] Moreover, nothing in the logic of the argument restricts its applicability to voting—as Olson and others have done us the service of demonstrating. It can be applied to voting and keeping informed, to political participation in general, and conceivably even to why the workers of the world have not united and organized to throw off their chains. It appears that this is not the paradox of voting alone, but the paradox of any action to further group goals, any socially responsible behavior. Morality, it seems, is not useful. That is why it is so useful to us that others practice it.

It should be noted that there have been various attempts to resolve these paradoxes. Yet unless we regard these as efforts to point out the *limitations* of the economic approach to democratic theory—typically this is not at all their purpose—then they have failed in one or both of two ways. Either in some way they manage to ignore or obscure the force of Olson's and Downs's telling point about the divergence of individual self-interest and desired collective outcomes, or they manage to so water down the concept of self-interest that the resulting theories lose their predictive grasp precisely as they extend their descriptive reach.[7]

Downs's solution to his own paradox is developed in terms of the utility of maintaining the entire system, which utility the rational individual will recognize. It is not convincing.[8] Even thieves can recognize their interest in everyone else continuing to observe the rules of respect for the property of others; but *their* interests, of course, lie elsewhere. Olson's solution to the paradox of political participation is slightly more satisfactory: the large groups which do manage to organize and pursue their goals are able to offer selective, individual benefits to their members. But this by no means accounts for all the large groups that have organized.[9] Wagner's attempt to resolve the paradox adds a Downsian twist to Olson's argument: organizations have leaders, and leaders are offered or obtain selective incentives. But this leaves out the followers, to whom Olson's careful analysis of the nonrationality of contributing time and money to the collective effort still applies.[10]

36   *Social Criticism, Political Science, and Democracy*

As Barry points out, another failed attempt to rescue self-interest is Coleman's effort to bring a sense of national identification under the utilitarian rubric.[11] Identification with the fate of the nation—and with it the understanding that voting, keeping informed, paying taxes, and generally good citizenship are essential to its good health and long life—is simply not sufficient cause for the rational individual to lift one finger. It may be virtuous for the individual to be a good citizen because he thinks of the democratic system as a whole as something in which he has an investment, but it is not rational, not as these theorists understand rationality. And is it not odd to describe virtue as an investment? Barry observes that "the condition of the investment is so little affected by the actions of one ordinary person that it would not pay to contribute to its upkeep."[12]

Let us leave these paradoxes and problems of voting and participation within a given constitutional framework for the moment and apply some of the same rigor and realism to the question of justifying the choice of the framework itself—that is, the choice among alternative ways of rendering collective decisions. For simplicity we will concentrate for the moment on majority rule. Political equality, Dahl and Lindblom argued in 1953, is an instrumental goal, instrumental in the pursuit of the "prime," personal goals of human beings in Western societies. They suggested that

> The democratic goal is twofold. It consists of a condition to be attained and a principle guiding the procedure for attaining it. The condition is political equality, which we define as follows: *Control over governmental decisions is shared so that the preferences of no one citizen are weighted more heavily than the preferences of any other one citizen.* The principle is majority rule, which we may define as follows: *Governmental decisions should be controlled by the greatest number expressing their preferences in the "last say."*[13]

A similar quotation from Downs suggests that their conception of democracy is not particularly idiosyncratic. Downs argues that government by consent of the governed consists of "decision-making in which the decider makes each choice on the basis of preferences of those affected by it and weights the preferences of each in proportion to the degree to which he is affected."[14]

These are tall orders, and it is questionable whether political equality and majority rule fill them. Even the relationship between political equality and majority rule is unclear. In 1956 Dahl suggested that it is "intuitively obvious" that majority rule follows from the assumptions of popular sovereignty and political equality, but nevertheless did offer a proof ("at the risk of presenting an essentially trivial demonstration of the logical relations involved . . . ").[15] By 1970 he limits himself to emphasizing the empirical correlation of beliefs in political equality and the practice of majority rule.[16] Let us look at some of the arguments which may have lead Dahl from proof to correlations.

If we take a naive view, "recognizing each other as equals" might merely imply that each person should get one and only one vote in whatever decision-making process is decided upon. This conception of political equality is basically one of anonymity, and as such it is compatible with a host of decision rules. Yet Dahl and Lindblom, and they are by no means alone in this, apparently think of formal political equality in terms of some kind of unspecified, perhaps unspecifiable, more substantial equality of *control*—or even results—wherein "the preferences of no one citizen are weighted more heavily than any other one citizen."[17] But of what does this equality of control consist? Why does majority rule produce it? And how could we ever ascertain whether it has been achieved?

When we say that minority rule involves weighting the preferences of individuals in the minority more than the preferences of individuals in the majority, what we have in mind is that under minority rule decisions will go against the majority. In each case, the majority and each of its members would have no control at all. Clearly, this is unequal weighting, whatever assumptions we may wish to make about how often different individuals are unfortunate enough to be in the majority, and thus be losers. What is disturbing about this objection to minority rule based on an analysis of outcomes, however, is that the same argument applies virtually word for word to majority rule, and the same objections obtain. Winners control decisions and losers do not.

It would be a mistake to conclude that the inequality embodied in majority rule is solely a result of the fact that the minority always loses. Let us take, for example, a decision-making rule which would consist of randomly choosing an individual from the polity and then abiding by that individual's choice on a particular issue, an issue, say, favored by a majority (M) and opposed by a minority (m). In the long run the minority would win some, but it would still lose M/m times as often as the majority. Reconciling even this with the notion of equal control or weighting of preferences is impossible. What should be clear from this elaborate glimpse into the obvious is that the inequality involved in any decision rule results from the collective decision itself, from the fact that people disagreed, thus making the decision necessary.

The inequality inherent in any decision has a dynamic counterpart labeled the problem of the standing minority. Typically the rationale for minority acceptance of majority rule makes reference to the minority's good sense in seeing that they are now, or might someday be, in the majority on some issues. As a justification of majority rule, this represents a considerable loss in generality. Here is an implicit admission that results *are* of the essence in determining whether preferences are or have been weighted equally, and that formal political equality under many circumstances might therefore lack significance. It conjures up the possibility of some kind of compensatory action for consistently outvoted minorities to insure real political equality. Only under highly specific assumptions about the pattern of preferences, how it will shift in the future, and so on, does this argument that the current standing minority should wait their turn gain much cogency. Otherwise it may well be prudent, or traditional, for the minority to accept majority rule, but to speak of it as instrumental to their goals is at very best unenlightening.[18]

Rae has offered a possible rationale for majority rule which helps spell out those special assumptions about preferences in the polity which a randomly selected individual would have to make in pondering the choice of alternative decision-rules.[19] Imagine an individual choosing a decision-rule for a polity in which he is to live and abide by its collective decisions, but choosing in ignorance of what the pattern of preferences in the polity will be. Suppose that over the long run he wants to minimize the sum of expected losses of two kinds: having a proposal which he favors voted down and having a proposal which he does not favor voted up. Under these assumptions, Rae demonstrates that only simple majority rule will satisfy the individual's requirements. Given that the analysis applies to any such hypothetical individual, simple majority rule represents a kind of joint optimization.

But the more interesting question is what this analysis implies for the choice of a decision-rule for an individual who knows in advance that he will be in a standing minority or majority on a certain class of issues, or perhaps on all issues of importance to him. Not surprisingly, the answer is that it depends on whether he stands more or less in the minority or the majority:

> The problem of the exploited faction is not a special difficulty of majority-rule, but a generic difficulty of all simple-decision rules. This is so because *any* rule will leave either the minority or the majority subject to one of three unhappy prospects: the unchecked imposition of unwanted policies; or the invariable veto of wanted policies; or both.[20]

There will not be agreement on the rule, so this is his conclusion:

> Even this much-too-brief consideration of factional conflict suggests that the effort to optimize individual values in collective choice must, in such instances, look beyond the choice of simple decision rules. No such rule will produce a joint optimization (as did majority-rule under the simple model). . . . Admitting that this consideration of the problem is far from exhaustive, I suspect that one must look away from formal institutional choices and *toward the standard civic virtues* [my emphasis] if individual values are to be optimized in factional strife. . . . these conclusions lead to one last conjecture: a constitutional choice can be made consensually only if uncertainty about the future makes appropriate a model analogous to our simple one. Once decision-rules are conceived as instruments in a *determinate* [my emphasis] conflict of interests, then the incentive for agreement on majority-rule (or any alternative to it) is destroyed, and unanimous consent seems improbable.[21]

Two features of his demonstration and conclusion merit special notice. One is that to the very end Rae continues to speak of virtue in terms of its usefulness to the individual, in "optimizing" "individual values" in factional strife. The other is that he comes perilously close to concluding that once we consider real people with real interests ("in a determinate conflict") in a real polity, the rationale for majority rule goes kaput.

Next consider a different rationale for majority rule. Condorcet demonstrated in 1785 that if some course of action is "right," but members of the polity have only a certain probability of knowing what is the right policy or decision, then majority rule will slightly enhance the probability that it will be chosen. At first glance the theorem seems to apply only when some outcome is transcendentally right or just. Yet it also applies to those situations in which everyone agrees on the desirability of certain results or outcomes and there is a correct or most efficient way of accomplishing the results, but the probability that the average person will know the proper means to the objective is less than one. Or there may be agreement on objectives and there may be one of two candidates who is the better equipped for the job of facilitating their attainment, and the individual electors each have a certain probability of knowing which of the candidates is "right." It is conceivable that majority rule derives some of its intuitive appeal from the fact that Condorcet's proposition is true, that under some circumstances a majority of heads is, for this reason, better than one. What must be strongly emphasized is the very special nature of the circumstances in which this rationale is applicable. Its applicability depends on a severe restriction on the amount of disagreement on the issue in question—that is, none.

Now let us try again to make sense of the notion that preferences should be weighted equally, given the simple circumstance of a small group trying to reach a decision. Assuming there is no consensus on what to do, one interpretation of the democratic decision might be that compromise which everyone regards as fair.[22] For a group of any size and heterogeneity, there is usually no such policy. But certainly this is one interpretation of the democratic ideal and sometimes it can be roughly approximated. Yet, as Plamenatz points out, to claim that this consists of an equal weighting of preferences adds little but confusion. Even in the simplest of cases, it is typically impossible to determine whether the resulting policy favors everyone equally, much less to settle the more difficult question of whether their control over the decision was equal.[23]

Similar questions will arise should the group decide it needs an agent or a representative to formulate some of its policies. Suppose we interpret equality as everyone having an equal chance to vote for "his" candidate, who if elected will vote and pursue his electors' interests exclusively. There is probably no way for the individual to foresee the range or identity of the issues his representative would have to deal with. But even if this were possible, his particular constellation of interests would probably not be perfectly represented by any candidate. Were there just four issues, with four possible positions on each, there would have to be 256 unique candidates (4x4x4x4) in order to insure that everyone gets a chance to vote for his "own." If by some fluke your candidate were elected, your control would then be considerably more equal than mine. Of course the representative may try to take account of everyone's interests or even to search for those compromise positions and policies which all his constituency considers fair. But here again we cannot tell from the policies themselves whether the results favor everyone equally, nor whether the process which took account of our interests granted us equal influence, weight or control. And the sense in which my representative is *mine* would certainly be lost in such arrangement.

Complicating the Democratic Game

Turn now to a different problem—determining the appropriate or most advantageous polity, irrespective of what decision-making rule is agreed upon. If the individual is really consistent and hard-nosed in his instrumental view of political institutions, then the decision-making rules may be of less concern than the results that are or are not being obtained under those rules. The results depend crucially on *where*, what level the decision-rules are applied, and who applies them. Suppose we agree with Dahl and Lindblom that "the greatest number" should express their preferences and have them honored in the "last say." Where is the last say said, and who says it? What is the relevant polity, and what is the relevant majority?

It is a familiar ambiguity. We encountered it in the tendency of the democratic critics to manipulate the level on which democratic authority should be exercised and to finesse the question of whose interests are actually involved in given social situations and policy decisions. Direct assaults on majority rule, whether by pluralists or their democratic critics, are rather rare.[24] The ambiguity is also involved in the question of whether public jurisdiction should be assumed at all, or left to personal choice. Clearly, Rae's hypothetical individual has to assess an even more complicated set of probabilities and expected frequencies of wins and losses.

As I suggested in criticizing the democratic critics, the individual may be willing to settle on an insignificant share in decisions of salience to him which have a higher probability of being decided in a manner favorable to his interests. Despite his small or even nonexistent share in these decisions, despite having to rely on representatives or experts, he may find that his "control" is actually more equal than his control elsewhere, though his share of the decision might be less. If results are of the essence, he might rationally relinquish his share of the decision altogether under certain circumstances, especially on matters requiring technical expertise. He might settle for a smaller share in decisions if jurisdiction can be assumed in a larger polity in which the majority is more sympathetic to his concerns. He might want no share at all in decisions properly relegated to trusted experts. Thus a concern with certain desired outcomes is inconsistent with simplistic advocacy of participation, centralization or decentralization, making more decisions public, or any one form of democratic authority—including majority rule.[25]

In the face of all this, the mind boggles at the prospect of determining the perfect strategy of the truly self-regarding person. The calculation is hopelessly complicated even for those persons who limit their possible strategies to those which are legal. (Their doing so is not a foregone conclusion, given that we learn so little about the abstract schemers which populate these analyses.) Or rather: the only thing that makes the individual's calculations manageable is the recognition that if he values his time he will probably forego some of the fancier strategies. So the mystery deepens. It began when we asked what majority rule has to do with weighting preferences equally. What has democracy to do with equality? More generally: what has democracy to do with fulfilling the demands impinging on it? The whole question of whether the system of authority is more or less democratic, at least when we pose it in these tough-minded instrumental terms, becomes increasingly problematic and unanswerable. Democratic theory becomes a contest to see who is most clever and opportunistic in manipulating the infinite possible permutations of different forms and levels and jurisdictions of democratic authority, together with the question of whose interests are legitimately affected by which circumstances and decisions and policies. Often, as we have seen, this exercise is performed by theorists with recognizably egalitarian sentiments and sympathies. But the expenditure of energy and ingenuity in their attempts to squeeze the last few drops of equality out of liberal democratic institutions and procedures—while fastidiously ignoring our actual beliefs concerning equality and the cultural obstacles to greater equality, as reflected in the demands impinging on those institutions —must surely be uneconomic.

There are other, much-discussed ways of further compounding these mysteries—notably, Kenneth Arrow's proof of the impossibility of devising any collective decision-rule which, given a moderate amount of heterogeneity of preferences, will satisfy a set of seemingly appropriate and innocuous postulates, including transitivity.[26] Arrow's theorem represents a generalization of the "paradox of voting" (not to be confused with Downs's paradox), which may occur anytime there are three or more voters choosing on a pairwise basis among three or more alternatives. What happens is that intransitive "social" orderings can be produced, of the sort that alternative A is preferred to B is preferred to C, but C is preferred to A. Arrow's theorem dispenses with the task of laboriously checking all conceivable decision-rules for this fatal flaw:

If we exclude the possibility of interpersonal comparisons of utility, then the only methods of passing from individual tastes to social preferences which will be satisfactory and which will be defined for a wide range of sets of individual orderings are either imposed or dictatorial.[27]

Apparently the very attempt to aggregate preferences, however we seek to do it, is subject to this radical incoherence, not to mention the other difficulties I have discussed. Our efforts to make sense of democracy in instrumentalist-utilitarian terms would appear to be doubly doomed.

In chapter 9 we will confront Arrow's bugbear (which, according to Riker and Ordeshook, "now looms so large in political theory"), but for the moment I suggest that our hands are already full—the simple and more basic complications have given us quite enough to ponder. This quest for tough-mindedness and axiomatic rigor in democratic theory, of which I have given a mere taste, seems to have made our ignorance of the rationale for democracy increasingly massive. Have we debunked democracy? Or have we debunked a certain approach to explaining and defending it?

I will subsequently argue that the latter is more nearly the case, and that the significant obstacles to greater equality, to distributive justice—and more generally, to the satisfaction of demands impinging on the political system—are ultimately cultural and human, not hidden in the esoteric demonstrations of axiomatic political theory, the paradoxes of the literature on collective decision-making, nor for the most part in institutional tinkering and strategic maneuvering. In order to do so we must take temporary leave of the vocabulary of democratic theory, narrowly defined, and look directly at the troublesome nature of the demands with which our institutions must deal—and at the cultural setting from which those demands and our problematic conceptions of man and democracy derive.

PART 2
Social Criticism, Psychology,
and Freedom

Any way of viewing the world, any mode of democratic theorizing, relies on a view of human nature, or philosophical anthropology, whether or not the reliance is self-conscious or explicit. Schematically speaking, it is simple enough to develop social criticism by reference to human nature. By observing individuals and cultures or by reflecting on the human condition we isolate certain basic human needs, developmental potentials, or imperatives of the human situation. We then use these as points of reference in criticizing social institutions or cultural demands, in suggesting alternatives, in reconceiving democracy. Unfortunately, the simplicity abruptly disappears once we leave this level of abstraction. Perhaps the only argument for engaging in such speculation is that, one way or another, we all do it anyway.

"There is only one philosophical anthropology, and it is the Marxist." The writer is Sartre, and either he is stretching the meaning of Marxist, or he is wrong. Nonetheless, it is appropriate to begin with some left and left-liberal social critics for whom Marxist philosophical anthropology, however unacknowledged or watered down and Americanized, is both a basic reference point and a source of intellectual sustenance. Thus it will be helpful to review the relevant aspects of the Marxist tradition from which they have drawn, however loosely and selectively.

The broad outlines of the Marxist view of man are clear and familiar, notwithstanding the apparently endless debates on the Left over details and emphases. As Lichtheim puts it, with Marx alienation became a sociological, no longer merely an ontological concept. Marx tied alienation to specific historical social structures, the destruction and transcendence of which would supposedly overcome alienation. The Marxist archetype of alienation is of course the worker's alienation under capitalism, from his products and the work process itself. Marx's interpretation of alienation

also included alienation from others and alienation from our species
and being as well. The reason he could lump together these apparently different, possibly independent or even opposed senses of
alienation was that his view of essential human qualities—man as
a productive, creative, social and sensuous being—enabled him to
argue that alienation from others, for example, was simultaneously
alienation from one's essential or "true" self.[1]

Berger stresses that Marx's essential human qualities are not human
nature in the sense of a fixed biological substratum which determines the manifold social manifestations. Rather, they are related
to a set of anthropological constants which include "world-openness," instinctual plasticity, sociality, and the necessity of externalization and objectification. Unlike other animals, man has no
home in the sense of an ambient determined by his instinctual
repertoire; his ongoing task is to construct and maintain a cultural
"home." Precisely because of his inherent plasticity and his world-
openness, he must construct and maintain a world to provide "clo-
sure." As Berger puts it, man thereby produces not only himself,
and a world, but also "himself in a world." Thus the human subject
first externalizes and then objectifies himself—it is his essential
human burden and privilege—in the simplest of products and tools
or the most complex of ideas and social institutions. This process
is unavoidably social, not merely because the individual must work
with and depend on cooperative others, but also because shared
meanings, symbols, customs, and language must be employed.
Man is more or less free to build a world, to make history, though
he must work collectively and with available tools—intellectual,
social, cultural, technological. When he no longer sees himself in
his products, however, when these become inhuman "facticities,"
he has become alienated. As Berger points out, human existence
cannot be conceived of in the absence of externalization and objectification. But alienation, or the rupture between producer and what
is produced, is merely a de facto aspect of the human condition. In
Marx's view, he "forgets" (or is encouraged, forced, or paid to
forget) his products, his contributions, actual and potential; the
human origins of the whole capitalist social and economic order;
and the human cooperation and acquiesence without which it would

cease to exist as presently constituted. And when (to introduce a more recent Marxian emphasis) "things" become the standard of all reality, when *as a human being* he lives and endures the life of an inert thing, his world and existence has become reified.[2]

Despite the fact that man is basically free (though again, not free to choose the instruments by which he expresses and extends his freedom) his "forgetting," and thus his further and unnecessary enslavement, is ubiquitous. Marxists are the first to admit it: "Everywhere and always social man is inventive, creative: everywhere and always he is in thrall to his own achievements."[3] Given that freedom, not forgetting, nor bad faith, and praxis, not passivity nor submission, are considered basic and praiseworthy, then alienation and reification can be condemned as inhuman and reprehensible. Similarly for the economic, social, political, religious institutions and attitudes that foster these maladies.

But how do we defend the proposition that exercising one's freedom is more basic than escaping from it? Examples of the latter probably outnumber the former. Why not say it is the nature of man to forget that everything is possible, to remember what he did yesterday and to think it necessary and natural to repeat it? Why not say man has a natural tendency (a developmental capacity?) to take on the qualities of an inert thing, to lose himself in social roles? He does it continually.

By contrast, the human starting point I emphasize here suggests that prior to the doctrine of praxis, or "man makes himself," or any other assertion about man, we have a basic dependence on our distinction-making potential and propensity—indeed, this "distinguishing" characteristic may be our distinguishing characteristic. And the harder we look at that potential and propensity, the more our human interests appear irreducibly ambivalent, or the more we see that we must necessarily see them this way.

The notion of humanly general ambivalence thus points toward a conception of alienation in which our humanity is implicated, and hopefully toward a better understanding of that dialectic by which human creations can be human-denying. It further suggests that alienation can be regarded as a protection against its apparent opposite, anomie, the other basic reprehensible human affliction—one given little attention by both Marxists and liberals—and that any effective analysis of alienation must simultaneously be an analysis of anomie.

Regarding the one-dimensionality of both liberal and Marxist conceptions of man and the naive analysis of alienation based on it, Weinstein and Platt assert that "in terms of advancing a convincing conception of internal processes, Marx had little more to offer than the liberal theorist."[4] This criticism applies with considerable force to a dominant strain of contemporary thought, Marxist as well as left-liberal, and even to much of the work of those who have sought to assimilate the perspectives of Freud (Marcuse, for example). The human starting point they propose is individual freedom, activity, change: Desan points out that it is almost as if, as in some of Sartre's earlier writings, any shared creed were by definition automatically oppressive. Of course if one were prepared to live in such a solipsistic, atomized world, alternating between chaos and oppression, this would be the end of it. But after all, such a conception of man is offered by those who have, or claim to have, collective concerns at heart. It therefore occurs to me that a Marxist (and those, like most of the left-liberal subjects of this study, who derive intellectual and moral sustenance from the Marxist tradition) proceeding from this conception of being human to his sociological critique and collectivistic prescriptions, is faced with two problematic alternatives. He can argue that alienation is total and must be totally eliminated; that all freedoms should be expanded; that change should never be blocked; that communication should be totally unrestricted, and so on.[5] Much of this is probably more liberal than left and, as Schaar suggests, no doubt unworkable anywhere outside the nursery. His other alternative, it seems, is to offer his collective goals and program as somehow extrinsic to his supposed view of man. Perhaps there is nothing inherently wrong with this as long as the discontinuity is explained and the gap closed in some other way. A Burkean appeal to tradition, perhaps: what we share, in a given culture, or might potentially share. But leftists and liberals alike generally regard such alternatives as unpalatable.

I will discuss several American examples of this common, modern, and disturbing schism. Mention of Sartre reminds us that while for Americans the gap is perhaps more obvious for our having less of a common leftist tradition and vocabulary, the dilemma is as much modern and Western as it is American.[6] Efforts to bridge the gap produce, in liberal and leftist circles, what might be called mere fads by other circles: ever-newer explanations of why and how we are alienated, act in bad faith, acquiesce in reification or inauthentic behavior, and so on. Alienation under capitalism is superseded by alienation under bureaucracy. Affluence disguises our alienation. The media lie to us, or render us passive and soporific. We are subjected to the dictates of technology, technological politics, technological thoughtways, or the tyrannies of logic itself. On the one hand we are told that alienation is related to concrete, historically-specific economic and social institutions: any suggestion that humans have anything remotely resembling psychological universals, much less that these somehow implicate us in our alienation and oppression, is anathema to all but a few Marxists.[7] On the other hand, new versions of the historic junctures and the alienating structures are continually being offered. But alienated we remain, apparently.

I begin here with some theorists who in various ways exhibit and underline these difficulties. Heavily if indirectly influenced by Marxism, particularly the Marxist concept and critique of alienation, they have turned to various psychologies in their attempts to give better accounts of what ails us and better prescriptions for our maladies. That they should turn to psychology for help is surely a most interesting and significant sign of the times—and a bit surprising. Several years ago, Judith Shklar remarked that there remains a great eagerness to deal with political questions in moral or prescriptive terms, but that steadily accumulating knowledge and insight, *particularly* from psychology and anthropology, have largely silenced the urge. "We know too much to be daring," she suggests. Yet what passes or should pass for knowledge is precisely what is at stake in an inquiry of this sort. Moreover, wisdom may well set limits on some kinds of knowledge, as Nietzsche asserts: some kinds of ignorance may well prove sublimely opportune. So let us begin with a brief look at some who *do* dare, temporarily reserving judgment concerning whether their courage is predicated on opportune, unacceptable, or dangerous ignorance.

3 The Leftist Literature of Freedom

The Phenomenon and Its Backdrop

Despite some obvious differences in vocabulary and perspective, the critics I will briefly consider here resemble each other in several important respects. First, they develop their social critiques by explicit reference to their conception of human nature or the human condition. Each reserves a place of prominence in his analysis for his conception of human beings, who represent something somehow superior to and independent of the social order. Second, all avoid the vocabulary of democratic theory, at least at the outset, despite the fact that the reorientation of democratic theory is central to their project. All admit that this society, whether democratic or not, seems to generate at least a limited sense of responsiveness, but all argue that something fundamental about human beings is being ignored or violated. Their analyses seek to supply what is basic and to explain how and why it is shortchanged. Their objectives and viewpoints are informed by a belief in the possibility and desirability of our assuming better collective control over our fate—and belief that justice demands a more equal distribution of life chances. While in this very loose sense they are "on the Left," they are prone to eclecticism in vocabulary and perspective, approach and prescription. Finally, despite their ostensible concern with collective goals and ideals, their emphasis on individual freedom is pronounced, and the connection between their general exhortations to expand freedoms and their collective concerns is not altogether clear.

It should be noted that there is nothing strikingly new about this project of building a social theory and critique from the (human) ground up, nor about the historical juncture out of which it springs. Hobbes comes to mind in connection with both the project and the context of fragmented authority. What may be new is the extent of the fragmentation and the decline of received authorities among the well-educated, comfortable, and intellectual classes in the industrial West. Granted that some analyses of whatever-is-happening-to-us have a myopic and exaggerated quality (prompting some of us to wonder whether certain intellectuals *are* the "intellectual crisis"); granted that whatever it is has more to do with how some of us think than how most of us continue to live. Still, something about the depth of the intellectual crisis may be historically unique. Institutions continue to have power over us, but their authority may be receding, and with it their intelligibility, even their reality. We may have driven the suspicion of given authorities to the point of questioning the very idea of authority, and this may be particularly true of Americans. It may simply be less obvious because, always having had less of a common culture to celebrate, especially on the left, we are more accustomed to doing without. More of us are prone to celebrate rather than to mourn the fragmentation. Some of us are even tempted, as Philip Rieff suggests, to confuse the fragmentation with culture itself.[1]

Whether we mourn or celebrate, our situation has to do with the passing of a common Christian conception of the world and all the questions this raises about whether everything is now permissible, whether society can hold together with any measure of peace, freedom, and justice.[2] It is likely that other "God-terms" are meeting a similar fate. Socialism has always been a kind of heir to Christianity, and with Christianity accumulating less and less emotional capital, the inheritance shows signs of becoming a pittance. More knowledge seems to purchase less belief: the failure of the revolution to occur where predicted and the failures of the revolutions which have occurred; the greater analytic and linguistic sophistication which makes it harder to believe that democracy, the general welfare, or the public interest are even remotely intelligible concepts, much less worthwhile ideals. The crucial failure of the proletariat god is entangled with perplexing questions about just who he is. Indeed, man himself—not just Marx's proletariat, but *any* shared conception of human nature—may be dying.

The critics I initially consider here—Amitai Etzioni, Christian Bay, Herbert Marcuse, and Henry Kariel—do not go quite so far. They are old-fashioned enough to want to put the world back together and to cling to collective visions and ideals. But they are by no means professional mourners, and they have undertaken the search for new foundations and vocabularies. If that collective vision must now be sold to the masses, and if the masses have become skeptical and sophisticated consumers and are no longer the embittered proletariat, then for maximum marketability one's language must be more modern, more congenial, and less preachy. So they couch their sales pitch in terms of what may be our last best object of devotion: our own sweet selves, however benign or perverse. In so doing, they are not without company, nor without competitors.[3]

Nor are they without precedent. Nietzsche pointed the way:

Our virtues? —it is probable that we, too, still have our virtues, although in all fairness they will not be the simpleminded and foursquare virtues for which we hold our grandfathers in honor— and at arm's length. We Europeans of the day after tomorrow, we firstborn of the twentieth century . . . *if* we should have virtues we shall presumably have only virtues which have learned to get along best with our most secret and cordial inclinations, with our most ardent needs. Well then, let us look for them in our labyrinths.[4]

Twentieth-century man may be too busy probing his labyrinths for virtues to go off into the bushes (as Nietzsche accused Kant's successors of doing) looking for this or that "moral faculty."[5] Perhaps his suspicion is that he would find nothing in the bushes but himself.

Peter Berger has put the point as follows:

What certainty there is must be dredged from within the subjective consciousness of the individual, since it can no longer be derived from the external, socially shared and taken-for-granted worlds. This "dredging up" can then be legitimized as a "discovery" of some alleged existential or psychological data.[6]

This prejudices matters by assuming that all such discoveries are inventions and by ignoring the possibility that we may discover a great deal by closely observing how and what we invent. But his basic point seems valid: what was once cosmology now shows definite signs of becoming psychology.

However, to say that individuals share the task (or glory) of dredging up their own individual certainties from their own labyrinths is to speak of sharing in a very loose and general sense. The only thing we really share, once we look within, might be our disagreements, including our disagreements concerning the nature of man. The critics I consider here are aware of this possibility. Nevertheless, there is an important sense in which they might be said to be, as Rieff expresses it, "poorly educated in the new learning." That is their willingness to generalize about human nature, to spell out what they think human beings share. This does set them apart from important if not dominant strains of modern speculation about man: for them, man is not yet dead.

Each of the following critics serves to introduce different facets of this intellectual project: Etzioni, the literature on basic human needs; Bay, the emphasis on human developmentals and the relationship of psychological and sociological modes of social criticism; Marcuse, the Freudian left and the idea of human ambivalence; Kariel, the point of views of those existentialists and existential Marxists who find little besides a radical freedom which is specifically human. The problems I see and direction in which the beginnings of solutions lie will be discussed after these critics have had their say.

Human Needs, Alienation, and Inauthenticity: Etzioni's Active Society

At the close of a lengthy book describing and recommending the "active" society, the sociologist Amitai Etzioni appears to discover a serious hiatus in his argument.[7] As he defines it, the active society is one in which the members are "conscious, committed, and hold a share of societal power." Its opposite is the alienating society (Etzioni takes the essence of alienation to be unresponsiveness), of which there have been two varieties. The first, he claims, was the alienated and alienating society of nineteenth-century capitalism. Etzioni argues that it was fundamentally unresponsive. Moreover, few of its members claimed and fewer still believed that it was responsive. The second and more recent variety is our own, the "inauthentic" society of advanced industrial states, which "generates a sense of responsiveness when in fact there is none." We are manipulated and lied to. It is, in a word, phony.

Yet Etzioni is faced with a society that is certainly busy and bustling, if not "active," and he is aware that many of its more fortunate members find their society quite responsive. He even assumes it can meaningfully be labeled a democratic society.[8] Thus he is eventually forced to search for some external point of reference and leverage with which to support his arguments that change is needed. His is a familiar dilemma. Faced with discontent and dissent, political authorities and social theorists always have the alternative of treating these as problems requiring better socialization and social control rather than problems necessitating social reform or revolution.

> There can be some lack of coordination between a society's socialization system and its productive and allocative structure or some time lag in the accommodation of personalities to changing societies; these factors could account for some unresponsiveness. But this responsiveness could, in principle, be eliminated as readily by changing socialization as by changing productive and allocative relations.[9]

Having argued that there can be such things as deviant societies, he needs a conception of what that society deviates from and how it frustrates its members no matter how effective its socialization process. He needs the concept of "basic human needs."

Etzioni's list of basic human needs apparently is derived from the literature that speculates on the existence and identity of such needs.[10] The results, apparently arrived at by collating other lists of supposed basic needs, are as follows: affection, recognition, the need for context (or meaning, or wholeness, or consistency), repeated gratification (more is better, up to a point), and two second order needs: some stability in the pattern of the distribution of rewards and some variance in the social structure. He suggests that these needs should be carefully distinguished from the wants induced by the socialization process, for reasons discussed above, and from the psychological needs common to man and animal, for reasons unclear. Thus the origin, the nature, and the exact status of the basic needs are rather obscure.

In any event the responsiveness of the active society is reformulated as responsiveness to the basic human needs of its members, and the alienation of the alienating or the inauthentic society becomes alienation from same. Somewhat tautologically, he suggests that "as a first crude approximation, it seems to hold that the more a societal structure allows for the satisfaction of the basic needs of its members, the less the structure will be alienating."[11]

Before we question how his concept buttresses his criticisms, two observations will be helpful. First, the notion of conflict between basic needs within the individual is generally either ignored or downplayed. In Etzioni's view, individuals either are not or need not be at war with themselves, despite the fact that a mere glance at his list of needs might lead you to think otherwise. Insofar as individuals *are* conflicted, the strong implication is that society is at fault. The one reference to the contrary is cursory and casual: "Complete gratification is not possible: the gratification of some needs reduces the ability to gratify others because of the limitations scarcity imposes on the capacity to satisfy even compatible needs and the devaluating effect of very frequent rewarding on the reward."[12]

The second point is that individuals, in pursuing their basic human needs, typically are not or will not be at war with others. The consideration of this possibility is also meager: "While the activation of some members of a society may increase rather than decrease the society's alienating character, we hold that if all the members of the society are activated, the society cannot help but become more responsive and authentic".[13]

The social criticisms his list of needs supposedly underpins represent a generalization of the Marxist analysis of alienation, involving not only a critique of the capitalist social structure but also of the bureaucratic institutions and the process of rationalization depicted by Weber:

> The post-modern society inherited from its predecessor an alienating structure—the product of modernity—especially industrialization, bureaucratization, and the legitimation of the priority of the logic of instruments (or "rationality"). . . . the post-modern society has added to this basically distorted structure an increased capacity for macroscopic manipulation.[14]

Such a society is alienating because it is not responsive to our basic needs; it is inauthentic because it leads us to believe otherwise. Etzioni outlines a research program designed to uncover the costs, measured in frustrated human needs, of the "structural distortions of modern and post-modern societies." On the individual level these can be assessed by methods probing the deepest layers of the personality; on the social level, by measuring the "social costs of socialization and social control."

Etzioni does not systematically relate how the present social structure violates the needs he describes, nor does he suggest which needs are shortchanged more often in more people than other needs. He does offer ad hoc hints ("To suggest that students are only transient members of a university and, hence, have no right to participate in its decision-making is not to respond to their basic need"[15]), but typically these passages do not mention what basic need is being frustrated.

There is one important exception to this silence concerning what particular needs our society frustrates. Etzioni explicitly denies that anomie, the "relative absence or confusion of values in a society or group," poses much of a problem. In this significant respect he agrees with the other critics under consideration here. "Modernization is said to have created anomie by its undermining of both micro- and macrocohesive units. We have already seen that this is not the case—that the old cohesive units have adapted and that new ones are created."[16] However, his list of needs does not totally neglect the possibility of anomie. It includes, after all, the need for context, for some stability of rewards, and for affection, all of which anomie might threaten. But once the needs are enumerated, most of the subsequent discussion concerns freedom. True, the freedom in question is the freedom to pursue goals that meet basic needs, but there is no specific discussion of the freedom to enjoy a context, for example, or the freedom to enjoy some stability of rewards: both might imply a critique of freedom as it is popularly conceived. Instead, freedom is either discussed abstractly or in ways that seem to exclude these kinds of freedoms and needs. Our community, locally and nationally, is not disintegrated, not anomic nor chaotic. It is repressive and inauthentic.

This suggests a final question: just what will we *do* in the active society? On this there is little. Perhaps the silence is appropriate, given that freedom is a large part of what the active society is all about. We do learn that "a much greater focus on symbols and on a purposive orientation is a prerequisite" for the active society. In general there will be more participation, especially at places of work, and a concomitant decrease in passive consumption, both of goods and ideas. This is because "a personal project that is materialistic and individualistic is most likely to increase inauthenticity, as it is likely to involve treatment of others as instruments."[17] Again Etzioni teeters on the brink of the tautological, and again finesses the crucial question of whether it is possible to authentically treat others as instruments.

If all this involves a series of value judgments on his part, Etzioni is reluctant to say. But in a sense it does not matter, since he contends we are already moving in this direction:

> It may be argued that the preference for a culturally and politically active life over the pursuit of consumption is a value judgment—an intellectual's projection of his preferences on the average citizen—and a Utopian projection. It should, hence, be added, first of all, that the preceding statement refers to changes which are on-going . . . . second, we hold that a society will move in the active direction as more of its members exhibit preferences for an authentic life; i.e., we expect that more people will live like intellectuals.[18]

On this happy note, let us turn to another critic.

Bay: Psychology and the Rebirth of Natural Law

Christian Bay, a political theorist heavily influenced by recent developments in humanistic or third-force psychology, believes in the "probable comeback of natural law in democratic theory."[19] Behavioralist researchers and pluralist-democratic theorists (apparently this includes practically everyone except the political philosopher Leo Strauss) have done yeoman service in demonstrating that the "classical theory of democracy is largely inoperative in the West." But in the process they have exposed their ideological slips. Lacking any reference point outside the data, they have been reduced to applauding the system for its stability and longevity. What we need instead is a "theory of democratic institutions as means to substantive ends." Referring to Strauss and his followers, Bay complains that "political philosophy . . . lately by default has become the almost exclusive domain of a neo-Aristotelian breed of political scientists."[20] So Bay suggests that we turn to our psychological knowledge of human development: "The dogmatic teachings of Strauss and his followers . . . will be replaced, or at least supplemented, by advances in research on human development."[21]

Bay's basic approach "is to analyze the proper scope and limits of majoritarianism and constitutionalism as instruments toward the maximization of individual freedom."[22] As with Etzioni, freedom is basic; its lack is the essential problem. But Bay's advocacy of freedom is constrained by his sensitivity to conflicts within and among individuals trying to exercise their freedoms, and by his admission that some individuals and groups make demands and espouse values not entirely consistent with "freedom demands" and values. Early in his argument he gives it an egalitarian twist by suggesting a distinction between human rights—freedoms which do not diminish when all share them—and privileges—freedoms which diminish as they are shared. And he repeatedly claims that humanistic depth psychology can and should guide us in determining which freedoms and rights are "more basic."

By now matters are confused, however, for it is not clear whether the distinction between human rights and unjustifiable privileges hinges on the question of the shareability of rights and freedoms or on psychological development and what thwarts or promotes it. The two approaches seem to point analysis, and with it social criticism, in two different directions. The first is a social consequences or social interaction analysis of the impact of different freedoms: the search is for freedoms that do not diminish themselves or other freedoms as we attempt to share them. This search has no obvious connection with the human needs which may be involved. By contrast the second approach tends to focus on the least free and relies on humanistic psychology to help determine what and whose needs are more basic and worthy of being met. The activities and freedoms of the more fortunate may be circumscribed or proscribed to help meet the more basic needs of the less fortunate, particularly if we can also confidently diagnose certain wants and demands of the more fortunate as being the products of sick psyches and improper development. Yet the relationship is never made clear between the freedoms that are shareable and those that are more consistent with human nature or development—between these two different approaches to declaring that some freedoms are more basic. Thus when Bay suggests that we must turn to research on the "basic, if empirically elusive, human nature," in order to determine which freedoms are basic human rights and which are privileges, some important threads of his argument are left dangling.

The solution he eventually settles on in *The Structure of Freedom* seems to give developmental psychology the back seat, in essence subjecting us to the very majoritarianism his whole human rights approach was supposed to guide and curb. He again contends that the distinction between freedoms and privileges should be based on (what I am calling) shareability and then admits that "general priorities between freedoms must ultimately be decided by majorities, however, since these are questions of value."[23] That is, he apparently abandons the effort to order freedom demands, to establish political values, by references to the stages of psychological growth. Instead, in this scenario the majority rank-orders various freedoms. Then at each stage of the process of extending these freedoms, absolute priority is given to extending a given freedom to every citizen before moving on to the next freedom in the rank-ordering.[24] Also, he specifically rejects an approach to establishing priorities among freedoms based on distinguishing sick from healthy demands, free and unfree expressions: "It is unnecessary . . . to go into the many dangerous consequences likely to ensue when a democratic government starts out on the road to discriminate between 'free' and 'unfree' opinions . . . I believe in the desirability of an equal freedom of expression, then, for 'neurotics' and 'normals' and for fanatics and skeptics."[25]

Elsewhere there are ambiguous hints that psychology will eventually provide more guidance. For example, it "will become possible to make judgments as to the comparative psychological importance of different institutional values."[26] In another passage, after restating his human rights approach to determining the proper scope and limits of majoritarianism and constitutionalism, he suggests that "as a second priority set of goals, a democracy should strive to enlarge freedom in the full sense employed here—a widening also of psychological freedom."[27] And his helpful discussion of the different dimensions of freedom (psychological, social, potential) relies in large part on humanistic psychology. Nevertheless, it is clear that he never settles the question of how psychological research is supposed to reorient democratic theory.[28]

Nor does he settle the related matter of which and whose research on human nature is most relevant and useful. At one point he argues that Abraham Maslow's conception of a hierarchy of human needs is the "best available point of departure."[29] Elsewhere he suggests using the "negative" model of stages of human development that Smith, Bruner, and White found in considering the functions political opinions serve for those who hold them. Full human development would then correspond to their stage of object appraisal, which is only possible after we are freed from ego defensive and social adjustment needs.[30] He also recommends Camus' "rebel" as a model. What all these conceptions have in common, Bay argues, is "their emphasis on man's potentiality for development," an emphasis he finds lacking in our models of the civic culture and pluralist democracy.[31]

By and large Bay has not responded to his own exhortations, and the supposed relevance of psychological research remains stuck at the stage of multiple reassertion. But he does add some important wrinkles to Etzioni's argument. The first is this idea of stages of growth toward full humanity, stages through which everyone must pass. This must be judged an improvement over Etzioni's basic needs, because the first task of any theory affirming the essential goodness of man—as both of theirs do—is to deal with his ubiquitous shortcomings and perversions. The second idea is a new slant on an old egalitarian theme: we should orient our democratic institutions toward helping others pass through these stages of development. In this way he seeks to mitigate, or at least to recognize, the conflict with equality which his pronounced commitment to expanding freedom generates, and to deepen our understanding of what it means to be deprived and unfree. His third contribution is to raise if not resolve the questions of what freedoms can be shared by all, how some freedoms collide with others, and how to handle disputes over contending "freedom values and demands." Finally, he introduces the question of the relationship between psychological analysis, particularly that of psychological development, to the analysis of the social consequences of the exercise of different freedoms, which is sociological in an important sense. The very ambiguities of his account pique our curiosity about the relationship of each of these to rational criticism of the society. What, in this important connection, can psychology tell sociology, and vice versa? And what can both contribute to social ethics and social criticism?

In Bay's view, psychological health is necessary, at the very least, to rational thought about society. In the meantime we will be plagued by "pseudopolitics," which is "activity that resembles political activity but is exclusively concerned with either the alleviation of personal neuroses or with promoting private or private-interest-group advantage, deterred by no articulate or disinterested conception of what would be just or fair to other groups."[32]

As in the case of Etzioni, little of the content of rational thought about society is revealed. But one thing is clear to Bay. The crucial aspect of the rational thought of the fully free will be a natural empathy for others: "I would start by defining 'human need' as any tendency whose continual suppression or blocking leads to pathology. . . . the destruction of self and others, whether fast or slow, presumably is . . . pathological."[33] Our most natural empathy is with the underdog: for Bay, as for Sartre, truth is in the eyes of the poor. Bay asserts that psychological well-being will free us to look them in the eye, so that the psychologically healthy, the fully free, will have a marked tendency to be outraged by oppression and injustice and to revolt against it wherever they find it. Moreover, all of us are potential rebels: "Every new human being is potentially a liberal animal and rebel; yet every social organization he will be up against, from the family to the state, is likely to 'socialize' him into a conveniently pliant conformist."[34]

Like Etzioni, Bay has no serious qualms about advocating that human needs be serviced and developed. Moving from the "is" of human nature to what ought to be done presents no problem, because both of them find so much strength and goodness in human nature itself. Nevertheless, Bay, no less than Etzioni, is a bit troubled by whether and in what way his argument is normative.[35] When the question comes up, he suggests the familiar expedient of converting it into an impeccably empirical question: whether or not we should develop in these directions, in any event it is likely that we will:

> I submit that it will help make sense of all the data reviewed in this paper if we consider Camus' rebel a developmental model—a probable type of person to develop to the extent that not only ego defensive but more mildly neurotic social acceptance anxieties are resolved or successfully faced up to . . . . the more secure and sheltered a person's infancy and childhood, and the more freedom that educational and other social processes have given him to develop according to his inner needs and potentialities, the more likely that a capacity for political rationality and independence will develop . . . . with a good start of this kind, such children may, when they approach adulthood, be able to resist the socializing of privilege-defending states, universities and other established institutional pillars of the status quo; if so, they become the student rebels, the civil rights workers, and the peace activists; a small minority, but a growing one in terms of influence among young people.[36]

And so by way of psychological developments if not by the teachings of a Strauss, natural law will supposedly stage its comeback, and democratic theory will be humanized.

Marcuse: A Biological Basis for Socialism?

It is arguable that Herbert Marcuse is out of place in this discussion because he often simply assumes the validity of leftist perspectives which the others feel obligated to underpin or justify more explicitly. He has typically used Freud to embellish or augment rather than to reconstruct or underpin Marxist theory, and just how seriously he takes Freud in either capacity is a question to which different answers might be given from year to year and publication to publication. Nevertheless he will serve us well in introducing the important phenomenon of the "Freudian left," and his intellectual gymnastics in trying to reconcile Freud with Marx are highly instructive.[37]

If Marcuse's flirtation with Freud has had its ups and downs, the basic utility of Freudian concepts to his critical project has remained constant and considerable. Like Etzioni's basic needs and Bay's developmental potentials, they provide the standard of health with respect to which a sick society can be judged sick: "As a tentative definition of 'sick society' we can say that a society is sick when its basic institutions and relations, its structure, are such that they do not permit the use of available material and intellectual resources for the optimal development and satisfaction of individual needs."[38]

The need to deal more directly and convincingly with the human material is particularly important and troublesome for those trained in the Marxist tradition. Their primary task is to explain certain overwhelming historical events—Nazism and the desertion of the Left by the German working class—and certain inescapable non-events—the virtual absence of revolutionary activity in the most advanced capitalist nation. In the process of explaining there has been a significant shift of focus: from class struggle to the struggle inside our heads, from objective class to subjective consciousness, from exploitation of the workers to the alienation of practically everyone, from class interests to general human interests. Jürgen Habermas has put the problem as follows: "The reflection that the new ideology calls for must penetrate beyond the level of particular class interests to disclose the fundamental interests of mankind *as such*, engaged in the process of self-constitution."[39] Conceivably, given the proper conception of human nature, not only can the Left interpret and justify and encourage what leftist dissent there is, but also explain its general absence and the reasons some people appear to embrace oppression. Perhaps they can render intelligible the utterly unrevolutionary average American, who would otherwise remain inscrutable to leftist émigrés. Knowing enough about human nature, they can say with Marcuse that "happiness is an objective condition" and that "only in the last analysis" can Americans judge for themselves whether they are happy, or free, or unexploited. "Do exploitation and domination cease to be what they are if they are no longer suffered, if they are compensated by previously unknown comforts? "[40] Marcuse thinks not, as one can gather from his loaded formulation of the question; and he is one of a significant minority of neo-Marxists who turn to Freud for help in convincing those who might not formulate the question in such a loaded fashion.

So as a working hypothesis Marcuse adopts Freud's final formulation of the instincts: Eros and death, a dualism at the deepest level of instinct.[41] The death instinct is typically found in the derivative form of aggression, and civilization is viewed fundamentally as a struggle between Eros, the building of ever-greater unities, and destructive aggression. But Marcuse introduces an important difference. In late Freudian metapsychology civilization borrows from Eros to bind aggression. Sexual repression, sexual in a broadly inclusive sense, increases (and with it the sense of guilt) in order to thwart aggression. Paradoxically, our sense of guilt increases as we become less guilty of actual aggression. Thus Freud viewed the history of civilization as the history of an ever-increasing sense of guilt.[42]

By contrast, in Marcuse's interpretation of the "hydraulic metaphor," repression proceeds apace with increased aggression and destructiveness. Where libidinal energy is withdrawn through sublimation, for whatever purposes, there destructive energy shall be. To keep aggression to a minimum, Eros must be liberated, even from sublimations with the best of intentions. Here Marcuse follows Wilhelm Reich, though this is inadequately acknowledged.[43] Liberated Eros also has a qualitative dimension: more varied, polymorphous sex, free from the "genital Tyranny" capitalism's Performance Principle exercises. Polymorphous is not perverse; here he departs from Reich and Freud alike. In both respects it is a familiar, congenially modern view. Saul Bellow expresses it succinctly: "The erotic must be admitted to its rightful place, at last, in an emancipated society which understands the relation of sexual repression to sickness, war, totalitarianism. . . . why, to get laid is . . . an act of citizenship."[44]

In this somewhat emasculated form, Marcuse holds fast to the Freudian dualism, however much he may have de-emphasized the antagonism of Eros and death since the gloomy days of *Eros and Civilization.* Perhaps this is because in the forseeable future analysts will need all the help they can muster in explaining the considerable aggression that remains with and in us. Now Marcuse clearly opts for Eros and its liberation. Somehow, Eros is more basic than aggression. Sadism is a perversion of love, not vice versa.

> Prior to all ethical behavior in accordance with specific social standards, prior to all ideological expression, morality as a "disposition" of the organism, perhaps rooted in the erotic drive to counter aggressiveness, to create and preserve ever greater unities of life. We . . . then have, this side of all values, an instinctual foundation for solidarity among human beings.[45]

Notice that, contrary to Freud, this passage tends to slight ("this side of all values") the instinctual foundation for division and conflict. Similarly, he speaks elsewhere of socially determined aggressive needs "sinking down" to the biological level, rather than, say, basic instinctual aggression receiving social expression, as would be more consistent with his dualistic position.[46] In another passage he argues that the revolution will be delayed until individuals change in "their very instincts and sensibilities."[47] Not only might this have the effect of delaying the revolution, it would also appear to rob the concept of instinct of much of its punch. Later on we find that freedom is instinctive as well: "Freedom is rooted in primary drives . . . . it is the vital need to enhance the life instincts."[48] But elsewhere he argues that freedom itself awaits emancipation: "Emancipation of senses would make freedom what it is not yet, a sensuous need, an objective of the Life Instincts (Eros)."[49]

Despite the vagaries of his account, in certain respects his basic position is intelligible enough. True morality is more or less instinctual. Most immorality is a product of socially-induced wants, however far these might "sink down" to the biological level. True freedom is not license but is intimately related to morality. It is "the vital need to enhance the life instincts," which probably contain a "moral disposition." And finally, true morality is disposed to be socialist.[50]

What this means is that Marcuse winds up some distance from his initial position of extolling freedom and uninhibited sexuality in carelessly general terms. Eventually he exhibits an old-fashioned preference for what, on the personality level, can only be called character, and for control and (socialist) order in society.[51] It is well known that Marcuse argues that advanced capitalism's Performance Principle (as contrasted with Freud's Reality Principle) demands Surplus Repression, much as the capitalist exacts surplus value from the output of the worker. In this way he embellishes the notion that since we are more affluent now, we need not work so hard, nor in general sublimate so much. Nonetheless, the concept of repressive desublimation also receives a great deal of attention in his writing, however muted it might be in his more popular works. Partly this is because of his understanding that desublimation can function in a repressive fashion by making the given regime all the more secure. And partly because it appears that Marcuse personally finds bread and circuses, even orgies rather distasteful.[52]

Character and self-control are especially important traits of personalities capable of dedicating themselves to the political struggle. For this reason Marcuse deplores what he sees as a growing absence of strong authority in the family. Though the "youth revolt," the "sexual revolution," and the "new cultural sensibility" obviously encouraged and innervated him, his attitude toward them quickly became ambivalent. In *Essay on Liberation*, for example, he praised the revolutionary potential of obscenity when used in ways which expose the *real* obscenities, those of the system. Two years later he writes: "another form of linguistic rebellion is the systematic use of obscenity. I stressed its supposed political potential; today, this potential is already ineffective."[53] After having flirted (in *One Dimensional Man*) with the position that logic itself is oppressive, he nevertheless argues that the radicalism of the cultural revolution is misguided because of the "anti-intellectualism which it shares with the most recent reactionary representatives of the Establishment; revolt against Reason—not only against the Reason of Capitalism, bourgeois society, and so on, but against Reason per se."[54] Having toyed with the idea that technology and technological thoughtways are inherently oppressive and destructive, and that some totally different, unimaginably new technology must take their place, he can nonetheless rather irritably exclaim:

Is it still necessary to state that not technology, not technique, not the machine are the engines of repression, but the presence, in the machine, of the masters who determine their number, their life span, their power, their place in life, and the need for them? Is it still necessary to repeat that science and technology are the great vehicles of liberation, and that it is only their use and restriction in the repressive society which makes them vehicles of domination?[55]

And he can chide Sartre and the existentialists for not recognizing that some reifications, after all, can have a liberating function—despite having misled many of his own followers on this score.

This preference for character and control extends to enemies as well as friends. Habermas offers an observation which probably applies to members of both camps: "Socio-psychologically, the era is typified less by the authoritarian personality than by the de-structuring of the super-ego".[56] Marcuse agrees, and likewise finds the fact perplexing. The new bourgeois ideology is harder to "re-flect," and therefore even its bourgeois character is in question. The new bourgeoisie has less ideological baggage, and therefore is more mobile, adaptable, and harder to pin down. It is even question-able whether they stand still long enough to stand *for* much of anything. So although Marcuse deplores guilt, he means real guilt, not the sense of it. One has the strong impression that he would appreciate meeting more American superegos with an old-fashioned sense of guilt, even if these superegos belonged to ruthless capitalists. At least their plundering might be more obvious and honest. And as for others, the better developed sense of guilt might be related, if not to revolutionary discipline, then at least to better manners.

As a Marxist Marcuse understands that one of his principal tasks is the critique of bourgeois freedom and anarchy, despite the fact that he depicts America as tightly controlled and "one-dimen-sional." Thus, after extolling freedom and condemning society in sweeping terms, he eventually affirms the necessity and desirability, even the attractiveness, of limits and controls. These include moral controls supposedly rooted in the organism and related controls necessary to putting capital and technology "in the service of the life instincts." What precisely these controls are, how much and whose repression will be involved in *their* application, Marcuse fails to say. No doubt this failure is an important key to his popularity. But it is to his credit that, after initially confusing matters, Marcuse finally affirms the crucial distinction between being truly emanci-pated and, as the saying goes, merely unbuttoned.

Kariel's "Expanded Political Present"

The political theorist Henry Kariel thinks that the "political present" is unduly constricted, and he wants to expand it.[57] His premise, the avowed basis of his social critique, is that nothing we have created, neither in religion nor politics, is really necessary. To think otherwise is to be guilty of bad faith, to do idealist violence to the world. His perspective has obvious affinities with existentialism of a Sartrean variety—plus some New World exuberance and minus some Old World gloom—and admirably displays the obstacles the leftist existentialist encounters as he moves his argument from radically free beginnings to socialist or quasi-socialist conclusions.[58]

While the basic form of his argument should be familiar from the preceding discussions, Kariel's perspective does offer a contrast with any conception of human nature that has an essentialist cast to it. The existentialist bases his social critique on his conception of the human situation, not of human nature as such. Human nature exists for him only on an irrelevantly grand level of abstraction, if at all. We need to free ourselves, as theorists and citizens alike, from basic human needs and instinctual demands, as well as institutional constraints. And presumably we can. Our human situation is that we are free, and that freedom includes forming our own conception of human nature, if we wish. Man makes, man chooses himself, his "nature." Nature, including human nature, is no guide at all, and Kariel thinks we should shout out the news. Because, first of all, such radical liberation is a fine and joyous occasion. "Everything is possible"; "reality can be appropriated"—what could be more intoxicating? —and secondly because, even though the social and intellectual world, including our conception of human nature, is obviously a human product, everyone is continually forgetting or denying the fact, as if it were frightening as well as exhilarating. Economic alienation and religious alienation are specific examples of forgetting, two among many. Intellectual alienation is another; its essence is denying or forgetting our creative role in formulating the ideas and systems we articulate.[59]

Given the pervasiveness of forgetfulness, all our products, whether social or economic institutions, intellectual constructions, or spiritual concoctions, have a tendency to confront their producers as

alien, seemingly immutable facticities. We are typically unaware of
the infinite dormant alternative realities that are ours for the
making. Like most existentialists, Kariel makes an issue of such
forgetfulness; and like most existentialists, he does not have much of
an explanation for it. He does suggest that some of us have been lied
to. Others suffer from an overdose of realities manufactured and
administered by the rich, the powerful, and their media henchmen.
These bad prescriptions keep us drugged, stupid, and submissive.

"Can men manage to act," he asks, "once they learn that nature
gives no final answer?"[60] Kariel thinks so: "Man could feel free to
make the formulas, myths, designs, languages, ideologies, and laws
that satisfied his needs."[61] Men are not really stupid: they are
burdened by an "excess of insinuating knowledge." We must help
ease the burden. We must "democratize creativity by extending and
intensifying experience." Privacy (for unexplained reasons) is
"self-destructive"; we must make a place in politics for "Protean"
man ("why settle for less?"). As social scientists our task should
be to suggest alternatives, and then "leave men alone." We should
affirm the "value of a phenomenological orientation which seeks
to give recognition to the repressed parts of the present—to causes
which are latent, unpopular, discredited, or lost."[62]

Presumably such causes are infinite in number, so Kariel is pro-
posing a heavy agenda indeed. Freedom is what it's all about, and
"there is no effort to say here: freedom for what." Thus, nothing
really being necessary, it is difficult to see how such a radical view
of freedom could justify anything other than ceaseless change.
Here again we are reminded of Sartre, for whom the epithet "bourgeois" loses much of its former Marxist reference to economic class
and economic oppression, and instead becomes virtually a synonym
for inertness and immobility. Whereas Marx's "false consciousness"
points to particular kinds of economic and political change, Sartre's
"bad faith"—any fibbing to ourselves that we are not free when in
fact we are—points us in all directions at once. This is generalization
by means of attenuation, and the price is confusion.[63]

While Kariel's argument seems to have these implications, by no
means does he actually have an infinite agenda in mind. A generous
if still ambiguous interpretation of what he is advocating is that
more people should be permitted to "appropriate" more reality

more of the time. This might involve new ways of thinking about those who are currently force-feeding ways of thinking that are so advantageous to their interests, new exposés of the ideological character of the "reality" they want us to accept. If so, appropriate the appropriators! It might even require (though Kariel does not pursue this explicitly) political action on behalf of the disadvantaged, in order to distribute the wealth more equitably: expropriating the appropriators! That is, the more closely we look at his argument, the more we see equality edging toward center-front of a stage on which freedom had been upstaging everything. Kariel may well believe that everything unconditional belongs to pathology, that convictions are prisons, and that we should avoid developing rigid superegos, constant convictions, and firm commitments whatever the cost.[64] But the pathology and prison of unfair inequalities are of particular concern to him, and he seems to be stuck with some egalitarian convictions of his own.[65]

"Reifications," he asserts, "serve to restrict politics to a few."[66] This debatable proposition requires defense but receives little. It is easy enough to interpret this statement generously, as meaning that certain reifications with which this particular society (bourgeois, or technological, or bureaucratic . . . Kariel touches all the bases) burdens us, make the race unfair and unequal. But this interpretation would require the analysis and vocabulary to become more straightforward and traditional. Instead of advocating "the democratization of creativity," we would be subjected to a tedious discussion of democratic theory. Talk of "oppressive reifications" would be replaced by discussion of more mundane oppression. Rather than inviting men to "move in and establish themselves" and "reduce self-destructive privacy," we might have to discuss the difficulties in maintaining our freedoms in the process of establishing socialist control of the economy. No doubt the resulting analysis would be altogether less zippy and modern, but then it would be easier to tell whether anything new had been said.

This is not to say that Kariel does not eventually get around to some specifics:

Men are kept underdeveloped by the dominant order of commitments: government by a plurality of elites, a functional division of labor, the distinction between private and public sectors, the system of fixed social and biological rules within hierarchical organizations, the market economy, the identification of security with military power, the achievement orientation, the separation of means from ends, and finally the organized repression of action and pleasure, of life and death, of politics and play.[67]

At times he strikes notes more recognizably Marxist, as when he suggests that "the fundamental economic institutions effectively govern the rhythm and texture, direction, and quality of everyday existence."[68] But he is also critical of these particular conceptions: "man as egotistical utility and power maximizer, public policy as interest group inputs, the economic sector as primary generator of community goods, governmental structures as hierarchical organizations, politics as a sacrifice of personal goods."[69] Nor should we "identify reality exclusively with such abstractions as 'balance of interest,' 'national honor,' 'private property.' "[70]

While this prodigious collection of criticisms is as eclectic as it is eccentric, most of them are familiar enough staples of the Left, Old and New. Despite his loose talk of appropriating reality and expanding freedoms at will, once he lists specific problems and issues he sweeps away the exhilarating fantasy that we can appropriate everything in sight and expand all freedoms of everyone at once. The obvious point, but one which certainly bears emphasis, is that fundamentally Kariel believes, like everyone else, that some freedoms of some people are more deserving of expansion. Similarly, some reifications are more pernicious or obnoxious than others. And other reifications, he implicitly suggests, may be downful useful.

Nevertheless, it may well be that Kariel has inadvertently prescribed madness for the individual and chaos or oppression for the society. Maybe individuals accept socially insinuated realities in order to avoid overdoses of raw reality. As for society: if Kariel is right that those with wealth and power currently appropriate all the reality, then his all-too-general exhortations to appropriate more reality are tantamount to open invitations to those who already possess the wherewithal to define reality advantageously to "move in and establish themselves" (in Kariel's own words) all the more securely. Others, in turn, might bridle and rebel at this. All in all, his may be a formula, not for expanding the political present, but for shrinking or even exploding it.

For the moment, it suffices to say that he has a strong tendency to undercut his own arguments. His difficulties should have a familiar ring. These representatives of what I will call the leftist literature of freedom have helped place some important items and significant dilemmas on the agenda. Let us now try to tease them out.

4 Getting the Agenda Straight

This chapter delineates what these representatives of the leftist literature of freedom have in common and suggests three important interrelated problems which plague their analyses. These problems include: their neglect of human ambivalence; their resulting focus on alienation, to the virtual exclusion of anomie; and their ambiguous account of the relationship of their conception of human nature to their social critique.

In the Beginning We Are Free

One basic similarity in their starting point has already received attention but merits special emphasis. It is that their conception of man fits squarely into what B. F. Skinner calls the literature of freedom.[1] As Skinner employs the phrase, the literature of freedom is the literature, whether fiction or psychology, which affirms and applauds the autonomy of the human subject and is hostile toward real or imagined threats to that autonomy. It is worthwhile to detail the respects in which this is true of these writers.

Throughout their analyses freedom is explicitly treated as the basic problem and concern. This is most obvious in the case of Kariel, who does not allow any generalizations about men—other than the contention that we are or should or can be free—to qualify his appeal to men to "move in and establish themselves." But this is likewise the case with the others. Etzioni, for example, begins with a very general conception of alienation as unresponsiveness. Later alienation is redefined as alienation from basic human needs, and by implication freedom becomes the freedom to pursue basic needs. Certain of these needs might seem to be irrelevant to any general call to expand freedoms—perhaps even in conflict, as I have suggested. But he goes on to stress freedom much more than the needs, especially those needs not obviously served by freedom, or by certain kinds of freedoms.

Similarly with Bay and Marcuse. The various models Bay suggests we look to are all more or less negative, suggesting what obstacles must be removed from the path to true freedom. True freedom and full humanity coincide for him. And in Marcuse's view there are no instinctual barriers to circumscribe or qualify or hedge his advocacy of freedom. Not because there are no instincts that true freedom must serve, but because freedom itself is instinctual. In both cases, the human stuff of which societies are made supposedly presents few or no impediments to their advocacy of freedom. On the contrary: it is part and parcel.

This brings us to their attitude toward society, another facet of the literature of freedom. Though their hostility is supposedly limited to certain forms of society, it is nonetheless surprisingly pervasive and uncompromising. Lionel Trilling has argued that the characteristic if not defining feature of the modern temper is that indicting society is virtually a category of thought, one of the organizing assumptions of modern knowledge and speculation. By this criterion, these critics are quite modern. They resemble those freethinkers against whom Nietzsche railed, "whose basic inclination is to find in the forms of the old society as it has existed so far just about the cause of *all* human misery and failure."[2] That this is true of Etzioni, the sociologist in the group, is interesting in light of the popular but dated conception that the role of sociologists is to demonstrate how everything that serves to maintain the given society is a good thing. But it is also important to emphasize that indicting society is logically possible for those who, like Marcuse and to a lesser extent Etzioni and Bay, postulate a basic instinctual human nature.

Approaching the matter naively, it is not clear why an emphasis on instinct should automatically lead to a conservatism and an attack on freedom, as is commonly alleged. As Trilling has written of Freud, "we must stop to consider whether this emphasis on biology is not so far from being a reactionary idea that it is actually a liberating idea. It proposes to us that culture is not all powerful."[3] A related point applies to the proposition that any doctrine of a common, specifically human nature, whether or not it is couched in terms of instincts, is a conservative agent of the social order. Without prejudging the issue, without supposing it either simple or settled, it is instructive to note that the most hideous visions of the future are typically predicated on the dubious hypothesis that human beings are utterly malleable. Yet these notions, these misconceptions, apparently underlie the antagonism most Marxists (not to mention liberals) exhibit toward anything that smacks of psychological universals. In particular this animates many of the objections to Freud.[4]

The final sense in which their work belongs to the literature of freedom has to do with their image of the society and what they castigate it *for.* I suggest that their primary focus, though not always made explicit, is on alienation, that state of unfreedom whose essence is that the individual accepts as immutable or experiences as other, separate, distant, that which is actually a human product and thus changeable, appropriable.[5] As my formulation of it suggests, their operative conception of alienation is as vague and romantic as Marx's, or even more so. (Marx repeatedly returned the discussion of alienation to the capital/labor context—after sporadically "wallowing in antitheses," as Kaufmann would have it—and in this context the analysis of alienation is much more specific and intelligible.) Without further guidance from these authors it is not always possible to determine who is supposed to be alienated from what or whom; nor is it always clear who or what are the culprits or obstacles. Kariel is deliberately vague and ambiguous: "everything is possible." Marcuse, perhaps because of his Marxist credentials, assumes that we know what he means by his general indictments of repressive bourgeois society. And while Etzioni eventually decides that alienation is actually unresponsiveness to basic human needs, he continues to operate with a very loose notion of alienation, as the unresponsiveness of social institutions to just about whatever it is anyone happens to desire.

Amid this confusion, one thing stands out with considerable clarity: society, or society as presently constituted, is at fault. As Kariel puts it, they wish to rescue us from unnecessary, socially imposed "humiliations." They characterize American society by means of images of excessive control, not images of anarchy nor chaos nor anomie.[6] Excessive, unnecessary, irrational, dehumanizing authority agitates them, not the absence of humanly meaningful authority, or the absence of all legitimate authority. Conformity disturbs them, not rampant, antisocial individualism. Socially imposed, false, arbitrary, alienated identities—not feelings of isolation or confusion, or the lack of stable identities at all. We are not ignorant because we are confused or conflicted or lacking in standards or guidelines, but because we are burdened by an excess of "socially insinuated" knowledge. We are not lonely, nor wandering aimlessly; indeed, we should be left alone more often, to find our own way. So say these representatives of the literature of freedom.

... But in the End We Are Leftist

While these writers all contribute to the literature of freedom, their contribution is of special sort. They represent what I am calling the *leftist* literature of freedom: their critiques and conclusions are leftist or liberal-leftist, however vaguely or belatedly so. The question is how a socialist order is to be reconciled with their carelessly general advocacy of freedom.

Kariel provides the sharpest before-and-after contrast. If, as he suggests, most social facts are "unnecessary," a close reading reveals that despite his feverish and sweeping indictment of society, he actually believes that some social facts, some reifications are more pernicious and humiliating than others. It is similar with Marcuse: *repressive* sublimations draw his ire; presumably there can be non-repressive, liberating sublimations, as he once suggested in criticizing Sartre. True freedom, not bourgeois freedom, is the goal; some freedoms are more desirable (more human?) than others, and the latter may have to be curtailed in order to achieve true liberation. Bay, for his part, starts out to circumscribe majoritarianisn and constitutionalism by the principle of maximizing freedoms, but then decides that some freedoms are actually undeserved privileges and should themselves be circumscribed. And Etzioni, though deploring certain kinds of control, writes a long book about an ideal society that takes charge of its own collective destiny in more substantial and profound ways than those entertained by pluralists and liberals, and "piecemeal" social engineers of all persuasions. Thus their indictment of society and social control is not absolute; nor, therefore, is their advocacy of change. Certain kinds of changes are preferred to others. And even those who proclaim to the last that "there is no effort here

to say—free for what" apparently discover that without some
glimpse of the "what" we have no way of knowing what makes us
more free. So the ultimate thrust of their critique is leftist or left-
liberal: affirming the desirability and the possibility of our society
assuming better control over its collective destiny.[7]

These collective or communal concerns are various and vague,
though when the subject comes up all affirm the central importance
of subordinating the economy to more humane purposes. Especially
vague are the means of control or coercion or persuasion by which
these objectives might be achieved. But the one common element to
their visions and proposals is egalitarianism, in one form or another.
Bay, most conscious of the tension between liberty and equality,
suggests special treatment for those who are disadvantaged because
they are in earlier stages of growth toward full humanity. The goal
for everyone remains freedom, but he wants everyone to have an
equal chance for it, and this implies preferential treatment for some.
Etzioni thinks his basic assumption (that there are common human
needs) is itself egalitarian, to the point of arguing that any doctrine
of human nature that does not affirm the existence of common
human needs is immediately open to racist interpretations (a questionable proposition). He also assumes that authentic exercises
of personal freedom will not involve the treatment of others as
instruments, and this assumption leads into the even more debatable
proposition (or escapist fantasy) that my freedom is never exercised
at the expense of yours. It is much the same with Marcuse, though
again the emphasis is primarily implicit. And there is even something
egalitarian in Kariel's ambiguous suggestion that everyone be allowed
to appropriate more reality more of the time. Whether or not their
dual emphasis on liberty and equality is compatible, eventually
both emphases are there.

There is something paradigmatically and poignantly modern about
this dilemma, this wish to have it both ways, and it seems to be
touching more and more of us. Perhaps it is the most important
facet of the dilemma of the left liberal, whose leftness typically
depends on generalized prescriptions for mankind which his liberal
side tends to deny. The recurring suspicion is that their collective
concerns and prescriptions, specifically their egalitarian concerns,

are irrelevant to their initial basic advocacy of individual freedom. Each would have us believe that the sole or primary basis of their critique is their view of human nature. But what does their individualistic psychology, with its pronounced concern with freedom, contribute to their quasi-Marxist ethics, their collective ideals?

No doubt these are questions which make many of us more than a little uneasy these days. For these critics, however, the tension is allayed by conveniently felicitous assumptions about how little conflict will remain within and between individuals once a society that speaks more adequately to our basic nature has been established.

Because It is a High-Synergy Cosmos

Harmony, within and between individuals, is not only possible, it is natural—or possible *because* it is natural. Contrary to Freud, man need not be a wolf to man. Individual interest and social duty, properly understood, need not conflict to a significant degree, at least not after the revolution. In essence these are their assumptions, and their way of finessing or obscuring a whole series of troublesome questions.

First, individuals need not be conflicted, need not work against themselves. This I infer from their omissions. There is not even much consideration of culturally induced ambivalence or conflict within individuals. Society and culture do not confuse us; or if they do, it is confusion only in that the one-dimensional roles and categories into which we are forced or finessed lead us to believe we are not actually free. Etzioni, for example, does not discuss the fact that the needs on his list are not obviously compatible with one another. Marcuse, with his initial assumption of instinctual dualism, is only a partial exception, because he renders the status of the aggressive instinct highly ambiguous by suggesting it has actually been "socially induced," having "sunk down" to the "biological level." And he generally soft-pedals the notion of internal warfare, whether instinctual or culturally induced.

Next there are two distinct assumptions which they have not distinguished very carefully. One is that the individual, in working for himself, naturally wants to work for others: good will is natural.

The second is that it is possible for him to do so: good will produces good deeds. This second assumption is one we might expect a sociologist to question first. The schism between individual intentions and social results is among the most serviceable emphases in sociological theory. Interestingly, Etzioni does not make any use of it here, possibly because of a kind of error which is more prone to occur among sociologists. This is the assumption that consensus and social conflict are inversely related.[8] The form it takes here is that if only we have the same basic needs or wants, conflict will thereby be mitigated or even eliminated. Of course the truth of such a proposition depends on the identity of the needs and wants. Not only can there be too much agreement on a bad thing (we may all agree to be rapaciously competitive) but there can also be too much of good things as well. This is one way of viewing congestion, as Thomas Schelling points out. That we share the same basic needs tells us little about whether conflict is necessarily reduced when all of us seek to fill those needs.[9] Or if it does, it is not intuitively obvious why it does.

Abraham Maslow has suggested the use of the term *synergy* to refer to the extent to which conflict is posited among men—by cultural values, or social institutions, or a doctrine of human nature, or particular goals or motives.[10] Synergy is a helpful concept because it shifts the focus from whether the individual is self-interested (or individualistic, or self-regarding, etc.) to whether, in pursuing his self-interest, he tends to defeat and frustrate others. The concept of self-interest, on the other hand, has the liability that it is capable of formal application to practically any action; the actions of an Albert Schweitzer may conceivably be self-interested, but to describe them in this way amounts to a kind of verbal-legislative fiat and is not very enlightening. Also, synergy tends to shift attention from whether actions are all of a kind to whether they can coexist and are complementary—to whether they are shareable, mutually satisfiable. It further suggests that the question of individual freedom or individualism is culturally relative. Different cultural definitions of individualism and freedom, together with corresponding social institutions, produce different results with respect to aggressiveness, conflict, and misery. A high-synergy society might be possible because human nature is high-synergetic, or because human nature is extremely malleable and we are clever enough to settle on some high-synergy cultural goals and social institutions with which to pursue the goals. A final brilliant stroke would be to call the resulting society "individualistic" or "free," if these happened to be traditionally honorific terms in our culture. Maybe there would be no way for anyone to tell the difference.

In the main, however, our critics prefer to get their synergy naturally, though Bay is a partial exception. Synergy is illogically associated with the fact that we all must work with basically the same human material. Moreover, the critics apparently assume that synergy on one level of society is positively correlated with synergy on other levels: contrary to Freud, we do not shower kindness on our friends only to rain destruction on our enemies. In short, the Golden Rule is desirable because it is an expression of human nature; not, as Freud maintained, because nothing could be more foreign to it. The desire for justice is not a reaction-formation. A socialist society is desirable because it will give a more adequate expression of our basic inclinations—not because nothing could be farther from our basic bestiality, nor because our nature is so undetermined that we would otherwise continually wreak havoc by accident.

But Will Nature Really Guide Us?

I have discussed how far these representatives of the leftist literature of freedom travel from their psychological beginnings to their social criticisms and prescriptions and how the journey is facilitated by pleasant though somewhat problematic assumptions about the enlightened way in which true freedom will be exercised. I want now to come full circle and return to their starting point, first focusing on how they got there and then on how or whether their views of human nature lend force to their critiques.

I have suggested that the origin, the derivation, and the status of the human material they postulate are not clear. We have seen that Etzioni deliberately severs his list of needs from both the biological and the social sciences; he extracts a list from previous lists of others who have speculated about human nature. Marcuse comes closer to a tighter definition of instinct by treating it as a biological, pre-emptory drive seeking one specific (sexual) outlet—but only in certain passages. Elsewhere he backs away by treating the whole Freudian apparatus as metaphorical. At one point he even complains about the instinctual plasticity that society is forever exploiting.[11] Bay attempts to derive our knowledge of developmental potentials from empirical observations of actual behavior. Following Maslow, the idea is to carefully observe the kinds of choices which are made . . . by the good choosers.[12] Like Maslow he admits that there are alternative paths to different potentials, and that some people just do not want to move at all. But he never justifies going all the way down the path to full humanity, nor is the direction of that path entirely clear. Kariel's apparent position is that everyone can be free and that moreover this is our most ardent desire. He does not concern himself with the ubiquitous exceptions, with people who wish to escape their burdensome freedoms, nor with the question of which wish, to find freedom or to escape it, is a perversion of which.

Philip Reiff, echoing Durkheim, has bluntly contended that "no doctrine of human nature has yet indicated its independence from the social order in which it has appeared."[13] The very words which are used to present our doctrine of human nature and argue its independence from the society are culturally derived. Nothing highlights the difficulty better than the fact that the critics' work has been prompted and to some extent legitimized in a specific cultural setting, by the eruption of leftist dissent in the middle and late sixties.[14] That dissent, that change in cultural climate, has made the language of basic needs, the notion of essential human qualities, the idea of the comeback of natural law in psychological guise, much more common and respectable.

So it is questionable whether anyone can obtain knowledge of human nature that is independent of society and its socialization processes. There is little doubt that in the strict sense this is impossible, but it would indeed be interesting if we found some universal invariants from individual to individual, culture to culture. As Yankelovitch and Barrett put the question: what can we know about an individual whom we do not know? As a member of the human race and not of a particular family or social location within a given culture? Possibly the only generalizations must be purchased by means of attenuation: for example, it is human nature to bewilder us with the variety of its manifestations.

And what can we do with a doctrine of human nature, once we have it? Why should basic human needs be met? The very word *basic* alerts us, on the one hand, to the possibility that we are being presented with a "persuasive definition," and on the other, to the existence of competing notions of our needs. But suppose that we could demonstrate the existence of some basic invariant human qualities. It would still not be clear why society should not try to frustrate or subordinate these human qualities rather than service them more adequately. Independence from society, in this sense, is not superiority. We might be able to say that under certain conditions it is more expedient or efficient to take account of basic needs, but this does not entitle us to say it is a moral obligation.[15]

This objection might not obtain, however, if our invariants included ways of thinking about *moral* questions. In this case moving from human nature to moral obligations would involve displaying the invariant elements of morality (or our thinking about moral questions) which had been before us all along.[16] Even the Kantian imperative may prove to have a hidden empirical base; all these critics seem to assume something of this sort, and it plays an important if unacknowledged role in their critiques. But once again there is the strong possibility that, in the very nature of the enterprise, we inevitably read our conception of the good into our conception of what human beings find basically good. Perhaps, as Nietzsche suggested, we are condemned to discovering our inventions.

Despite these deep difficulties in pursuing a cross-cultural, transhistorical conception of human nature, I consider the enterprise both meaningful and important.[17] But I shall argue that these representatives of the leftist literature of freedom have propounded a view of human nature and freedom that fails to take sufficient account of human ambivalence, that peculiar tendency of our most important human truths to come in apparently contradictory pairs; that this, in turn, results or is reflected in their neglect and underestimation of anomie and its relationship to alienation; and that both of these difficulties help confuse the question of whether and to what extent appeals to human nature lie at the basis of their critical perspectives. I shall also sketch the alternative analysis implicit in these criticisms.

In the meantime we have been introduced to modern echoes of a kind of Enlightenment faith. This time around, however, the faith has more to do with our basic human potential to "self-actualize", or with "life instincts awaiting liberation" than with exercising the power of sovereign Reason or pursuing a tedious analysis of the secrets of capitalist accumulation. This time around, natural law and democratic theory will be more securely underpinned by knowledge of basic needs and psychological laws of development, and we may learn to discharge our responsibilities to others by first being responsive to our own innermost selves. No one knows for sure what personal certainties will be dredged up in the process, nor what this new liberated man of theirs will *know*. But since they are convinced his learning and liberation are crucially dependent on his "getting himself together" in one sense or another, let us pull ourselves together and proceed.

5 Ambivalence, Alienation, and Anomie

As we have seen, one of the crucial aspects of the leftist literature of freedom concerns the focus on alienation. I contend that such a focus contrasts significantly with an emphasis on anomie, its threat or presence. Since Marx and Durkheim alienation and anomie have often been confused, both with each other and, as Nisbet has suggested, with timeless metaphysical yearnings that no conceivable society could accommodate. It will nevertheless be most helpful to resurrect and carefully scrutinize the opposition between Marx's concept of alienation and Durkheim's concept of anomie.[1] If—as our critics, following Marx, suggest—alienation implies excessive or illegitimate social control and the denial of individual autonomy and self-realization, then anomie involves the sociological state of rulelessness, and subjective anomie, the feelings of isolation or confusion or egoism or loneliness associated with this absence or confusion of normative guidelines. What I suggest is that much (though not all) of our alienation can be regarded as a protection against anomie, once both phenomena are suitably reinterpreted; and that because or as a reflection of human ambivalence, we are all vulnerable to both these seemingly opposite maladies.

Before leaving our left-liberal critics it should be pointed out that it is easy to see why they avoid the proposition that we are often alienated as a protection against the anomie we fear. There is obvious conservative potential here, and its conservative uses are well documented. This suggests that we may need or even enjoy our chains, and it thereby appears to absolve society of any responsibility for our imprisonment. We are lied to; but maybe we fib to ourselves that the lies are true, or develop conveniently faulty memories. We are coerced and manipulated and constrained; but we do need guides and guidelines. In short, we may have very human reasons for forgetting that "nothing we have created . . . neither in religion nor politics nor literature," is really necessary: it may be

humanly necessary to do so. There may be human inhibition and inertia and submission, as well as social unresponsiveness and oppression.

If the alienation they deplore is a human response to anomie, this
might prove fatal to their social critique, or indeed to any social
critique. Perhaps this is their intuition. I will argue, however, that
the reverse is more nearly true, and that those concerned with
human freedom must pay more attention to our ambivalent interest
in freedom. But I will also argue (beginning with chapter six) that
human nature is a less certain guide than they sometimes assume. Already we have seen that these critics, particularly Bay, occasionally
offer arguments and experiment with modes of analysis that have no
immediate or obvious connection with human nature and what is
humanly satisfying, and instead deal with the question of what
freedoms and goals are shareable. Knowledge of what a conception
of human nature cannot tell us might prove to be a most important
kind of knowledge, especially for the social critic.

As for what it *can* tell us, I propose that we approach this question
indirectly, by means of a look at our most human habit of drawing
distinctions and positing opposites. Since classical Greece and until
recently in the history of Western thought, the fundamental faith
in opposites and opposite values has been generally shared by the
lowliest commoners and the keenest metaphysicians.[2] The com-
moner may be forgiven for not always recognizing this intellectual
kinship, given the often arcane qualities of metaphysics and the
personal eccentricities of the metaphysicians. Indeed, Nietzsche
accused Kant of setting out to prove to the common man that the
common man is right, but in a way calculated to mystify him.
While my purpose here is not to mystify, I will nevertheless suggest
that those common men and metaphysicians who hold such a faith
are, in an important way, deeply wrong—at least as concerns the
nature of human nature. Less mysteriously: I wish to explore what
distinction-making and the positing of opposites might tell us about
our human, emotional repertoire; to explore the emotional corre-
lates of this most primitive thought-act. The result of this inquiry is
the notion of humanly general ambivalence, and the effort to think
of human nature in terms of apparently opposite tendencies or
qualities whose simultaneous presence is difficult yet crucially im-

portant to affirm. Among the most salient oppositions, I argue, are precisely those apparently opposed concerns that underlie our concern with alienation and anomie. In this way the notion of human ambivalence connects with the reinterpretation of alienation and anomie as opposites. Then I proceed to discuss some of the reasons we fail to appreciate the presence and implications of common shared ambivalences and suggest a conception of psychological development that stresses the "self-overcoming" of these inevitable personal polarities.

Primal Contradictions and Primal Ambivalence

At this point I am not concerned with the genesis or developmental aspects of the process of distinction-making, nor with the question of which cultures emphasize which distinctions to what extent. Nor am I suggesting that our emotional realities necessarily cause the distinctions we observe or distinction-making in general. Instead, my approach is purely descriptive, and many of the connections I draw between the way we think and the way we are may be, or seem to be, the product of free association. But at this late post-Freudian date we should not delude ourselves by thinking that free association is perfectly free.

The description, or series of free associations, concerns the emotions and desires that attend our human tendency to make distinctions and thereby to populate our world with self-identical things: a modest exercise in the psychoanalysis, if you will, not of particular things, but of our tendency to attribute "thinghood" to our world. Alternatively, a psychoanalysis of distinction- and opposition-making: not only why particular differences make a difference for us, but why differences do. Putting it the first way highlights what might be called the integrative aspect; the second emphasizes differentiation. Thinking about thinking in terms of these apparent opposites may be both appropriate and unavoidable, given the way we think.

Whatever particular or bizarre way we might conceive of our world, it is a thingful world that we must conceive. For all A, in our particular view of the world, A is equal to A. Any particular A may not survive a change in perspective or taxonomic scheme, but "thinghood" or "thingness" does, and this seems intimately bound up with our ability to reason.[3] As a matter of logic, we conjure up a universe in which, for all A, A and not-A are mutually exclusive: the equality of A to itself implies and depends on the equality of the not-A to itself. How might we describe what we have done when we set A equal to itself? What might this reveal about us?

We might begin by describing this thought-act as integrating (or equalizing, synthesizing, unitizing), in that we impose a possibily fictitious unity or identity on what was previously formless. It is as if we had requested or even demanded the component parts of A to subdue themselves, to behave to whatever extent is necessary to maintain the fiction of A's essential unity. Of course it is permissible to name the component parts or allow them to assert themselves so long as they do not get out of hand. These component parts would themselves have to get their component parts to behave, and so forth. As Nietzsche said, all equality is an equality of cooperation and organization.

Yet the cooperation and organization are Janus-faced. Again, the equality of something to itself depends on the existence of a self-identical not-that-something (perhaps an opposite, or a whole collection of different things). So this is cooperation and organization, too: we require that A's external boundary be respected both by not-A and by A. Thus in setting A equal to itself, in integrating or pulling A together, we simultaneously perform an act of differentiation or separation: we have applied the knife, as Pirsig puts it, and have distinguished A. Thus we appear to integrate by differentiating, and vice versa. We *distinguish* things; we distinguish *things*.

Now let us have another go at it, employing terms more emotionally rich and resonant, with a view to what distinction-making and the reactions it provokes may reflect about us. Suppose we say, with Nietzsche, that the essential feature of our thought is to make equal and familiar what may actually be formless and always new. If our most primitive thought-act is to attribute thinghood where previously there may have been none, to set something equal to itself, then it is only reasonable to suppose that this reflects an interest in equality, unity, order, security, familiarity. These concepts, and the reader can supply additional ones, do suggest and resonate with each other. Perhaps they can be put in a still broader context. The prejudice of reason, Nietzsche writes, is "to posit unity, identity, permanence, substance, cause, thinghood."[4] This *hemiplegia* of our knowledge (as he once referred to it) is apparently universal, and the psychological universals that underlie it, whatever we may name them, conjure up a creature cowering in abject terror in the face of a constant threat of chaos, disintegration, anomie.

But hemiplegia is only half the story. We have already seen that in creating the equal we simultaneously create or assume the unequal. Differentiation and separation are always involved in making equal. From this point of view Nietzsche's oft-repeated contention that "the inventive force that invented categories labors in the service of our needs, namely our need for security . . ." itself appears one-sided.[5] How can we defend this subordination of inventive forces to our need for security? Why not say that our taxonomizing labors in the service of our need to assert ourselves, to reach out, to invent—to be autonomous, perhaps. The order that we establish may be merely the tool of our need for invention, rather than our invention being the tool of our need for order. This, too, rings true.

In similar fashion we can view the postulate of causality, or our readiness to employ it, as a quest for familiarity, for order, for security. It can be thought of as a kind of dynamic analogue of our belief in things. Its purpose is "to fit the new material into old schemes."[6] If everything is actually new, and changing to the point of there being nothing distinct left to change, then our taxonomies, our logic, our belief in causes, would represent, as Nietzsche said, a kind of *ressentiment* against reality, suggesting a conservative, defensive posture on our part.

Yet ressentiment is certainly a prejudicial term with which to discuss the prejudices of reason. The equality (or familiarity, order, and so forth) that we posit is itself presumably new—an imposed, asserted equality of familiarity. So if we try to designate whatever it was that characterized the situation before we arrived with our equality, our order, our causes, our taxonomies, as a situation of becoming, then the paradox is that we can only conceive of imposing being on becoming as *itself* a kind of becoming. And Nietzsche admits as much. Viewed in this way, then, ours is a more offensive, assertive, outreaching posture. Once again we have come full circle.

Let us pause for a moment. It is a peculiarly modern mess, this cursed self-conscious inability to make any of our distinctions really stick. We make distinctions—here, concerning distinction-making itself and what this says about human beings—yet we do not really believe in the differences. We postulate oppositions only to see them dissolve into one another before our coldly modern Oedipal stare. After our short-lived delight, a kind of vertigo or nausea ensues, and to combat it we make new distinctions, posit new opposites, in that self-conscious way that increases the anxiety and virtually assures their short-lived authority. We draw our lines about what is me and what is you, what is individual and what is social, what is reason and what is emotion, mind and body . . . yet we cannot stop the traffic across these boundaries. And, if we are honest, we have increasing difficulties ignoring it, despite our obvious wish to do so. Whether we see and think truth in ones, twos, or fistfuls, we see and know too much to be really fooled. We begin to suspect, with Nietzsche, that our truth, the truth of irrefutability, says as much about our limitations as it does about the truth. It is a Protean universe, to repeat Hannah Arendt's poignant complaint, "where everything at any moment can become almost anything else."

But enough. I assume we will stay afloat, if at all, by simultaneously affirming the necessity of distinctions and oppositions, and our inability to ever consciously "think" contradictions—but also by recognizing their necessary limitations and disturbing as well as comforting qualities.[7] We may have to cultivate a lack of seriousness, a playfulness about our distinctions, in order to avoid getting stuck with a set of rigid, false and inhuman distinctions, or in that swamp of cynicism and unintelligibility in which no differences are seen in any distinctions. On the other hand, getting out must necessarily involve the deft use of helpful distinctions, as for example between dwelling momentarily in this mess and wallowing in it. Distinction-making is the way we progress, we distinguish ourselves.

So I submit that reflecting on the process of distinction-making and our reactions to it—and to the fantasized extremes of a rigidly

fragmented, divided world on the one hand, and an undifferentiated, primordial muck on the other—suggests that human nature is
fundamentally, primally ambivalent. Or rather: it suggests that we
should try to think of it in terms of apparently contradictory needs
and tendencies. Paradoxically, it may be precisely because reality,
or what is most human, does *not* know any distinctions, much less
our distinctions and oppositions, that we must try to maintain the
simultaneous truth of apparently contradictory truths about ourselves. Because we must necessarily traffic in distinctions and oppositions; apparently we have no alternative.[8] In the interest of being
more fully human, we may have to actively combat an equally
human myopia induced by our distinction- and thing-making. In
order to avoid seeing things too distinctly, too clearly—too *soon*—we
may have to cultivate a kind of multiple vision. And for crucially
human matters: double vision.

Why double vision? Human truth does not come exclusively in
opposed pairs, nor in the set of permutations of these pairs. Certainly it does not come in one such pair. Still, many significant
human truths seem to, at least in Western culture. Why should this
be so? What are dualisms affectively charged, alternately seducing
and disturbing us? Why, indeed, do some concepts have opposites,
or near-opposites, and others do not? What, in any case, is an opposite?

Dictionaries are not much help. Evidently opposites are things
that emphatically and adamantly insist that they are not each
other.[9] In order for any *A* we designate to stay equal to itself, I
suggest, it requires the cooperation of the not-*A* (whether not-*A*
is an opposite or a whole host of other things). But opposites are
special in that they depend heavily on each other for their existence,
as if they fed on or off each other. Viewed psychoanalytically, they
look suspiciously like mutual reaction-formations against the truth
of the other: things we have trouble keeping straight, separate, so
we take special notice of their difference. So when there is more at
stake, humanly speaking, opposites are likely to be postulated or
employed.

What this implies is that we will be more prone to rigidly oppose
this truth to that truth, and thus to exclude important opposite

human truths, precisely when we are dealing with important human truths. Or, given our confusion and ambivalence in the matter, to oscillate between rigidly held opposites. When not so much is at stake, we do not need to protest so much, and thus we can be more playful, pragmatic, nimble-footed and sophisticated in multiplying and employing fine distinctions and dispensing with opposites. Paradoxically, we may have less trouble keeping straight those distinctions that make less difference to us. I would therefore expect a rough correlation of concepts which have opposites; concepts touching on important human truths; and concepts (opposites) which, the harder and more honestly we scrutinize them, the harder they are to keep straight. Oppositions and dualisms may be, not of the essence of being human—on the contrary—but our crude essential way of attempting to express the essence, at least with the grammatical tools available to us in this culture. Maybe it is precisely because we are *not* primally ambivalent that we need to think of ourselves this way, to entertain primal contradictions.

But which ambivalence, which opposition? There is no shortage of candidates, nor followers of each, for whom this or that difference makes all the difference in the world. Nevertheless, I suggest that the concerns I have uncovered in scrutinizing human distinction-making are crucially human. These include, on the one hand, the wish to distinguish, to separate, to assert and realize oneself; and on the other the desire to belong, to be included, to make and be equal; the desire for the secure, the orderly, the familiar.[10] Moreover, I contend that these are precisely the opposed human concerns that underlie and animate our concern with alienation and anomie, respectively. Either we are ambivalent creatures to the very core, and subject to apparently opposite maladies of alienation and anomie, or we must necessarily try to think of ourselves in this unaccustomed and uncomfortable way.[11]

The idea that alienation and anomie are opposite maladies is not altogether new to the careers of these concepts, although anomie, if it is distinguished from alienation at all, is usually regarded as a variety or dimension of alienation.[12] What is new here, and controversial, is to see these opposed maladies in the context of human ambivalence, and to see the desire to "self-overcome" or accommodate personal polarities at the bottom of these concerns. Walter Kaufmann apparently puts forward a version of the first idea in his critique of Marx's treatment of alienation.[13] Kaufmann argues that in most of his writings Marx implicitly defined alienation as the antonym of autonomy and self-realization, and that he misled himself in doing so. Not only did this mean that Marx stretched the term to cover what might be more usefully labeled dehumanization or moronization, but it had the further effect of seducing Marx with the notion that when alienation, again in the sense of self-alienation from one's productive and creative powers, is eliminated, no sense of isolation or insecurity from others or from the culture will remain. And this seems to imply that anomie also is reduced as alienation is reduced—which is probably another way of saying that Marx failed to distinguish the two concepts.

If the quest for self-realization and autonomy is in fact the positive aspiration behind our concern with alienation (as I believe it is, and as Marx seems to treat it), then reducing this self-alienation may well increase the sense of isolation and distance from the many members of that self-alienated, conformist, uncreative crowd (who may experience far less alienation than we do from pop culture, its mindless pap, and from each other). As self-alienation decreases, anomia or isolation or marginality may increase. But to simply state (or implicitly assume, as Kaufmann does) the opposition of alienation and anomie and be done with it is to be done with only half of it. To do so ignores our interest in combating both anomie and alienation, and the necessity of doing so simultaneously. It ignores the practical, political, and theoretical tasks of taking both seriously. And finally it ignores significant areas of human experience in which we do simultaneously speak to both kinds of concerns and combat both kinds of maladies: as in friendships and loving relationships in which the very basis of the relationship is an appreciation of differences; as when social roles and social order help provide the security without which we could not be so bold; or when we use social roles and institutions as vehicles for our creativity and self-realization, giving up our freedom on one level only to have it returned with interest on another; or when submission to legitimate authority is a means of fending off illegitimate authorities, and so on.

Marx appears to make the opposite mistake, in effect *assuming* a reconciliation of concepts and needs that must be *achieved*. (This is an example of what Erich Fromm calls a "regressive" or "downward" union, as opposed to a true synthesis. It does not respect the integrity and thus the apparent opposition of the parts—in this case alienation and anomie, and the opposed human needs they reflect and symbolize.) This has nothing directly to do with the proletarian revolution, or the advent of the communist utopia. While the revolution might improve the prospects of overcoming both anomie and alienation, the theoretical and practical task of doing so would remain. So if a handful of theorists—Lukes, Hortan, Verder, Kaufmann—take the opposition of alienation and anomie too seriously, then Marx, and most Marxists, neo-Marxists, liberals, and conservatives alike, do not take it seriously enough.[14]

What needs to be done is to place this opposition in the context of human ambivalence, as revealed by our vulnerability to and our desire and attempts to overcome both maladies. If autonomy and self-realization are indeed the goals, then we will not seek to "extirpate" (as Nietzsche put it) our communal-conservative needs to belong, to be included, to feel at home—but rather to tame, use, and accommodate them so that they will follow us henceforth "like good servants." Otherwise, when unacknowledged and unsatisfied, they will likely dog our every step in pursuit of autonomy and make us more vulnerable to those conformist, consuming, patriotic pseudocommunities that are the very antithesis and nemesis of self-realization. If both kinds of needs, to belong and to distinguish ourselves, are crucially human, then we must concern ourselves with the kind of community in which what is shared is itself the basis for the toleration, appreciation, and even encouragement of individual differences and individual transcendence of received social roles, institutions, and realities. That is what the liberal democratic community, as I shall call it, is all about.

I will try to show that these hackneyed categories, looked at in this unconventional way, still have a great deal to contribute to social criticism and to democratic theory. Yet even if we could somehow agree that the particular split or ambivalence I have discussed is fundamental, or even that all others could be satisfactorily sub-sumed under it, we would still have reason to suspect the splitting itself is fundamentally in error. Or that there is something basic in us that protests as well as engages in the splitting. For we may have intruded upon what was essentially a unity or continuum by our very way of thinking about it; and our inability or unwillingness to seriously consider or characterize ourselves in terms of one such polar attribute without invoking its apparent opposite heightens our suspicions.[15] And once again: the more humanly important an opposition is—like alienation and anomie, and the opposed human needs reflected in the wish to overcome both—the more prone we will be to err by choosing one of these polar truths at the expense of the other.

But if there are some needs that are crucially human, we need to think of and discuss them in terms of these contradictory attributes whose simultaneous truth seems difficult or impossible to affirm. This is the profound and exhilarating insight behind Nietzsche's contention that all opposites derive from one another.

And disturbing as well. In suggesting that we are, at bottom, con-tradictory creatures, that we must attempt to simultaneously affirm apparently contradictory human truths, we apparently have pushed the modern desire not to be fooled to the point of not wanting to be fooled by our very criterion of foolery. In the face of the resulting anxiety, the possibly pernicious Dionysian implications of such notions—and mindful of those who, dwelling on similar truths have achieved only confusion and unintelligibility at best[16]—it is tempting to once again fool ourselves in the usual, defensive, time-honored way, by applying the knife to our image of man by radi-cally segregating our opposed attributes. There is this human truth and that one, the truth of alienation and the truth of anomie, in-dividual truth and communal truth, the truths of Marxism, liberal-ism, conservatism. Or our world, our conception of ourselves and others can be split in additional, not yet imagined ways: after all, is this not the way we think, proceed, progress?

in the beginning when the world was young there were a great many thoughts but no such thing as a truth. Man made the truths himself and each truth was a composite of a great many vague thoughts. All about the world were the truths and they were all beautiful. The old man had listed hundreds of truths in his book. I will not try to tell you all of them. There was the truth of virginity and the truth of passion, the truth of wealth and of poverty, of thrift and profligacy, of carelessness and abandon. Hundreds and hundreds were the truths and they were all beautiful. And then the people came along. Each . . . snatched up one of the truths and some who were quite strong snatched up a dozen of them. It was the truths that made the people grotesques. The old man had quite an elaborate theory concerning the matter. It was his notion that the moment one of his people took one of the truths to himself, called it his truth, and tried to live his life by it, he became a grotesque and the truth he embraced became a falsehood.[17]

The old man's truths became falsehoods as a result of their false opposition to, their separation from other truths. Taking "their" truth too seriously they took their other, contradictory truths, and thus themselves not seriously enough. This in turn was the basis for not taking one another seriously. In psychoanalytic terms, their truths, their separate sides, were compartmentalized, with inadequate or no communication with one another. When carried to excess this can be regarded as grotesque and schizoid, and such schizophrenia is a disease that menaces both individuals and cultures. It produces divisions between the Sorels and the McNamaras, as political theorist John Schaar puts it. That is, such opposites can be unhealthy and destructive, and there is good reason to believe that they depend on each other for their existence.

No one knows who will live in this cage in the future, or whether at the end of this tremendous development entirely new prophets will arise, or there will be a great rebirth of old ideas and ideals, or, if neither, mechanized petrification, embellished with a sort of convulsive self-importance. For of the last stage of this cultural development, it might well be truly said: specialists without spirit, sensualists without heart; this nullity imagines that it has attained a level of civilization never before achieved.[18]

But this is not for us good Westerners, as Nietzsche would say. We must imagine those specialists and sensualists in illicit alliance, stalking the land and spreading destruction and misery. And we must imagine that they will do so roughly in proportion to their radical innocence of the fact that all of us carry both the specialist and the sensualist around in us.

Ambivalence, Its Vicissitudes, and Its Accommodation

Failing to appreciate the implications or even the presence of common shared ambivalences probably stems, first, from the complexity and variety of sociocultural contexts and vehicles in which they can be expressed and compartmentalized; and second from our desire, born ultimately of the need to escape anomic terror, to present excessively simple (or precise, certain or secure) images of ourselves and others, to ourselves and others. And indeed, to believe them. The two can go hand in hand. A complex society may effectively segregate different personal polarities in space and time, thereby contributing to simplistic notions that this man is completely independent, another lacks all normal feeling, and so on. Social complexity is also *utilized* by various psychic mechanisms, like projection and displacement—ways of helping us appear more simple than we are. Thus Nietzsche said, we take our rest.

In order to take his rest, the individual may employ a number of psychological devices. First, he may project: that is, attribute something that is his to someone or something else. He may project his freedom, his independence, his creativity, his potency onto his God, his car, his technology, or his president, or perhaps onto all of these at once. His weakness and dependency and submissiveness he may attribute to blacks, or women, or children, or dogs. Projection can be viewed as a way of indulging in something without getting caught, even by oneself. And if the impulse or need that is involved is sufficiently weak, then vicarious thrills may suffice.

Next, think of the sum total of fantasies counter to what we are actually doing or thinking, counter to the way we see or define ourselves—and more generally counter to the way we think, and the distinctions and oppositions that are thereby produced. Think of all this as the unconscious. It may receive expression in daydreams, nightmares, projections, slips of the tongue, and so on. The careful clinician will even be tempted to postulate it, name it, and file it away in some handy and secure and simple location. But it is not a thing, nor a receptacle, nor is it located anywhere.[19] Instead, it is an attempt to avoid the denial of our human rights by mentally rein- stating the contradictory desires and truths we have repressed. More- over, the unconscious is not inaccessible to consciousness, not by definition at least. It is a matter of just how smug we are about the adequacy of our consciousness, how ignorant of the limitations of conscious, differentiating modes of thought. The unconscious can be a form of revenge that reality visits upon anyone who takes his particular, differentiated view of reality too seriously. One im- portant way of taking ourselves not seriously is to take too seriously our often simplistic image of ourselves and the differentiated mode of thinking such images reflect.[20]

Finally, there is the related principle, long the stock-in-trade of dramatists, poets, and writers of fiction, that one must be suspect if one protests too much: that is, the best place to find negatives is behind exaggerated positives, and vice versa. Following Slater, let us think of this by expressing a person's ambivalence—say, between independence and dependence needs—in terms of percentages.[21] If the person has a preponderance or majority of independence needs (say 75 percent /25 percent), we might expect his dependence needs to be expressed in limited, specific, well-defined contexts—at home, for example, or at parties—the better to be free of them in the business and bureaucratic world, where they might be inappro- priate and might trap him. He may appear to integrate these appar- ently contradictory qualities into a coherent identity, so that their opposition is apparently overcome, so that he seems to us much more, and much more consistent, than the mere sum of these contradictions. An equally stable pattern might obtain were he to have a preponderance of dependence needs, though this might mean he would appear less than manly in many contexts. The key to stability in either case is, as Slater points out, the decisive relative strength of one of the affects or tendencies. A person who knows he is this, and not that, often is more tolerant of that which is in in him and others. He tends to make less rigid distinctions between the two qualities and between "this" people and "that" people. He is less likely to bore us and arouse our suspicions with elaborate protest that he is emphatically not like that, not like them.

But a curious thing happens as we approach a situation of even strength of the affects. The affect in the slight majority is exaggerated, perhaps in both word and deed; the person has less and less ability to express the apparently large minority directly. As Slater has suggested, it is as though the majority were tyrannizing the minority because of the minority's strength, appropriating that strength while forbidding any direct participation in the regime. And as we move still closer to an apparent position of equal strength, the minority gets increasingly unruly (that is, from the psychoanalytic observer's point of view) and increasingly inadmissable to the person himself. We see the security or authority he craves in his protestations of extreme independence, or his exaggerated and conveniently abstract emphasis on personal freedom, especially if we watch closely for allied phenomena of displacement, scapegoating, and projection. He may be prone to alternating between apparent extremes or behaving radically different in different contexts. In many respects these extremes resemble each other more than anything else; they also depend heavily on one another. (To use the familiar example: the censor and the pornographer seem to have more in common with each other than with those who, whatever their position on pornography, are not particularly agitated over the issue. Their common interests, up to and including keeping each other employed, are scandalous.) Our most rigid self-conceptions and self-distinctions are precisely those we have the hardest time keeping straight; the rigidity and the brittleness aggravate one another, and are of a piece.[22] Indeed, I suggest that our conceptual and emotional oppositions are intimately related, and that this phenomenon is characteristic of all our most precious distinctions and sacred oppositions, whether or not these are directly concerned with self and self-conception.

Of course if the excessive extremes are avoided, then a great deal of unidirectional, single-minded energy can be derived from the resultant flattening or one-dimensionalization of motivation, experience, reality. Once again the advantage lies not merely in having a focus, or a simple identity, or well-defined goals, though none of this should be underestimated. The utility of our false conceptions of self and others also derives from the fact that the action on the basis of these ideas can be fueled by the suspicion that they are not really true!—quite a bonus to receive because of our errors. No doubt this is the way the West was won, by good cowboys from obviously bad Indians, though admittedly the bonus was one-sided.

As the example suggests, the social consequences of such hemiplegia might be pernicious indeed, irrespective of what the effect on the individual might be. Yet it is likely that those who attempt to deny their contradictory natures will not rest easy, entirely aside from whether they allow others to rest in peace. Not recognizing or coping with ambivalence involves three interrelated problems: the choice of means and goals contradictory to ambivalent needs, to the sides of our ambivalence we repress; the inferiority of substitute gratifications of contradictory needs, whether these are sought through vicarious thrills, projections, or whatever; and the resulting problem of sheer manageability.

In light of these problems the image of the individual who does accommodate himself or is accommodated, begins to emerge. Accommodation implies a mode of psychic economy whereby we attempt to make servants of all our conflicting impulses rather than futilely trying to destroy any of them:

> Overcoming of the affects?—No, if what is implied is their weakening and extirpation. But employing them: which may also mean subjecting them to a protracted tyranny. . . . at last they love as good servants and go voluntarily wherever our best interests lie.[23]

As to how these affects, whatever their nature, will manifest themselves, there is little certainty. We have every reason to believe that, as Philip Rieff has put it, man has the terrible capacity to express everything. Whatever affects we may have, and however few in number, it is indeterminate how they will receive expression, at least prior to specifying what social-institutional channels are available to us. We have, in this sense, an unfortunate lack of instinctual guidance.[24]

But as to the *kinds* of affects, I suggest that we can say more. For Rieff (and even Nietzsche) are also speaking of or implying possible limits to this human plasticity. Or limits beyond which we may go, but must pay. Our assertive, expansive side makes chaos possible; our other side makes it terrible: a form of servitude, Camus said. And not simply because we tend to bungle when we do not recognize the necessity of hard choices, and choices among criteria for choices. Chaos may be unsatisfactory as well as unworkable. We must accommodate our desires for order, security, familiarity, being included as well as our needs to separate and distinguish ourselves. Otherwise we have failed to provide a comfortable home and may seek out any foreign port in a storm. To neglect our anomic state, to deny that we are lost, alone, adrift, is the shortest, swiftest route to finding ourselves there, alienated, in an alien port.

We might say, then, that man has the terrible capacity to express everything . . . and its opposite as well. He must therefore, Rieff puts it, "stabilize his ambivalences." Ironically, the modern wise man, after seeing through and denouncing distinctions without a difference, categorical this and categorical that, the (bourgeois, Marxist, Christian, and so on) Yes and No and the "grotesques" these produce, must nevertheless have *his* Yes and his No, his system of controls and releases from controls.[25] But he must avoid taking them, or even the battle for them, too seriously, lest he take himself not seriously enough. We have little reason to believe that such self-overcoming of personal oppositions is anything but hard work, especially since the self-consciousness it entails is what made the task necessary in the first place and what promises to heighten its difficulty in the second place.

Getting ourselves together in this sense, however, may prove to be our first responsibility to others. As a general proposition (though stripped, usually, of the emphasis on human ambivalence) this is a common and congenially modern article of faith, as I noted in discussing the left literature of freedom. As the sole basis of a left-liberal social ethic and critique, it is inadequate, as I also suggested in criticizing those critics. Just how and why this is so are the subjects of the next chapter.

6 The Humanly Satisfying and the Socially Shareable

I have suggested that the left literature of freedom tends to neglect human ambivalence, that these critics thereby neglect the problem of anomie and fail to clarify the role their model of man plays in their social ethics and critique. This chapter seeks, first, to establish what direction the notion of human ambivalence, and the loose model of psychological health and development based on it, takes social criticism. This I introduce in connection with Philip Rieff's analysis of the "therapeutic culture," which relies heavily on the idea of ambivalence. Secondly, I suggest the limitations of this mode of criticism, specifically its failure to directly confront the question of what goals are socially possible and shareable, irrespective of whether they satisfy, or are in some sense more human. This question is introduced in connection with a brief discussion of the work of Lawrence Kohlberg on the stages of moral development, work which suggests that a concern with goals and freedoms which are shareable, mutually satisfiable, may in fact be a part of everyone's potential cognitive development. After discussing his findings, and their possible connections with the notion of human ambivalence, I suggest that left-liberal social ethics and social criticism should simultaneously concern itself with the satisfying, the shareable, and their relationship to one another.

The Failure of the Therapeutic

We are indebted to Philip Rieff for a series of provocative speculations concerning the possible emergence of a supremely individualistic "postcommunal" culture in the Western world.[1] Rieff suggests that culture will be populated by psychological man, a close modern relative of Nietzsche's free spirits. Rieff's man differs primarily in not feeling the desire for heroic solitude so keenly. Nor is he inclined to be so hard on himself. These, too, he realizes, can be traps.

But for psychological man and free spirits alike, the central problem is coping with ambivalence—as Rieff puts it, establishing some stable workable pattern of controls and releases—in a world in which, increasingly, this must be done self-consciously, with fewer sociocultural supports, ready-made or sacred justifications for suppressing impulses and delaying gratifications. Discipline and authority must be reinvented in a climate increasingly suspicious, as Arendt suggests, of the very idea of authority. Thus both Rieff and Nietzsche affirm the saving nature of authority and character, while recognizing that the old authorities and controls now function primarily to make us sick.[2]

If we train our conscience, Nietzsche said, it will kiss us as it hurts us. Nowadays, our conscience seems to be kissing less and hurting more, and it was the genius of Nietzsche and Freud to recognize this fact. It is not so much that Christianity, for example, is untrue: rather, its errors have ceased to be beneficial. Our heavy-footed ironfisted pursuit of militant collective and character ideals must be replaced by nimble dancing among commitments instrumental to a most radically enlightened self-interest. Commitments must be dropped beyond the point of diminishing returns. The returns do diminish because we are simply not that simple. And now we know it. Any dream, any ideal, any one-dimensionalization of ourselves, taken too seriously for too long, frustrates our ambivalent needs, and thus is neurotic. Psychological man, Rieff imagines, will therefore hedge his bets, whether he bets on God or love: nothing, not even sex, is sacred to him. Son of economic man, he betrays his ancestry by his shrewd economizing, and displays his superiority to it by putting even economics in its place. His self-interest is so enlightened that he can see that hedonism, too, can be a trap. According to a Chinese proverb, a crazy dancer will make us wise again. Psychological man adds some skill, discipline, even moderation to this formula, but only up to the point that they begin to spoil his fun. He may even add a bit of reverence.

The postcommunal, therapeutic culture (and Rieff assumes that America is farthest along in this respect) will be predicated on the belief that individuals can dispense with faith, and with it communal purpose. With the projected advent of mass affluence, the business of life need no longer be business, but for the first time in history can be life itself: psychological man can supercede economic man. With affluence there may come proximate equality, and psychological man may be more interested in the quality of his life than the quantity of his income. Public passions will decline, as Tocqueville predicted. Classical problems of legitimacy and public policy will no longer be salient, and political man will be rare, a rather quaint anachronism. Public passions, any passion not obviously instrumental to the individual's self-interest will be considered vaguely suspect. Faith, commitment, group activity, belonging, love will be just so many therapeutic tools, to be used accordingly, judiciously. Their purpose, and the purpose of therapy proper, will not be to integrate or reintegrate the individual into the larger community but rather, as Rieff puts it, to help him define and further his private purposes at less cost, psychic and otherwise. Community, even culture in the traditional sense, will not even exist.[3]

Less love may mean less hate, Rieff contends. Instead of loving or hating your neighbor: thou shalt understand him, even as thyself. Or at worst, benign indifference will prevail. Morality, at least in the limited sense of reciprocal toleration between those who actually encounter each other, may be improved by less rigid distinctions between the good and the evil. In Nietzsche's terms: the opposition of good and evil may give way to the softer opposition of good and bad. With fewer pure hearts, with a bit of the rogue in each of us, there may be less ruthlessness. Relationships may be detached, fleeting, impersonal, but not binding and suffocating. People may be superficial and fickle, but less aggressive. What aggression remains may be more honest, aboveboard, instrumental to specific purposes, and perhaps more manageable. As Slater suggests, we may learn to get love, love, and leave love quickly and expeditiously. Less love may mean less hate.

It is a vision at once both exciting and disturbing, beguiling and offensive. Many of us are no doubt testing the water of this innocent affluent technological Eden while obstinately keeping the other foot shored up on faith, however tenuous that foothold has become.[4] If we knew that Rieff's projection were truly a historical inevitability, then we could regard our ambivalent reaction as transitional, historically speaking. We transitional types, we modern amphibians, could at least feel superior to those walking anachronisms, those doomed dinosaurs, who still take their beliefs, objects of devotion, their loves so very seriously.

Yet if the human race is eternally ambivalent, so that part of us remains always adolescent, then what is really adolescent is to think otherwise. Nietzsche answers himself (and the Rieff who does not really believe in the viability of the therapeutic culture) in the following passage:

> When one is young, one venerates and despises without that art of nuances which constitutes the best gain of life, and it is only fair that one has to pay dearly for having assaulted man and things in this manner with Yes and No. Everything is arranged so that the worst of tastes, the taste for the unconditional, should be cruelly fooled and abused. . . . Later, when the young soul, tortured by all kinds of disappointments, finally turns suspiciously against itself, still hot and wild, even in its suspicion and pangs of conscience—how wroth it is with itself now! how it tears itself to pieces, impatiently! how it takes its revenge for its long self-delusion, just as if it had been a deliberate blindness! . . . above all one takes sides, takes sides on principle, *against* "youth"—ten years later one comprehends that all this, too—was still youth.[5]

And again:

> Perhaps the day will come when the most solemn concepts which have caused the most fights and suffering, the concepts "God" and "sin", will seem no more important to us than a child's toy and a child's pain seem to an old man—and perhaps the "old man" will then be in need of another toy and another pain—still child enough, an eternal child![6]

Only within limits, Nietzsche contends, can the youthful craving for authority, and its "taste for the unconditional" be subdued: it was the apostle and exemplar of a radically new and modern freedom who made this point, over and over. And in the final analysis, Rieff, too, cannot convince himself otherwise.[7] We have seen that on occasion he argues that no doctrine of human nature is independent

of the social order that produces it. But implicitly he makes an
exception of his own doctrine: man has the capacity to express
anything and everything, and this is emotionally terrifying. Apparently he does not regard this as a transitional, or a culturally relative
truth.[8] Culture must militate against the constant possibility of
anomic terror. The absence of horizons, as romanticized by Kariel,
spells madness, not liberation. Always and everywhere, liberty and
authority are inseparable. Though the crosses of authority that we
carry weigh us down, they also support, like backbones, a flesh
that is otherwise too weak.[9]

So we should be skeptical of modern claims to have dispensed
with authority. That is to say: we should listen *carefully*:

> The eagerness and subtlety . . . with which the problem of "the
> real and the apparent world" is today attacked all over Europe
> makes one think and wonder; and anyone who hears nothing in
> the background except a "will to truth" certainly does not have
> the best of ears . . . when they side *against* appearance, and speak
> of "perspective" with a new arrogance . . . who knows if they are
> not trying at bottom to win back something that was formerly an
> even securer possession, something of the ancient domain of
> the faith of former times, perhaps the "immortal soul", perhaps
> the "old God", in short, ideas by which could live better, that is
> to say, more vigorously and cheerfully, than by "modern ideas"?
> There is mistrust of these modern ideas in this attitude, a disbelief
> in all that has been constructed yesterday and today.[10]

What may distinguish us moderns is the unprecedented variety
and bizarre identity of our ever-newer objects of belief, and the
rapidity with which they are dropped for still-newer terror-assuaging
beliefs. The measure of the underlying terror may be the obsessive
quality of the search. Perhaps no one really wants the forcible rebirth of collective ideals: most of us would more likely feel smoth-
ered than comforted, certainly in the long run. Freedom, as leftists
and liberals alike remind us, *is* the point. But even psychological
man has ambivalent needs, and a culture that consistently misnames
and one-dimensionalizes his malady, that does not speak adequately
to his need to be comforted, if not ruled—a culture that carries
its antinomianism, as Trilling has put it, beyond culture itself—risks

the forcible imposition of ancient or modern ideals, or at very least vulnerability to the latest fads.

Thus Rieff—in sharp contrast with most representatives of the left literature of freedom—has implicitly put forth a persuasive argument for the unworkability of the therapeutic culture he sketches with such halfhearted brilliance. In a deep human sense, he suggests, it would fail to satisfy. And thus, he concludes, would prove impossible. The radical freedom, the exaggerated individualism it posits may self-destruct, and the triumph of the therapeutic might prove a disaster.

But in the process Rieff has inadvertently raised questions about the impossibility of such a culture that have no obvious connection with what is humanly frustrating or therapeutic. Such a culture may fail to satisfy, but it may also encourage everyone to do things that are simply impossible for everyone to do simultaneously. This kind of question is of equal importance to a fuller understanding of the impossibility of the "impossible" culture and the different criticisms directed toward it. It is, for want of a better term, the question of *shareability* or *satisfiability*: what kinds of goals, or patterns of goals, can we successfully pursue simultaneously? What kinds of freedoms, and combinations of freedoms, can be extended to all?[11] For a culture in which equality and radical individualism are somehow supposed to coexist, this question would seem to be of fundamental importance.

The Promises and Perils of Higher Moralizing

Rieff's analysis helps establish the direction and emphases of a mode of social criticism relying on the notion of human ambivalence, seeking a healthier society, and therefore concerned with anomie and its relationship to the alienation that we more commonly protest. However, on closer examination it likewise suggests the limitations of such appeals to what is human, and humanly desirable or satisfying, and suggests another approach which stresses the problems and exigencies of social interaction, seeks a more reasonable, rational society, and is concerned with goals and freedoms that are shareable or satisfiable. The work of Lawrence Kohlberg is particularly relevant to the latter mode, and will serve well to introduce it.

Early on we saw that when the radical social critics with whom I began the discussion ask themselves whether their model of man and their social criticisms and prescriptions are normative, they commonly assert that in any event we are moving in their preferred direction anyway. There is, or soon will be, a factual connection between the Is of psychological development and the Ought of moral obligation. In a series of studies based on the cognitive-developmental theory of Jean Piaget, Lawrence Kohlberg has made a major contribution to our understanding of the development of moral thinking.[12] In the process he has suggested that, psychohistorically speaking, in our thinking about moral questions and possibly our behavior as well, we may all be headed in a distinctly Kantian direction.

Through an analysis of the responses of children of various ages to hypothetical moral dilemmas, Kohlberg isolated a number of different aspects of moral thought, each of which apparently develops through at least six stages. The first two stages are the *premoral* level, in which there is conformity to rules based on gaining favors and rewards or avoiding punishment; what is right is what benefits the individual, whatever its impact on others. The next two stages are *conventional role conformity*. These involve understanding and some adjusting to the point of view of others, either to please others (stage three) or out of respect for authority (stage four). The fifth and sixth stages, of special interest here, comprise the morality of *self-accepted moral principles*. The individual is prepared to go against the wishes and expectations of others or to defy authority if his principles so dictate. The fifth state stresses rights of individuals and contractual obligations: individuals recognize that all others have rights that are independent of their social status. And the final, most mature, and most Kantian stage is the morality of *individual principles of conscience*:

> Stage 6: Conscience or principle orientation. Orientation not only to actually ordained social rules but to principles of choice involving appeal to logical universality and consistency. Orientation to conscience as a directing agent and to mutual respect and trust[13]

Kohlberg has not only shown that these stages follow the same sequence in widely differing cultures, but has also demonstrated that a child who is at a given stage in one aspect of morality will also tend to be at the same or neighboring stages in other aspects.

By no means does everyone reach stage six: Kohlberg's data suggest that most Americans never reach stage five.[14] What is particularly interesting is the possibility, reminiscent of those speculative assertions of the social critics discussed above, that sociocultural and historical trends will make it increasingly likely that more and more come to think of moral matters and dilemmas in these advanced ways. Keniston speculates as follows:

> Three social factors that may stimulate moral development in youth are . . . continuing disengagement from adult institutions, confrontations with alternative moral viewpoints, and the discovery of corruption in the world. There is reason to believe that all three of these conditions obtain to an unusual degree today. In the extension of higher education, the cross-cultural implosion, and the pervasive reductionism of our age we have created important new catalysts, for better and for worse, for higher levels of ethicality, as well as for more marked moral regressions.[15]

It is a fascinating prospect, this possibility of a historically unprecedented approach to moral questions, at once both radically individualistic and communal, to be employed by ever-increasing numbers. Three questions become particularly interesting and pressing. First: does other, more speculative evidence support Kohlberg's contentions, particularly concerning the natural progression to stage six reasoning and the willingness to universalize one's personal code of conduct? Second: if this seems to be the case, then why so? And third: what implications and consequences might it have? Or are these indeterminate? I suggest that adequate answers to these questions lead us back to the notion of human ambivalence, and that, in effect, social ethics and social criticism must take both the Kantian-Kohlbergian and Freudian-Nietzschean emphasis seriously.[16]

There does seem to be a surprising degree of universality of this willingness to contemplate the generalization of one's principles of behavior, at least once the willingness to justify one's behavior at all is present. When people do seek to justify their actions and their lives, again and again they come up with something that can be interpreted as a crude approximation of the Kantian or Kohlbergian answer. When people will moral choices, they automatically seem to do so universally—subject, of course, to the size of their universe. Consider the following from Sartre, who in other contexts challenges conventionality so vigorously and relentlessly:

> When we say that man is responsible for himself, we do not mean that he is responsible only for his own individuality, but that he is responsible for all men. . . . in choosing for himself he chooses for all men . . . nothing can be better for us unless it is better for all. . . . I am obliged at every instant to perform actions which are examples. . . .[17]

This implies an intense life indeed. Furthermore:

> I can pronounce a moral judgment . . . we will freedom for freedom's sake, in and through particular circumstances. And in thus willing freedom, we discover that it depends entirely upon the freedom of others, and the freedom of others depends on our own. Obviously, freedom as a definition of man does not depend on others, but as soon as there is a commitment, I am obliged to will the liberty of others at the same time as my own. I cannot make liberty my own unless I make that of others equally be my aim . . . I cannot not will the freedom of others.[18]

It would be a mistake to attribute this view (which actually goes beyond Kant in willing something specific, freedom, to be universalized) to the histrionic tendencies of yet another French rationalist. For we find it as well in Camus, commonly regarded as a much more naturalistic thinker.

If we look carefully we find that this passion for consistency is widespread. The affinity of the categorical imperative and the Golden Rule, for example, is clear. Erikson assumes, without argument, that they are virtually synonymous, and points to the resemblance of both to moral maxims basic to most cultures.[19] Arnold Brecht has argued that a similar appeal to logical consistency is central to all theories of justice, as well.[20]

Once people justify their actions, deliberate inconsistency is a surprisingly rare phenomenon. Much of it turns out to be in the eye of the observer and not in what is observed. Similar considerations apply to the phenomenon of outright hypocrisy and cynicism, which is probably rarer than is commonly believed. Hypocrisy is often hypocrisy to the outside observer, not the reputed hypocrite. Many alleged hypocrites can honestly offer arguments that explain why it is necessary that they appear hypocritical to others under certain circumstances. If asked about it, they may be able to defend the principles by which they are proceeding as a refinement of the categorical imperative, not its denial. Of course where there is a will to immorality, there is often the ingenuity with which to justify self-serving actions by describing them in a moral way. Nevertheless, a noteworthy feature of such vices is their implicit tribute to virtue, in the specific form of attempting to render those actions morally reasonable.

There is another source of the contention that people do not care to be consistent: people use the tools that are available. If the regime in power has monopolized the tools and trappings of rationality and objectivity, when the universe of discourse has been thereby corrupted, then reason may dictate opposition in irrational terms. When a Pentagon spokesman explains calmly and dispassion-ately that the bombing of Hanoi oil dumps was not escalation but "merely an incremental adjustment to meet a new stimulus level"; or when lies are described as "inoperative truths," then some of us may be forgiven for wondering whether rationality and objectivity are not in fact part of the problem. As Hobbes phrased it: when reason is against man, man will be against reason.

To summarize these speculative addenda to Kohlberg's findings: there may be something about human beings that causes their judgments to move both inward and outward, in the sense formal-ized in Kant's categorical imperative and exemplified by stage-six moralists. With Kant, with Sartre, we exhibit a concern for making absolute judgments which we believe will not negate themselves when made universal practice.[21] Even the judgment that everyone should just "do his own thing" may reflect this desire. Such judg-ments may be dead wrong in their implicit belief in their univer-salizability. They can, of course, be refined or sophisticated, or crude and naive. And some folks' horizons are severely limited. But much of the apparent unwillingness to universalize principles of conduct may be the result of smaller universes, limited intelligence, limited education, and limited exposure to other views, as Keniston suggests. In Kohlberg's stages there is apparently a logical progression from stage to stage, as if, after certain threshold points, the quantity of experience and the distance of horizons turns into qualitative differences in moral reasoning. Maybe we have all been trying all along to conceptualize moral questions in the sophisticated way of Kohlberg's stage-six moralists.[22] Certainly the fact that we often fail to do so, and that some of us do not always try very hard, should not be interpreted as convincing evidence to the contrary.

Thus it is conceivable that, given optimal circumstances, such reasoning in matters of morals is universally human, or potentially so. But if so: why so? The political theorist Ellen Wood suggests a possible explanation based on her reading of Piaget, on whose work Kohlberg's research is also in large part based.[23] Piaget argues that our consciousness of self and others develops out of an original childish egocentrism, which involves a thoroughgoing confusion of ego with the external world. Thus, egocentrism or egoism is a result or a reflection of the *lack* of ego-consciousness.[24] True self consciousness and ego strength are both derived from and conducive to sociality: true individuality and sociality are inevitably, intimately related. Wood suggests, following Rousseau, that the crucial psychological mechanism involved, at once mental and emotional, is compassion for others, a natural consequence of love of self and the perception of similarities with others.

In a similar vein, George Herbert Mead convincingly argues that we only come to know ourselves by perceiving ourselves through the eyes of significant others, and ultimately through the eyes of the larger community, the "Generalized Other," and that therefore mind, self, and society are "co-emergent."[25] This may help explain why it is troubling to advocate something for others which, when the circumstances are similar, we are unwilling to comply with ourselves. If our conception of self is based on our ability to view ourselves as a social, socially situated object, with associated roles and rules and responsibilities and their accompanying logic, then it is psychologically painful to opt out of the judgments we offer: it is much easier to generalize the prescription, at least to the outer limit of the community we recognize, and to believe what we advocate. Here again, mature individuality and genuine sociality are nearly synonomous. Rieff has gone so far to suggest that the related perspective of Charles Horton Cooley demonstrates that the Golden Rule is simply "routine psychological dynamics."[26]

This brings us to the third pressing question suggested by Kohlberg's work: what implications and consequences might the mass achievement of Kohlberg's stage-six moral reasoning have? In particular, what does it imply for social criticism and social ethics? Kohlberg himself seems undecided concerning whether his stages have implications beyond indicating how a person will conceptualize moral dilemmas and rationalize his answers and solutions. Individuals are placed in different stages, not according to whether their answers are Yes or No to the various moral dilemmas described in the text, but according to how they explain their answers.[27] Even so, it is difficult to believe that there are no right answers to his moral dilemmas. I was left with the strong impression, for example, that a stage-six individual will or should argue that the husband should steal the drug which alone can save his dying, cancer-ridden wife, after having his desperate pleas for credit turned down by an inexplicably hardhearted druggist. And when Kohlberg turns to the real world, it is clear that he thinks an individual's stage classification has specific consequences for his behavior.[28] Keniston, discussing some of the applications of the Kohlberg test, is even less restrained, bluntly asserting that "the level of moral reasoning is associated with the actual morality of behavior."[29]

But even Keniston refrains from equating moral thinking with "real ethicality":

whether the highest stages of moral reasoning lead to destructive zealotry or real ethicality depends upon the extent to which moral development is matched by development in other sectors. The critical related sectors of development, I submit, are those which involve compassion, love, or empathic identification with others....[30]

Keniston's solution is a common one, however difficult it is to determine the difference between destructive zealotry and genuine ethicality. Kant's solution is not enough, many feel: necessary but not sufficient to insure real ethicality. Where is love, or compassion, or empathy, or the proper attitude? Where is human nature? Indeed, in one way or another, one critic after another suggests that what is natural and human has been too radically dissociated from what is reasonable, and that the result can be a dissociation of moral thinking from real ethicality, and a society which is both unnatural or inhuman and unreasonable.

Without pretending that the notion of human ambivalence resolves all these difficulties, and without assuming that this is really what Keniston and the others have in mind as a supplement to the Kohlbergian-Kantian emphases, I would nevertheless contend that an adequate answer to this question leads us back to the idea of ambivalence. Social ethics and social criticism should combine a concern with the socially possible or satisfiable or shareable, and the humanly satisfying in the sense suggested by the notion of ambivalence. Put negatively, the resulting imperative would be: do not attempt to universalize, to base a culture upon, principles of conduct, conceptions of freedom, sets of goals that do not adequately accommodate human ambivalence, human polarities and the desire to overcome these polarities. This will likely prove impossible because it is humanly unsatisfactory, as a close examination of the egoism of Rieff's therapeutic culture and psychological man (whose needs are not exclusively egoistic) suggested. Those cultures that hold out goals, encourage the pursuit of freedoms, entertain conceptions of individualism which do not speak to our ambivalent needs are more likely to see their goals unrealized, their freedoms self-destructed, their individualism dissolved in conformity. This is not merely because certain goals and certain freedoms, irrespective of human psychology, human ambivalence, and what is humanly satisfying, cannot be exercised by all, and diminish as they are extended to all. It is because freedom may have natural limits as well as limits based on the requirements of social interaction and the necessity of sharing social space.

At the same time, as I suggested in criticizing both Rieff and the radical critics, the question of shareability is not reducible to the question of satisfaction, the exercise of essential human powers, or the self-overcoming of personal polarities. Given the plasticity of the human subject, the many ways in which ambivalences may be expressed and distributed and stabilized, there seems little doubt that the category of what is human in this sense contains more than the category of what is socially shareable or satisfiable. On the other hand, the multiplicity of ways of expressing and being human make it conceivable that a subset of what is human might also be shareable.[31]

In any event the following attempt to reinterpret and redirect left-liberal social criticism is the result of trying to take both concerns seriously. I argue that both kinds of concerns are in important respects sociological, and I try to indicate what such a sociological or psychoanalytic-sociological critique involves.

PART 3
Social Criticism, Sociology,
and Community

I have suggested that the left literature of freedom fails to take adequate account of human ambivalence; and that this failure is associated with the failure to appreciate the significance of anomie and its relationship to alienation, and to unambiguously specify how appeals to human nature underpin social criticism. I have developed this argument in connection with what may be our distinguishing characteristic, the making of distinctions. I have argued that to make distinctions and posit opposites may be a necessary, necessarily human kind of erring, more or less shrewd, and that there are points beyond which error overtakes shrewdness. Applied to our reflections on the nature of human nature, this implies the notion of human ambivalence, and the unceasing attempt to simultaneously affirm apparently contradictory human truths, particularly of an individualistic or liberal sort on the one hand, and a communal or conservative-communal sort on the other. These distinctions will hopefully prove helpful in redressing the imbalance we encounter in our fundamentally liberal culture, in combating its particular form of gratuitous support for the very human errors to which we are prone. But if the argument suggests anything, it suggests that the opposition between the liberal perspective and a communal or sociological perspective can itself be overdone. The task is to affirm such oppositions, to work to overcome them, and to avoid ever assuming this has been fully accomplished.

With this in mind, then, consider a different and more sociological image of this society and its ailments, one which contrasts sharply with the image implicit in the literature of freedom. It depicts a society that is anomic, even anarchic, almost as if we were discussing a different place altogether. In this view, or frame of mind, talk of freedom conjures up confusion, or loneliness, even madness or suicide. Basically the country is out of control, whether we ascribe this state of affairs to the bourgeoisie, to technology, bureaucracy, or sheer automony of process. Maybe that is why it seems so repressive. In some sense we have too much freedom, and somehow this seems to result in less freedom than is possible. Our ideology of freedom and individualism amounts to a hopeless escapist attempt to ignore relationships to others and to the environment; thus, thoroughly unprepared for their impact on us and our vulnerability to them, we produce less freedom and few individuals. Freedoms must be defined more carefully, or redefined. And if we are alienated, separated from what we could do and be, then at bottom it may be because we are really in a state of anomie—plagued by unadmitted, inadmissible communal needs but presented by this most liberal culture with a most one-dimensional notion of what is really troubling us. This culture promotes the notion that liberty and authority, individual and community are almost always in opposition. No doubt this is in the best interests of some—we shall have reason to explore the economic and political beneficiaries. But the proposition is unhealthy on the individual level, and unreasonable or irresponsible on the social level. And perhaps: essentially untrue on both levels, as if individuality and sociality were not so radically different. The literature of freedom, even its leftist version, naively accepts this pervasive simplistic cultural misinterpretation of what ails us. When the culture succeeds in convincing us to misinterpret accordingly, as often it does, then we take our rightful places as part of the problem.

Two variants of the argument have been tentatively distinguished. The first I have introduced in connection with a conception of what is humanly satisfying or desirable. The point of that development is freedom, and a radically new freedom, historically speaking. Paradoxically, however, this notion of human development, given its suspicion that opposites, and emotional opposites, are fundamentally false; given its recognition, therefore, that our interest in freedom is fundamentally ambivalent, leads us to an apparently conservative sociological concern with anomie. This is especially appropriate in certain cultural settings. This we saw in discussing Rieff's supremely individualistic, postcommunal culture. Sufficiently exaggerated, freedom, individualism, egoism may prove emotionally untenable, and impossible to sustain and make adequate use of.

The other variant relates to what is socially possible or satisfiable or generalizable: the exercise of some freedoms, the pursuit of some goals, may not be unnatural at all, but merely unworkable, disruptive, or disastrous. And in some cases impossible, especially if we all attempt to pursue them.

In many ways the first variant of the argument calls to mind the great turn-of-century sociologists—Weber, Durkheim, Simmel, Toennies—and in some ways Tocqueville. It is arguable that concern with community, authority, social order, identity—with anomie—is *the* sociological tradition.[1] In any event most sociologists have been keen and anxious observers of the French and Industrial Revolutions. Many have occupied themselves—one thinks of Comte, Durkheim, Parsons—with picking up the pieces, with finding possible secular equivalents to a Christian community.[2]

These historical sociologists were therefore preoccupied with the costs and benefits of progress, and their greatness lies in their sometimes heroic refusal to ignore either. The costs and benefits have to do with the emergence of large-scale societies, which are increasingly industrialized, urbanized, bureaucratized, complex, differentiated, and secularized. Their names are associated with different facets of the same basic social-structural changes: Weber with rationalization and bureaucratization, Simmel with urbanization and monetization, Durkheim with individualism and the division of labor.[3] What these changes mean for the individual best sums up their historic significance: the individual emerges from history, as a historic fact, as the product of a particular kind of society. He becomes increasingly individuated. Apparently we are only beginning to understand the full implications of this fact. As we would expect from the previous discussion, his emergence is a process both exciting and painful. And so, especially under extreme conditions of economic hardship and social dislocation, the individual may choose to escape his new freedom, to deny his tiresome, even frightening individuality.

Out of this intellectual tradition came the thesis, formulated in response to Nazism, that the processes of industrial transformation produce social disorganization and disintegration, destroy communal ties, atomize society, and produce a society populated by anomic mass men in need of charismatic leaders and ripe for participation in totalitarian movements.[4] In its least subtle and most deterministic form, this might be called the theory of mass society. None of the historical sociologists subscribed to mass society theory in this crude form, and probably would not have done so even if they had lived to experience Nazism. But central to the magnificent tension informing their work and marking its superiority to that of their successors is the conviction that anomie is neither a trivial nor transitional human concern. And for this reason, progress is problematic, always and everywhere.

Yet if we emphasize the social origin of individual demands and needs, then it is not clear why the problem of the lonely, rootless, and isolated individual should not be transitional, however serious it might be. Contrary to Etzioni (see above, chap. 3), Weber does not assume the existence of basic human needs, not as Etzioni conceives them. Nor, certainly, does Durkheim. So the way was open to their sociologist successors, particularly Durkheim's, to treat anomie as generally less serious and more temporary. Or as a temporary problem that has already been solved, as Etzioni himself argues. Both paths have been taken. There may be normative inconsistencies and disparities between individual demands and social deliveries, but in light of the basic malleability of human material this is temporary or transitional, and amenable to better socialization. Progress becomes completely progressive. Hence a significant difference: the notion of humanly general ambivalence confronts the more jingoistic advocates of progress (as individuation, specialization, and so forth) with the possibility that such progress may be *permanently* problematic. And this is because certain patterns of social demands may be humanly unsatisfactory, irrespective of how efficient the agents and methods of socialization and social control may be. For the moment, let us leave it at that.

The intellectual affinities of the other variant are more diverse, but this variant can also be labeled sociological. The concern with shareability and with the exigencies of social interaction owes a great deal to the concept of unintended social consequences, whereby results different from or even contrary to what was intended by individuals or groups obtain once all the results are in. It has affinities with functional analysis, or that variety of functional analysis which is willing to consider functions that are actually dysfunctions. It is linked to the traditional concern of political philosophers with the concept of authority—its necessity, its character, and particularly the consequences of its absence. More recently, it has received expression in the disciplines of systems theory, cybernetics, and ecology, and through many of the critics of technology and economic growth whatever their specific perspective or discipline.[5]

These perspectives provide the basis for a different sociological indictment of this advanced industrial society. The concern here is more with those principles of behavior, cultural goals, with those freedoms that are socially unreasonable, which cannot be pursued together without negating themselves or wreaking havoc, in the long if not short run. As Bay puts it, freedoms which diminish as we attempt to share them. Thus the questions at stake here relate to satisfiability or shareability, and possibly to equality, and less to what is human or humanly satisfying per se. On the whole, cultural norms, what sorts of things people try and are encouraged to try to do, and to some extent institutions and institutional practices, seem more relevant here than human nature.

Nevertheless, both approaches—one dealing with question of satisfaction, the other with questions of shareability or satisfiability—tend to imply or issue in critiques of this industrial society and its dominant cultural goals from a standpoint I will call communal. Moreover, we have reason to believe that the two kinds of critiques are closely related, and possibly complementary.

But all this requires argument, and I will proceed by offering a reinterpretation of anomie which draws on both approaches, both kinds of sociological concerns in attempting to explain why we in this culture do not always prefer our apparent preferences. In so doing I suggest that it is a form of rulelessness in this society which is, paradoxically, in control; and that our confusion concerning anomie and our intellectual failure to appreciate its many manifestations and consequences is itself anomic. As Rieff suggests, many of us are prone to equate the absence of culture with culture itself, and to elevate rulelessness to the status of a rule. I will try to point out three crucial but by no means exhaustive aspects of this rulelessness; to suggest, largely by implication, three corresponding aspects of community; and to explain, by reference to the notion of human ambivalence, the ways in which our essential human attributes are involved.

7 Anomie in America: Yet Another Interpretation

I suggest here an extension and reinterpretation of the concept of anomie. I begin with Durkheim because he made anomie one of his principal concerns, contributed heavily to making it one of the principal concerns of all subsequent sociology, and appears to have asked the right questions. Then, turning to Merton's reformulation of anomie as a disjunction between cultural success goals and social-institutional means of achieving these goals, I suggest that our appreciation of that disjunction, that gap between what is promised and what is delivered, can be deepened and extended by reference to the themes of human ambivalence and cultural contradictions; alienation as a protection against anomie; and the close connections between what is humanly satisfactory and socially shareable.

Individuation and Anomie: Durkheim

Durkheim interpreted the course of industrialization primarily in terms of increased individuation, a theme on which all the great turn-of-the-century sociologists played variations. Industrial societies are characterized, for him, by the division of labor. For this reason, they are more complex, and the upshot of societal complexity is the growth of individuality. The average individual must assume an increased number of specialized roles, and he thereby becomes more and more unique. The net effect of this, Durkheim feared, might be a reduction in the amount of social control over the individual. Not only is such progress not necessarily reflected in increased comfort, he warned that such changes can be downright dangerous for the individual. In *Suicide*, he argues that "egoistic" or "anomic" suicide can result if the individual's ties to society become sufficiently attenuated.[1]

Yet his conclusions in an earlier work, *Division of Labor in Society,* had been cautiously optimistic. There he foresaw the possibility of "organic solidarity," a new harmony and a higher morality based on the increased interdependence of individuals, and their increasing recognition of that interdependence. In a society so blessed there would be a proper, nonanomic amount of specialization and individualization. Thus the cure for anomie in industrializing societies was not the reversal of these processes of social transformation, but their extension and perfection in the form of organic solidarity.

Yet his treatment of the possibility of "Anomic Forms of the Division of Labor" is surprisingly thin.[2]   The problems are two, but closely related. The first is his inadequate treatment of the cultural context in which his social-structural changes proceed, and with this the possibility that cultural emphases and biases can be inimical to organic solidarity. The second, as Slater has stressed, concerns the possibility that human psychology might place limits on individuation and the division of labor.

Consider first the cultural context. Durkheim dealt inadequately with those aspects of conflict that seem inherent in the complexity of industrial societies, or perhaps in all societies. Sociologists, even those firmly within the Durkheimian tradition, are well aware of these conflicts; but many, taking their cue from Durkheim, view them as transitional, and in the long run not particularly serious.[3] Society's normative inconsistencies and our conflicts and ambivalences are attributed to the uneven pace of the processes of change. Ultimately they stress the mutual consistency (and the functionality) as well as the multiplicity of the new institutions, roles, and ties.[4]

There is a minimal sense in which the assumption of mutual consistency is necessarily, even tautologically true in a society not obviously or rapidly disintegrating. Opposed to this happy scenario, however, is the possibility that some important contradictions in society and culture are not transitional, not historical accidents or holdovers. I have previously argued this in psychological terms. But there is a sociological version of the same argument, stressing how the functional requisites of a stable society, one which preserves and reproduces itself, are responsible for—or at least perpetuate—these conflicting tendencies and persuasions. Any society, for example, must depend on cooperation as well as allow some competition. Any society must provide a measure of stability as well as allow some change . . . and so on.[5] These contradictory functions, as the division of labor proceeds and the society becomes more complex, tend to be split off into separate social structures or institutions of their own, whereas formerly they had been fused together, or ascripted. This fragmentation threatens the society with dissolution, deadlock, or paralysis—just as differentiation of formerly ascripted parts of our personality can threaten our personal integration.

Whatever the source of these contradictions, in the interests of unity, or survival, or effective functioning (or because the human mind is intolerant of ambiguity, of contradiction) cultural belief systems arise that tend to stress one or the other of a pair of contradictory polar tendencies or requirements. Competition over cooperation, individualism over group loyalties, are the obvious American examples. The minority requirement of cooperation, equally vital socially (and psychologically), assumes a less prominent, official, or dominant status. It is associated with certain minority social institutions, while most social institutions are tailored to the majority, dominant requirements.[6] These requirements, plus their associated goals, needs, truths, demands, motives, are made "socially general," as Simmel put it. Therefore by "cultural contradictions" I will indicate the necessary presence of conflicting cultural demands. This reminds us that cultural systems can exhibit the same myopia, the same tendency to one-dimensionalize themselves, as individuals do. No doubt this is aggravated by that same human inability to *think* contradictions, whether about ourselves, other individuals, cultures, or whatever. So on both the individual and the cultural levels, double vision will often be essential in helping us to avoid seeing things too simply.

Contradictions are to culture as ambivalence is to the individual. As with the culture, so with the individual, it is less enlightening, as Slater observes, to speak of the presence or absence of certain fixed traits than the manner in which tensions between paired opposite needs, desires, emotions, motives, are resolved or coped with. Here, too, an oft noted strain toward consistency, toward overcoming or ignoring antagonisms and conflicting tendencies is operative. For convenience, for peace of mind, in order to act or to "take our rest," we tend to exaggerate the difference between each thought, each feeling and its opposite.

So the minority feeling is repressed, often in the strict sense of denying or being unaware of its presence altogether. Moreover, we try to generalize our majority characteristics into some kind of regime, some integrated and coherent and consistent self-image, and to insist on those boundaries which insure that we coincide with ourselves. In the process we necessarily oversimplify ourselves and others in like manner. We may be especially prone to this kind of myopia about ourselves, others, and our culture when we are products of a myopic culture that encourages as well as exhibits this sort of error.

In what way do these considerations challenge Durkheim's analysis and his optimism? Let us begin by agreeing, contrary to the leftist literature of freedom and most left-liberal critics, that the socio-structural changes he depicts do lead to an expansion in the range of personal choice open to the average member of the society. Individuals do become more individualized, whether or not they perceive matters this way or experience their new freedoms as constraints. Over his lifetime the average individual has the opportunity to put together a relatively unique collection of roles. He has, indeed, the task of doing so. The reduction in ascribed guides to behavior entails this fact.

But Durkheim's cautious optimism concerning these changes is based on his neglect of certain crucial aspects of the cultural context in which the change takes place, and on a psychology which largely ignores human ambivalence. The critical feature of that psychology is that it enables him to assume that the elaboration of individual differences (at least in a society characterized by organic solidarity) does less violence to personality than conditions of life in a society whose "mechanical" solidarity is based on individual similarities. Durkheim makes this very clear:

But does not the division of labor by making each of us an incomplete being bring on the diminution of individual personality?

That is the reproach which has often been leveled at it. . . . Let us first of all remark that it is difficult to see why it would be more in keeping with the logic of human nature to develop superficially rather than profoundly. Why should there be more dignity in being complete and mediocre, rather than in living a more specialized, but more intense life, particularly if it is thus possible for us to find what we have lost in this specialization, through our association with other beings who have what we lack and who complete us? We take off from the principle that man ought to realize his nature as man . . . but this nature does not remain constant throughout history; it is modified with societies . . . in advanced societies, his nature is, in large part, to be an organ of society and his proper duty, consequently, is to play his role as an organ. . . . Moreover, far from being trammeled by the progress of specialization, individual personality develops with the division of labor.[7]

Here Durkheim asks us to accept his largely unexamined postulate that human beings are, or can be, more different than similar, along with his assumption that to be many-sided is necessarily to be superficial. Personality development is virtually equated with specialization of task. Insofar as the two are not equivalent, presumably there will always be some other specialist around to complete us.

However, if ambivalence is humanly general—and if, as Slater puts it, we share a limited repertoire of bipolar needs and tendencies—the Durkheimian movement toward individuation and specialization may do violence to our emotional economies, to our personalities. Especially this may be so in certain cultural contexts, as I suggested in the initial look at American culture in chapter 6. By becoming more individual in such contexts, we may become less human: emotional hemiplegics. Maybe this is the key to understanding the sometimes limited use we make of our increased freedoms; why some experience freedom as constraint, view the proliferation of choice as a bore at best and an intolerable burden at worst, and fall back as quickly as possible on the nearest conformist, alienated mode of being; and why progress does not always seem so progressive. Maybe this is why certain social critics continue to insist on calling good things bad names.

Anomie as a Disjunction of Culture and Society: Merton

Robert Merton adds to Durkheim's conception of anomie by bringing into sharper focus the cultural context in which Durkheim's social-structural changes take place. He suggests that anomie results from our cultural overemphasis on success coupled with the inadequacy of the social-institutional avenues for pursuing success.[8] Merton emphasizes the simple but powerful idea that socially generated needs and wants can be socially frustrated, and suggests the way in which this is true of American society. But his conception of this rulelessness, this disjunction between what this society promises (its cultural goals) and what it delivers can be broadened, and his view of why individuals choose deviant means or goals can be improved, by reference to individual ambivalence and cultural contradictions. What I will suggest, first, is that Merton underestimates the gap between dominant cultural success goals and the opportunity or ability of all to pursue these successfully; and second, that he neglects the presence and the frustration of communal concerns counter to those success goals. Thus, not only is there a conflict between society and culture, but also a conflict *within* the culture, and within our minds and hearts. Not only is there a conflict between our conventional wants and what most of us can reasonably expect to realize, but also a conflict between what we want and what else we want.

In effect Merton suggests that the worst cliché concerning American culture is the best starting point in characterizing it: namely, this is an extremely individualistic, competitive, success-oriented society. The specialization of task which Durkheim stresses is not for the purpose of self-realization, or personality development, but is in the service of productivity and profit, as Adam Smith vividly pointed out in the opening pages of *The Wealth of Nations*. So Merton begins here his reinterpretation of anomie.[9] He admits that other societies exhibit a cultural emphasis on success, often with the American emphasis on acquiring possessions and wealth. But what is unique about this society, he argues, is the extent to which we inculcate and spread wide the need to succeed. Even vastly more successful countrymen are not generally viewed as people apart. Instead, the people apart are those who drop out, who stop trying, or are suspected of it. This oft noted feeling of social equality, in connection with the relative underemphasis on the legitimate means to achieve success, produces a strong temptation to cheat, to use the technically most expedient means, whether or not these happen to be legitimate, lawful, or fair. Merton therefore attributes anomie to a cultural overemphasis on success goals coupled with a relative lack of emphasis on the legitimate means by which success is supposed to be achieved. He then discusses how a differentiated or stratified social structure will channel adaptation to this pressure, causing particular social strata to adapt and deviate in characteristic ways.[10]

By stressing the competitive context in which the division of labor proceeds, Merton makes of anomie a more serious if not more permanent affair. He finds a social structure characterized by increasing individuation in a cultural context characterized by competitive, possessive individualism. Durkheim did not ignore competition, but he assumed, by noting the adaptation of different species of animals to situations involving scarce resources, that the division of labor among human beings would reduce competition.[11] This neglects the fact that the competitive context has a life of its own. Moreover, human beings have the knack, encouraged and exploited in this culture, of imagining that things are scarce even when this is not necessarily the case, thereby rendering them really scarce. Furthermore, Durkheim's analogy is suspect because human beings are one species, and therefore might be expected to want or need similar things. Expecially this might be so if they are all influenced by the same culture, and even more so if the culture had strong egalitarian emphases.

But Merton fails to pursue this question of what goals are impossible to successfully pursue together, and he thereby understates the extent to which we have planted that rulelessness or disjunction at the very foundation of our cultural prescriptions. He implies that anomie would be reduced if only we developed the proper avenues for attaining success and placed more stress on their use. This slights the fact that most of the games we are taught to play require losers. Success, when defined in relative terms, requires a backdrop of failures. There is abundant evidence that Americans define it this way. Fame is typically obtained at someone else's expense. In Maslow's terms: our cultural goals tend to be low-

synergetic or unreasonable, in the sense of shareability or universalizability. As Slater suggests, this is either inherent in the goals as
in the case of fame, or it results from defining them in a relative
way, as in success and wealth. These goals, coupled with the motives
they mobilize, posit much conflict or zero-summedness between individuals and others. Moreover, these attitudes and conflicts are not
easily confined to strictly economic spheres.[12]

So the egalitarianism that Merton stresses, while undoubtedly
genuine, is peculiarly escapist. Contrary to what he implies, it is
not merely the social structure (more rigidly stratified than we are
led to believe) which produces the losers, but rather the nature
of the goals and games, which posit conflict among individuals
and demand winners and losers, particularly the latter. Equality
and opportunity work at cross-purposes when the opportunity in
question is the chance to become unequal. But of course this is a
fact that gross inequality of opportunity and our preoccupation
with equalizing opportunities have a way of obscuring.[13]

These considerations apply to whether cultural goals are shareable,
mutually satisfiable when everyone pursues them. The further
difficulties with Merton's analysis relate to the question of satisfaction. As in the case of Durkheim, they stem from a simplistic psychology and a view of culture that is excessively monolithic—that is,
he neglects individual ambivalence and cultural contradictions.
Merton correctly points to and places deserved emphasis on our
dominant cultural orientation and how it pervades most spheres of
our lives. But in so doing he manages to capture only the dominant,
majority aspect of our beliefs and goals. He neglects those minority
orientations I have argued are necessarily present in both the individual and culture. Thus he neglects their frustration as well.

This can be seen most clearly by asking why it is that certain
individuals or social strata reject the dominant cultural goals, the
legitimate social means, or both. Merton's explanation amounts to
the contention that some people cannot be successful in the conventional sense, not if they are forced to use legitimate means.
Their failure is primarily due to their disadvantaged social location,
and the inadequate and rocky social roads leading from where they
are to where they want to be. I have suggested that there are other

obstacles in the very nature of the demands. But other individuals do not even seem to want to succeed, especially once we examine their failures more closely. Or better: they are ambivalent toward success and what succeeding entails. And under certain personal, social, and historical circumstances the other sides of their ambivalence can receive expression. How many fail because they wish to do so, however incoherent or inarticulate or preconscious their implicit appeal to other desires, goals, ideals? Merton is therefore particularly hard pressed to deal with his important deviant category of rebellion. In terms of his paradigm, the emergence of goals and needs and demands in opposition to those generally emphasized (as opposed to radical demands to be dealt a better hand in the given competition) is peculiarly inexplicable. It is his treatment of the culture as monolithic and individuals as one-dimensional, I suggest, that causes the trouble.[14]

Yet the idea that anomie results from or amounts to a disjunction, a ruleless gap, between the culture and the society—between what is promised, and therefore demanded, and what is delivered—is a pregnant one, rich in its implications for social criticism and democratic theory. Let us develop the idea of disjunction by first elaborating the socially generally requirements for making it in America; and second, by means of a better characterization of American culture: what Americans want, and what else they want. For in addition to the disjunction between culture and society on which Merton has focused, there is a disjunction or contradiction within the culture, and within individual psyches.

Making It in America

Whatever else we Americans want, we want success. I will argue later that our psyches are more complicated, but in the meantime we must not confuse the complications with the basic monomania. The complications I will introduce at this point concern Merton's account of the difficulties and requirements of upward mobility and success in America. Merton places deserved emphasis on the failure to develop and encourage the use of legitimate social means for pursuing cultural success goals. This puts the focus on social stratification (though not necessarily on class or class conflict, as Marxists would be quick to note) and the obstacles individuals from some social locations encounter in their pursuit of success. Here I will try to complement that emphasis by devoting attention to some of the obstacles the society presents at its best, most progressive— that is, most meritocratic. In the long run the average American may have as much to fear from the ideal American society as he does from the actual, flawed one. Then I will turn from this account of what it really takes to succeed to an expanded account of what Americans really want.

"The characteristic style of this industrial society," to quote Daniel Bell, "is based on the principles of economics and economizing." According to Parsons its basic attitude is "instrumental activism," which consistently "favors increasing the level of adaptive flexibility through increase in knowledge and economic production." In short, in some ways this is the industrial society par excellence. It probably places fewer psychological and social obstacles in the path of economic change, if not economic growth, than any society in history. (This may be compatible with a low growth rate; growth may require more cooperation than most Americans are capable of in peacetime, or more intrinsic interest in work, pride of craftsmanship, or devotion to duty, and so forth.) The industrial revolution, far from being over, shows every sign of accelerating. It is possible that the postindustrial society will be even more highly rationalized, characterized by the "generalized application of organized efficiency." At its best and most progressive, the society emphasizes "functional rationality, technocratic decision-making, and meritocratic rewards," Bell points out. It is an ever more specialized society, subject in many respects to rapid and ceaseless change, especially in the economic sphere. And most of these socially general characteristics can be traced to the fact that the social structure is dominated by technology, typically developed and employed in the service of profit-propelled economic activity.

From such characteristics derive the requirements for competing well. These extend far beyond a mere willingness to compete, and beyond the social advantages and disadvantages on which Merton concentrates. Standards of performance are higher, requiring longer periods of education and training: the decline in challenge that some observers find characteristic of this age refers primarily to matters of physical work and survival. (More speculatively, it amounts to an oblique commentary on a society that for some reason does not seem exciting anymore.) Moreover, the supposed decline in competition either refers to the decline of some of its more virulent, robber-baron forms, or is quite mythical, revealing more about our secret desires than our society. The standards are more specialized, and different in nature as well. Increasingly, the characteristic demands placed on the individual are cognitive, and predicated on the repression of emotion and on delayed and indirect gratification. We must, in most social settings, be "affectively neutral," to use Parsons's affectively neutral phrase. Therefore these demands issue, not from Freud's harsh, punitive superego, but from what Keniston has called the "technological ego." Even so, they can be harsh and punishing.

It will be instructive to dwell for a moment on the personality characteristics and quirks of this modal man-most-likely-to-make-it (without delving, at this point, into what really makes him go). As already implied, he is likely to be a he, and one of the most important if not defining aspects of his masculinity is his ability to make distinctions and separations. Indeed, distinguishing *himself* from others, and from whatever is seeking to distract or sway him from his course or slow or bog him down, is an important key to his achieving personal distinction.[15] He is also likely to be, as Parsons indicates, a specialist in the separation of affect and intellect, in establishing emotional distance—a crucial element in the development of symbol systems and powers of abstraction, since these depend on our not being trapped or duped by immediate, concrete, senuous particulars.

Suffice to say that to compete well involves much more than the competitive spirit.[16] And in this larger context the meaning of equality of opportunity, so important to Merton's argument, must be reexamined. As Schaar argues, the definition of merit is always and everywhere relative to certain kinds of abilities. Applying scientific criteria of merit, however universally we do so, always discriminates against other abilities and qualities.[17] In American society it is the masculine, the aggressive, the young (to a point), the affectively neutral, the cognitively skilled who are generally favored over the feminine, the meek, the older, the more affectively charged and cognitively deprived. With Marx, Merton quite validly argues that social location has much to do with determining the identity of the losers. We must stress the simple point, however, that our games also demand losers, and that all barriers to winning cannot be ascribed to the fact that certain advantaged social locations give others a head start. In light of the rules and requirements of the game, for all practical purposes many may be quite lame. Others, eminently sane, may be quite crazy for practical purposes.

If this account of some of the prerequisites of advancement and success has any validity, it suggests the disturbing possibility that we may have managed to construct the worst of worlds, in a certain sense—a more pessimistic version of the already unattractive scenario sketched by Freud in *Civilization and Its Discontents.* Freud tied repression of instinctual impulses to the work of Eros, by which individuals and whole civilizations are bound together in ever greater and more effective unities. Presumably this process was to include repression of the impulse to exclude the less fortunately situated and the less gifted from the ever-greater community, or the impulse to trample over them. The sense of guilt, product of the never-satisfied superego and based on repression, was supposed to increase because real guilt—that is, for aggressive, antisocial, excluding behavior—decreased. There were to be communal dividends for the human costs of instinctual repression. But what we may have demonstrated is that repression of impulse need not be in the service of Eros: trampling over your neighbor can also be hard work, involving much dedication and delay of gratification. Not doing so can even be a source of a sense of guilt. Perhaps it is possible, although a dubious achievement, to increase repression of impulse, the sense of guilt, and real guilt simultaneously. Repression in the service of low-synergy goals can actually contribute to that "psychological poverty of group life," about which Freud warned America. It can also contribute to neglecting the poverty of the real poor as well, and to the general tendency to step and spill things on each other, as I shall argue shortly. So there is, as Slater has pointed out, a double paradox at work here: our individual controls may themselves be out of control; and this helps explain why the society is out of control. Paradoxically, this is what contributes to the widespread notion that what control we have is excessive and repressive.

Of course excessive control is not what Americans want: Americans want their *freedom*, do they not? Let us now turn to a closer look at what Americans want, and then at what they really want.

The Cultural Contradictions of America

Some wit has observed that the field of national character analysis has more critics than practitioners. What I wish to do here falls somewhere between practice and criticism. My "data" are analyses and impressions of American character and culture, including some impressions of my own.[18] What I seek is an interpretation of what has been said in many ways in many contexts by many observers, particularly those observations and propositions that have been generally agreed upon. My interpretation revolves around human ambivalence and cultural contradictions. "It is a commonplace," Erikson writes,

> to state that whatever one may come to consider a truly American trait can be shown to have its equally characteristic opposite. This, one suspects, is true of all "national characters" . . .—so true, in fact, that one may begin rather than end with the proposition that a nation's identity is derived from the ways in which history has, as it were, counterpointed certain opposite potentialities; the ways in which it lifts this counterpoint to a unique style of civilization or lets it disintegrate into mere contradiction.[19]

Comprehending these contradictions is the first step, then, beyond the faulty expedient of ascribing all contradictions to the existence of contradictory subcultures, and beyond acquiescing in the disintegration of our opposed tendencies and potentials into mere contradictions.

Let us add another cliché to our account of American character. Americans want their freedom, everyone seems to agree. Americans are great individualists: on this proposition there is far less agreement; nor does it ring quite so true. This bears investigation. Maybe the apparent contradiction is due to what *else* we Americans want.

David Potter suggests a distinction between individualism defined as self-reliance and individualism in the sense of nonconformity. Americans subscribe to the former, he argues, but are not known for their hospitality to eccentrics and nonconformists. But let us not be hasty: to observe that Americans fail to achieve nonconformity (and sometimes punish it severely) does not demonstrate that we do not want to.

Potter's distinction calls to mind the related distinction Simmel draws between eighteenth- and nineteenth-century individualism.[21] The first of these focuses on the supposed general human characteristics that would be revealed once arbitrary social barriers and distinctions among men had been struck down. It received its ultimate philosophic expression, he argues, in Kant. He calls it the individualism of singleness (*Einzelheit*). It is the "ideal of fundamentally equal, even if wholly free and self-responsible personalities."[22] The corresponding notion of individual freedom is the freedom to express what is actually in all of us. It is, I suggest, very American.

By contrast with the freedom to be alike, nineteenth-century individualism, according to Simmel, is the individualism of difference, incomparability or uniqueness (*Einzigheit*), "in which each individual finds the sense of his existence . . . only in contrast with others, in the personal uniqueness of his nature and his activities."[23] Motivationally speaking, Americans appear to be individualistic in this sense, in apparent contradiction to Potter's contention. That we often or even typically fail to achieve incomparability, distinction, or nonconformity should not necessarily be a reflection on our aspirations.

But it would appear that Americans have gone one stage beyond the individualism of incomparability. In Simmel's conception, individuality-as-incomparability is linked, much as in Durkheim, to a differentiated social role in a society characterized by increasing division of labor. Or this is potentially the case: "The metaphysical foundation of the division of labor was discovered with the individualism of difference, with the deepening of the individuality to the point of the individual's incomparability, to which he is 'called' both in his nature and in his achievement."[24] But there is no necessary connection between individuality-as-incomparability on the one hand and the responsible performance of a social role on the other, and Americans have little use for what is unnecessary. Our individualism, as Braybrooke asserts, does not take seriously the division of labor, and the cooperation implicit in this principle. The idea of a calling tends to get confused, in the American mind, with the exhortation to go West, young man. To be called is to be called away! Lacking a conception of what is better, Americans settle for what is different, more, somewhere else, or merely their own. That is, onto individualism-as-incomparability Americans have superimposed what might be called individualism-as-*escapism*. This in turn might be called twentieth-century individualism. Images of release seem to control the modern American psyche and to dominate American culture. Americans, F. Scott Fitzgerald observed, have always believed in the Green Light, and they often pull away from it like they had just seen a ghost.

It should be quickly added, however, that particular directions of movement are preferred and encouraged: American individualism, if we wish to use the term, has specific qualities and outlets, surprisingly narrow limits. As Tocqueville suggested, "men living in democratic times have many passions, but most of their passions either end in the love of riches or proceed from it."[25] This is the reason that "they will be surprised at length to find themselves collected at the same spot."[26] Of course there is pervasive cultural conditioning involved. Of course, as Marxists and liberals alike are quick to remind us, there are often oppressive, coercive institutional constraints on our conceptions and exercise of individualism. But it is doubtful whether this is the whole story. The feebleness of our sometimes frenzied exercises in eccentricity, independence, self-realization is also a good rough measure of the emotional untenability of that total release and total freedom so often romanticized in song, in folklore—in theory, as we have seen—and above all in advertisements. Thus we "have it our way" at Burger King—along with millions of others.

Such qualifications to the assertion that Americans are an

individualistic people are embarrassing in force and number. On the other hand, as I have already suggested, the contention that Americans are basically conformist does not quite ring true, either. The suspicion therefore grows that these apparently opposite contentions about Americans are both in some sense true, and not merely of different individuals and social strata. In this way we wind our way back to the genuine contradictions in American culture and the American psyche. We begin to see what is unsatisfactory about the individualism of incomparability and escape, and approach a better understanding of why, in the final analysis, a people who exalt freedom of choice wind up with a relatively short cultural menu of choices, despite the superficial surface variety; a surprising rigidity, despite the general and growing emphasis on staying cool and loose; and a remarkable willingness on critical occasions to impose its choices on minorities of various kinds. For Americans do want agreement. We do want to be included and accepted. We do eventually define freedom rather narrowly, and are tempted to do so for others as well, and not merely because our culture conditions us and our institutions sometimes force us to do so. We do want to lay down our burden on something solid, substantial, certain, and secure. Anyone who hears only the pleas for more freedom, for more distinction and incomparability, is just not listening carefully. Or perhaps, as Nietzsche suggested in making a similar point, he "does not have the best of ears."

What really makes us run? Philip Slater has remarked that the American tendency to deny the necessary and normal desire for authority and dependence in human relationships resembles that of the schizophrenic. Robert Lifton has noted that Americans, especially young Americans, virtually equate nurturance with the loss of autonomy. To see unfreedom everywhere we look is suspicious: as Nietzsche said, "the person betrays himself." So I venture the hypothesis that behind our obsession with freedom and our apotheosis of egoism—and the human needs to distinguish, separate, assert, and realize ourselves these engage and further—there lurk apparently opposed needs to be accepted and included, opposed desires for the secure, the orderly, and the familiar.[27] That is, what is behind our concern with alienation, and what indeed bloats our preoccupation with alienation, is the opposite concern with anomie. And what makes our liberalism so exaggerated and so brittle, what makes us so vulnerable to the alienation we so hotly protest, is precisely that state of anomie and the frustration of those communal concerns. As I argued earlier, it is as though our liberal concerns were in slight majority, and therefore were tyrannizing the communal minority because of its very strength, appropriating that strength while forbidding any direct participation in the regime.

Again, these supposedly opposite needs can be seen in our exaggerations. Even in exaggerated self-reliance and escapism there is a desire for security, however sick and self-defeating it may become. The suburb is an escape, but there is security and a kind of community in it, too. Perhaps there is more security in some other suburb, though the search itself may create sufficient anxiety to defeat its purpose. Similarly, the automobiles that take us there are vehicles for security as well as mobility, for being included in the fraternity of the stylish and the successful as well as distinguishing and distancing ourselves.

In like manner, the typical use we make of our technology is to facilitate our escape—from each other, external nature, even ourselves—but technology simultaneously functions to make us feel more security, at least for the moment. There is a precious (however piddling or precarious) measure of identity to be derived from each new product, at least until next year's model arrives to aggravate our ontological insecurity once again. There is a desire for acceptance and affection underlying our pursuit of individual success and distinction, though if the pursuit is successful we may destroy the context in which alone acceptance and affection are meaningful or possible. We may distinguish ourselves, but all too well, so that our accomplishments and triumphs are painfully private and difficult to share.

What keeps us running and escaping, then, is the fantasy that there is a place of perfect peace and comfort over the next hill, a familiar, warm, accepting place—"there'll be no distinctions there," as the old Gospel hymn puts it—and the equally naive belief that we would enjoy it for very long. (Such crude opposites, Kaufmann has observed, "deserve each other.") This is of a piece with the notion that all we really want is to distance and distinguish ourselves, to assert ourselves, and to be left alone. Granted, such innocence can be eminently functional to a certain kind of society. It does keep us running. But it can also make us vulnerable, particularly in dealing with certain economic men who still know, or at least think they know, what they want. It can make us dependent on their conception of what we should want, and thus we may not manage to escape them at all.

Of course, all this has been pursued in the name of individualism, freedom, expansion, release, and so on, and on first look the psychology of all the scurrying about does appear profoundly liberal or agentic. But surely more is involved. As Slater has pointed out: if rats in a cage should move about as frenetically as most of us do in this society, the rat-psychologist would feel a professional obligation to provide a full explanation of what is bugging *them*. And what seems to be the case, on closer look at the society, is that much of the energy for this activity has been appropriated from the communal or communal-conservative desire to make the world orderly, secure, familiar. Nietzsche makes the point, appropriately enough, in discussing the motivations (and paradoxical results) of science:

> The development of science resolves the "familiar" more and more into the unfamiliar—it desires, however, the reverse, and proceeds from the instinct to trace the unfamiliar back to the familiar. . . . thus science is preparing a sovereign ignorance. . . .[28]

The ostensible, obvious purposes of our culture, as epitomized by our magnificent science, have been mastery, adventure, the satisfaction of disinterested curiosity, pushing back the frontiers of knowledge no matter what—expansive, fearless, liberal purposes. Cowboy purposes. But mastery for what? We have been trained to think that the answer is simple and obvious—as if *we* were so simple. The fact is that we also wish to make the world familiar, warm, certain, secure, orderly—a most fearful, defensive, conservative posture. Meanwhile, the world seems to become less familiar, less comforting, less orderly. And in the well-worn words of another Gospel hymn: we "can't feel at home in this world anymore."

Moreover, what is tabooed returns to inflate the world-winning, mountain-moving, Faustian propensities of the Western mind and spirit. The less than satisfactory, indirect, substitute gratifications which narcissistic individualistic success offer gets translated, via a cultural misinterpretation or one-dimensionalization of what we really want, into ever more frenzied and self-defeating activity. The results seem increasingly unsatisfactory and unmanageable; the society seems both unnatural and unreasonable. Maybe it is both.

Thus our exaggerations betray us, betray a close ambivalence toward the liberal goals of this apparently liberal culture—however elusive the concept of exaggeration, however difficult a direct, conclusive, empirical demonstration of its presence. But there is another place to observe close ambivalence, as I argued before—in alternation between apparent extremes.[29] Individualism and conformity provide the obvious example. There is apparently no way of telling whether the basic American psychopathology is, to use Erikson's terms, identity diffusion or identity foreclosure. Or in our terms, acute anomie or acute alienation. Both appear to be manifestations of the same virus: uncertainty concerning who we are too often forecloses the possibilities of what we might be. As Slater has observed, Americans appear to vacillate between an infinite suggestibility and a brittle absolutism, between an exaggerated, compulsive individualism and an astonishing vulnerability to the latest fad, a consumer's mentality seemingly devoid of all taste, imagination and creativity. Or take attitudes toward technology. We cannot seem to decide whether technology will eventually do it all for us, or will inevitably do us all in. As one of his critics points out, Norman Mailer, who has deftly probed the American psyche on many occasions, spends the better part of his *Of a Fire on the Moon* agonizing over whether the first moon walk was the best or the worst thing that has ever happened to mankind—a question, needless to say, he does not resolve. It is hard to miss the hubris involved in posing such grand alternatives: American technology must be absolutely the greatest disaster the world has ever seen! ("Whoever despises himself still respects himself," Nietzsche said, "as one who despises.") And there is something puritanical about it: either we Americans are the Children of Light, or we must surely be the Children of Darkness.

On this last score, too—whether Americans are moral or religious—

observers reach seemingly opposite conclusions. Americans do have a strong "moral orientation," Robin Williams reports.[30] Most observers agree that Americans are relatively incapable of cynicism: American innocence and idealism have always been rich sources of our most charming and ludicrous behavior. Any account of our fabled callous competitiveness and greed must be complemented by mention of our fabled generosity. The generosity may be directly expressed only in severely limited or inconsequential contexts, and often in ways, like private charity and welfare, which emphasize as much as reduce the gap between benefactor and beneficiary. But however indirect, ineffectual, or escapist, it is genuine. For America is the place where businessmen must talk like preachers, and vice versa, even though it is usually clear who is co-opting whom. Even sex gets shamelessly moralized, whether the argument is pro or con: Americans oscillate between sounding like failed hedonists and failed Puritans. Maudlin sentimentality alternates with quick-draw, two-fisted shrewdness, the cowboy mentality, and an incredible pre-occupation with and romanticization of violence. Americans are *not* selfish, not cynical nor cruel. Each for himself and God for us all, the elephant said, as he danced among the chickens.

However, to suggest that we oscillate is not to suggest that anything goes, that nothing whatsoever is characteristic of this culture. Some observers seem to have fallen into this error. Philip Rieff suggests that the difficulty with this culture, with changing it, is that it really does not stand for anything: this is the key to its unyielding plasticity. While his point has considerable force, it blithely ignores the basically bourgeois and bureaucratic limits to what yields and what does not. On the contrary: this culture does stand for a few things, and our conceptions and practice of freedom and individualism, despite our sometimes loose rhetoric, are usually tailored accordingly. Admittedly the culture does not seem to stand still, and its bourgeois ideology is harder to reflect, as the Marxists say, because the new nimble-footed bourgeoisie move so fast that, like vampires, they cast no reflections in our mirrors. This culture does stand for certain things, however. Particular wants are pursued, allowed, and encouraged, and these have most of all to do with economics and technology, products and profit. As in any culture that prolongs itself, releases from these dominant controls can be and are used to make the controls all the more secure. This is the repressive desublimation of which Marcuse has often made an issue, and with good cause. But the dominant controls are actually in the nature of releases: a type of bourgeois anarchy is in control—not the nihilism which Kristol, Bell, and others, following Schumpeter, imagine they see, nor the total repression imaginatively conjured up by many Marxists.

For this reason any analysis of the dominant culture's still remarkable staying power, its amazing absorptive capacity, must focus first on attempts (however misguided or disguised) to overcome this anomie, so instrumental to alienation and so profitable to bourgeois interests; and second, on the way attempts are often subverted, and what began as protest becomes just another part of the alienated scene. Moreover, it must resist the tempting notion that the whole process can be accounted for by the ubiquity of social-ization messages, the undoubted genius of Madison Avenue, or the coercive constraints of present social institutions.

Two recent cultural phenomena will be useful in illustrating how this works. The first concerns the idea of personal identity, the quest for it, and the false notion that it can someday, somewhere, some-how be found. Clearly there are conservative impulses at work here. Identity is an updated version of what used to be called character, and applauded as such. It expresses the desire for that saving measure of security and authority afforded by well-defined personal bound-aries. This can be especially liberating in a culture whose stress on freedom and release tempts us with worrisome possibilities of going anywhere, expressing everything, being anybody. It is the product of some weariness, and the wish to take a rest from defining ourselves every moment by painfully self-conscious decisions. This is all very human. Differentiating self-identical things is fundamental to thought, to communication, to culture: but it begins at home, with us. Sus-tained difficulty in equating ourselves with ourselves is at best quite tiresome and at worst nightmarish.

On the other hand, serious or prolonged inability to allow traffic across the useful fictions that are our ego boundaries is probably an epistemological error and certainly a deprivation, an alienation. The "contact barriers" we need must also serve as points of access. Thus it is especially conservative and unrealistic to entertain the notion that identity is something fixed, out there somewhere, that can be adopted or put on like new clothes—or bought, perhaps—as opposed to something that must be created, developed, and sustained by means of hard work and constant vigilance. This mistake represents the peculiar revenge our mind takes on itself for generally having to believe, as part of a cultural prejudice, that we can dispense with identity, that we need not and should not place barriers between ourselves and our possibilities of being and doing anything and everything. Thus some people talk as though they expected to find their identity on their doorsteps one morning along with the newspaper. Others speak as though it were a mighty oak already fully formed inside their little individual acorn, needing only some magic fertilizer to send it bursting forth full-bloom, full-grown, overnight. All of this quickly becomes a psychic variation on a standard American get-rich-quick scheme. And waiting in the wings are veritable armies of emotional engineers, reckless but shrewd, eager to really get rich quick, to exploit this innocent belief of ours in magic products, slogans, and techniques.

The obsession with identity amounts to a telling indictment of a society that falsely leads us to believe that we can do without one. It is a most human response. But observe what happens. We conclude that identity can be found. This represents a curious fragmentation of our thinking into equally untenable and unrealistic alternatives—unceasing quest, blind breathless activity, insecurity and anomie on the one hand, and utter rest, passivity, and the life of an inert thing on the other. And notice the consequences. The false notion that identity can be found keeps us going, keeps us mobile and loose, though within basically bourgeois limits. This mobility, in the language of the sociological clinician, is functional to a certain kind of society. In economic terms, it is profitable: indirectly to the identity-seeker, who gains the detachment necessary to grab or purchase the next opportunity and to abandon the last; directly to all those businessmen who detach him from his money.[31] Whole industries arise to peddle and service still newer conceptions of style, of identity, of human nature itself. And it is all done with a seriousness that would be laughable if it were not that, at bottom, these are serious and often sad matters indeed. Somewhere along the line, what started out as implicit criticism of the culture became another expression of what was originally being criticized.

Next consider nostalgia, and the nostalgia craze. It represents authentic dissatisfaction with restless, unstructured, and meaningless change, with the ever-new, with modernity itself. "There is mistrust of these modern ideas in this attitude, a disbelief in all that has been constructed yesterday and today."[32] Though generally trained to be disdainful of the past (and condescending to our outdated elders) we must wonder from time to time whether, without the vivid presence of the past, without the context that Etzioni suggests as a basic human need, the present has much meaning. Sometimes, as a friend has suggested, it seems that the only justification for this frantic activity in the present is to create a past to look back on. But that very activity prevents us from seeing, from even having time to look back. We begin to wonder, with Berger, whether society and personality themselves might be, in the last analysis, *memories.*

The attraction of the past, as Berger suggests, is its massivity, its inevitability, and not necessarily its attractiveness. The past is simply *there*, and seems to be less easily tinkered or tampered with. It can thereby provide a kind of liberating security or resistance to our restlessness. This is reflected in the fact that precisely what happened in the past, and whether those were happy times, sometimes seems relatively unimportant and incidental. The characters in Larry McMurtry's *The Last Picture Show*, a good recent beneficiary of nostalgia, are themselves nostalgic for a small-town-cowboy Texas existence that had already passed away by 1950, when the story takes place. And nostalgic for men of integrity and character, the likes of whom supposedly existed before postwar affluence put everyone on wheels and then ruined their virtue in the backseat or at big city parties. Nostalgia within nostalgia. Soon we will be sitting around reminiscing about how we used to sit around reminiscing.

Somehow it is a bit perverse: not really what we had in mind. (Part of the perversion is that planned obsolescence, in products and ideas, has its costs in dollars and depleted resources. It has its unworkable, unreasonable, wasteful side, apart from questions of

motivation and satisfaction; the nostalgia craze is inseparable from
the nostalgia industry. But here we are concentrating on wasted
emotions.) It all begins with unacknowledged fear and confusion,
seeking security in a frantic search to be up-to-date and stylish. The
resulting chaotic flow of products and ideas produces additional
fear, additional insecurity, which produces still more apparent
variety. But little real variety is produced, with even less tolerance or
appreciation for what variety there is. Instead, fear leads to boredom
and the blasé attitude appropriate to stimulus overload.[33] There is a
vague dissatisfaction, an ill-defined malaise and melancholy. What
would really be new in such a context would be more substantial
and sacred, not rendered obsolete by next year's model. What would
be new would be . . . old, past, settled. Enter nostalgia. But also
enter those who understand that there are profits to be turned in
continually redefining the past. The past can be appropriated, as
Kariel might say, just like any other reality: any temporary society
worth its label has a temporary past. But the beneficiaries, the *real*
appropriators, have a distinctly bourgeois look. In the end nothing is
really new in this concern with the old. What once was intended,
however unconsciously, as protest becomes just part of the scene, as
restless, as escapist, as that which it sought to escape and to overcome.

The reader is invited to question what is similar and dissimilar
about the rise and fall of other protest phenomena—as for example
the supposedly new cultural sensibility and political radicalism of the
1960s. To misinterpret maladies is to risk taking one's place as one
of the symptoms; and once that protest movement degenerated into
"doing your own thing," it became clear that the grand American
traditions of doing, owning, and things still had plenty of life in
them. Additional examples of this process, with similar interwoven
patterns of exploited innocence, blunted aspirations, and reaped
profits (deferring discussion of the social chaos that may accompany
it) can be multiplied indefinitely. If it is a conspiracy, let us admit
that most of us—or parts of all of us—are part of it. When we are
struck, as Tocqueville observed, "by that strange melancholy which
oftentimes will haunt the inhabitants of democratic countries in the
midst of their abundance," from the very depths of our cultural

heritage, and not only from Madison Avenue, we receive the counsel that the problem is them, others, too much order, too much conformity, a lack of freedom from society, culture, even nature. So we renew our efforts, as Simmel put it, to "summon the utmost in uniqueness and particularization" in order to "remain audible" to ourselves. Overdoing the distinction between ourselves and others, we find nothing much to share (certainly not our distinction, our success!), and our much-touted freedom becomes, as in Kris Kristofferson's song, "just another word for nothin' left to lose." What was the purpose in distinguishing and distancing ourselves so radically? Perhaps the point, we belatedly discover, was to be accepted and included.

I have suggested that ambivalence is humanly general. I prefer to sidestep extended discussion of the specific ways particular institutions in this society inculcate and frustrate our ambivalent needs. The argument is easily "oversociologized," and then we are tempted to see the presence of cultural contradictions and individual ambivalence as a transitional problem to be eliminated by improved measures of socialization and social control. (This is not to suggest that we should not concern ourselves with narrowing the gap between promises and deliveries, but rather that we must simultaneously be concerned with the nature of the goals involved, and whether these are humanly satisfying.) As to the source of our close ambivalences, Margaret Mead pointed the way when she suggested that in this culture the yearning for success was planted in our breasts by our mothers' "conditional smiles."[34] Maybe it is to recapture love and approval that we keep the treadmill going. Maybe it is in the attempt to *re*create some perfect state of dependence, nurture, warmth, and security that we so radically distinguish ourselves from what is, that we see reality as consistently inferior, and thereby frantically create a world in which we are more abandoned and homeless than we need be.[35] Social climbing begins at home, as Slater contends: its underlying intention may be to end up at home as well, at peace, at one. But let us not blame Mother for everything, and let us keep in mind that society may channel or dispose or frustrate our ambivalent needs, but does not destroy them.

Whatever the specific sources, Americans seem to be closely

ambivalent as between liberal, individualistic success versus communal or conservative-communal needs and dispositions. This is an
important key (in addition to the blandishments of Madison Avenue
and to dictates of specific institutions) to understanding the
exaggerated (conservatively) liberal, Lockean, bourgeois quality of
our dominant cultural goals and orientations. The culture has ways
of assimilating and emasculating its communal opposition, ways that
are at least as effective as outright repression—principally by means
of a one-dimensionalization of what it is we think we want. Thus we
are returned to much the same alienations, and we seem to resemble
ourselves more the more we change. Our innocence concerning what
we want, our own one-dimensionalization of our wants, is the chief
ally of the dominant culture and its principal beneficiaries in insuring that protest becomes part of the alienated scene. Without denying for a moment that there are significant and pervasive social- and
economic-institutional constraints impinging upon us—external barriers to self-expression and self-realization, institutional sources of
alienation—we must not mistake this popular and congenial view of
alienation and its sources for the whole picture.

Anomie Reinterpreted

I began this reinterpretation of anomie with Robert Merton's
interpretation, which defines anomie as a disjunction of culture and
society resulting from a cultural overemphasis on success goals and
an underemphasis on the social-institutional means by which success
is supposed to be pursued and achieved.

I have sought to improve Merton's conception of this disjunction
in two ways. The first focuses on the difficulties of succeeding, and
amounts to an elaboration of his conception of the disjunction
between dominant cultural goals and social-institutional means of
attaining them. Merton ascribes these difficulties primarily to the
barriers to success that social stratification and ascripted advantage
place in the path of individuals from certain social groups and classes.
But he misses the extent to which our games and goals and the
motivations they assume are low-synergetic: that is, they assume,
they demand, and they regularly and reliably produce losers. They

are, in this sense, unsatisfiable or unshareable. And this is more serious because we successfully spread wide the desire to succeed. The culture is genuinely egalitarian in suggesting that each of us has the chance and indeed the responsibility of making himself unequally successful, and escapist egalitarian in not facing up to the consequences of this emphasis. I further argued that the difficulties involve more than the question of whether the wish to compete and advance is present, more than not being handicapped by social circumstances, and I have tried to elaborate some of these requirements and demands on the individual. In the process I suggested that, contrary to Freud, considerable delay and repression of impulse need not be in the service of Eros or communal values but instead can be in the service of egoistic goals. Even perfect equality of opportunity in Merton's sense—the absence of social barriers to advancement—favors some skills, styles, and propensities and discriminates against others. Criteria of merit may be applied universally, but there are no universal criteria of merit.

These considerations augment Merton's concern with the shareability or satisfiability of our cultural goals, while retaining his basic conception of the disjunction. My second line of criticism extends the notion of disjunction, and the concept of anomie, by addressing the conflict between those cultural success goals and those individual inclinations or inabilities that are useless or inimical to culturally dominant goals. This involves the consideration of cultural contradictions and individual ambivalence: the idea of contradictions within the culture, the notion of mixed motives and conflicting desires, and thus the question of whether these dominant cultural goals are satisfying, whatever the extent to which they can be satisfied.

Thus I have tried to improve Merton's view of American culture by discussing genuine cultural contradictions and how these relate to individual ambivalences, suggesting further reasons why the losers lose and ways in which even the winners lose, and we are all touched by anomie. In apparent contradiction to those dominant goals and motivations stressed by Merton—individualism, success orientation, activism, competitiveness—Americans simultaneously have, and are taught and encouraged to have, aspirations I have chosen to call communal. The latter needs and aspirations can be detected in the exaggerations of the former, in our rapid oscillation between apparent extremes, and even in the peculiar plasticity by which the dominant culture and its chief beneficiaries manage to absorb, transform, and emasculate the opposition. This argument aids in understanding how one side of us is implicated in what the other side finds oppressive. It also helps in understanding why some individuals reject cultural goals, legitimate social means, or both, and why others exhibit wish-generated inabilities to make it.

Anomie, then, is this disjunction, this rulelessness. It suggests a critical perspective that not only questions dominant American cultural emphases, but also questions prevailing conceptions of democracy that naively reflect these emphases. This conception of anomie suggests that those leftist and left-liberal critics who find the sole source of our alienation in omnipresent and coercive social institutions have indeed "stood truth happily on her head." It questions the culture and the analyses of these critics both from the standpoints of human satisfaction and the satisfiability or shareability of our goals. Nor is its application limited to those who deviate or fail: we are all touched by anomie, and to focus on deviants (as Merton and others tend to do) is a mistake, especially when we compound the error by focusing exclusively on deviants who do not have the resources necessary to cheat and cut corners in multimillion-dollar style. Nor does this concept of anomie imply, as Merton's seems to, that our condition can be dealt with merely by means of better socialization agencies and messages. On the contrary: part of the problem is that most Americans know damn well what the society is all about.

The two kinds of questions, shareability and satisfaction, are closely related but by no means synonymous, contrary to what many social critics imply. The question of shareability would not be settled by goals that would satisfy if only we could achieve them. The genuinely egalitarian strain in American culture and in American conceptions of individualism make such a question increasingly pressing; Kohlberg's research suggests that more and more of us will give this kind of question more explicit attention; and historical circumstances may be conspiring to make such questions increasingly unavoidable. Be this as it may, I have tried to suggest that in fully accounting for what is unreasonable or unworkable about this society and culture, it is important to recognize that we have ambivalent needs and motivations; that communal as well as success needs are frustrated; that it is our anomie, as well as coercive, constraining institutions, that leads so often to our alienation; and that we misinterpret our dissatisfaction only to exacerbate the symptoms.

Anomie and the critical perspective it entails are inevitably bound up with both shareability and satisfaction, both approaches to explaining why Americans may not really want what we think we want. Let us keep both approaches in mind as we further pursue the notion of anomie in connection with the question of inequality and the spillovers of economic growth and technological innovation.

8 The Inherently Unsatisfactory, the Downright Unfair, and the Merely Unworkable

Here I suggest the relevance of anomie to justifying distributive shares and coping with the spillovers of economic activity, especially economic growth and technology in the service of profit. Significantly, these concerns are usually dealt with singly, and not in this context, but I will try to show the usefulness of seeing them in relationship to the anomie which underlies and aggravates them.

Distributive Justice as a Collective Issue

As Daniel Bell has pointed out, no one votes on the overall pattern of rewards in this society, yet human beings require a rationale, democratic or not, for differences in rewards. This is especially acute in a cultural context that is egalitarian in significant respects. What is the rationale for differences in rewards meted out by a system of private enterprise, prices, and markets?[1]

Look first at the production side: according to the liberal economist, individuals should be compensated according to their productivity. More precisely, compensation should be equal to the marginal value-product of the individual's labor, or the other factors of production he may own. In any event this should be true of pre-tax distributive shares. If each factor is paid its marginal contribution, it can be demonstrated that the market economy is efficient in the sense of being Pareto-optimal. In this context, Pareto-optimality means that no further rearrangement of distributive shares can help at least one individual without taking from others.[2] Because I am involved in a joint process of production, I may be better off than I would otherwise be (in the absence of compensation according to marginal principles) because someone somewhere else in the process is better off than I am.

Payment according to the marginal value-product of factors reminds us that the demand for the individual's labor is a demand derived from the product he assists in producing. Contrary to Marx and Ricardo, no iron law of wages specifies a necessary long-run relationship, certainly not an equivalence between his wage and the subsistence wage.[3] Wages simply reflect relative demand for different products, in conjunction with supply of various kinds of labor. On the supply side there can be ascripted social advantage, inherent genetic advantage, not to mention persistence, initiative, daring, dedication, and the sheer disposition to work hard. From a cosmic point of view, this can be seen as a social, genetic, and dispositional lottery in which elements of accident and luck loom large, especially when compounded by the luck of being strategically located with skills or resources with which to provide something that happens to be in demand.[4]

It may be objected that the designation "luck" ignores the fact that people have freely voted with their dollars to establish the pattern of demand, and (ideally) are free to vote with their feet by moving to more attractive or lucrative jobs. But the analogy with voting is specious. It leads us directly back to the initial distribution of income and wealth, which largely determines the pattern of demand. Moreover, it affects the ability to provide labor skills in great demand, to compensate for genetic or dispositional disadvantages, and to take advantage of distant opportunities. Even insofar as merit determines the ability to meet the demand, this is tantamount to determining merit, and with it distributive shares, by means of the initial distribution. This, too, is circular reasoning. Voting with dollars is plutocracy, maybe, but not democracy: relative scarcities do not add up to distributive justice.

Now let us approach the same matter from the consumption side, an approach which leads to utility theory. Utility was introduced into economic discourse to explain the difference between value and price, or value-in-use and value-in-exchange.[5] Adam Smith posed the problem in connection with the relative prices of water, so essential but so cheap, and diamonds, hardly essential but expensive. This is counterintuitive: it does not do justice to water. The solution, as articulated by Alfred Marshall, is that water is less expensive than diamonds because the marginal utility of that last drop of water consumed is less than the marginal utility of that last diamond, given the relative abundance of water. On the other hand, water's total utility, given its essentiality to life, is infinite. Marshall argued that "the law of human nature on which this is based is the law of satiable wants."

As Joan Robinson has pointed out, utility theory was intended and interpreted by many as a mainstay of the argument that individuals should be left alone to dispose of their income as they see fit and therefore as a defense of the rewards distributed by the market. Left alone, the individual consumer is free to arrive at a pattern of consumption in which the last dollar spent on each item adds the same amount to his welfare. Any other allocation of his consumption expenditures means that a net gain in welfare can be obtained by shifting expenditures to items whose marginal utility per dollar is higher. Once he reaches this optimal point, the last dollar spent on his various consumption items yields a common marginal utility of income.

For the individual to allocate expenditures in this way is little more than refined common sense. Yet the use of this argument in justifying a given pretax distribution of income is another matter. If our interest is in maximizing society's total utility, then defending a given distribution amounts to assuming that the last dollar spent by each member is as valuable to him as the last dollar spent by others. Until there is a common marginal utility of income for all the members of the society, total welfare can be increased through redistribution. Thus in spite of itself, utility theory reveals its egalitarian undercurrent. Marshall himself did not shrink from it. While his law of satiable wants does not necessarily imply declining marginal utility of income as one's income increases—since satiability in one want does not necessarily imply that another want cannot be found—Marshall thought the stronger form of the proposition was self-evident, too: "A shilling is the measure of less pleasure, or satisfaction of any kind, to a rich man than to a poor one."[6]

Theoretically, there are at least three ways of avoiding this egalitarian potential in utility theory. The first and somewhat dated approach is frankly elitist: individuals, or whole classes or races or nationalities, may differ in their capacity for pleasure, happiness, and pain: "For, if sentients differ in *Capacity for Happiness*—under similar circumstances some classes of sentients experiencing on an average more pleasure (for example, of imagination and sympathy) and less pain (for example, of fatigue) than others—there is no assumption that equality of circumstances is the most felicitous arrangement."[7] Or to put it more bluntly: "How do I know that it hurts you more to have your leg cut off than it hurts me to be pricked by a pin?"[8]

We now think of these as matters of belief, not knowledge, and from all appearances such beliefs are no longer seriously entertained. Or at least they are rarely argued in public. Insofar as vestiges of the argument are heard, we likewise hear considerable disagreement concerning just who should be pricked and who should be cut. After all, to justify present inequalities in this way requires an argument that these inequalities accurately reflect different capacities for happiness. But who believes that the distribution of such capacities is as skewed as the distribution of wealth and income? Insofar as this is the case, who believes that capacities for happiness determine inequalities, and not vice versa?

We seldom hear such a frontal assault on equality, not from utility theorists.[9] The neoclassical economists, and the generations of economists who have followed them have proceeded in two other closely related ways. One, perhaps the orthodox position in modern liberal economics, denies that interpersonal comparisons of utility can be made. One way of supporting inequality is to shroud your brief on behalf of it in a profession of ignorance of what others feel and experience. This destroys the rationale for redistribution; but it likewise destroys the rationale for the existing distribution. The latter implication has received less attention. The second way of proceeding is to focus on aggregate production and the problem of increasing it. More is better. Not "soak the rich," but "deal me in": the American attitude, David Potter has argued. Your percentage share of the pie may not increase, but your slice gets larger as the pie does. And maybe (a backhanded concession to the theory of declining marginal utility) the rich will become more careless or generous with the crumbs.

On closer look the argument has both a static and dynamic version. Aside from the question of growth, how much change in a poor man's income would result from the most extreme redistribution? Surprisingly little, it is argued. Compounding the problem, there are the possible disincentive effects of high taxes on the initiative and effort of the highly productive rich, and also those lower middle classes who measure their progress by their distance from the poor. Once these effects work themselves out, it is possible that the least well-off in a society characterized by considerable inequality may be better off than if they were in a situation of perfect equality.[10] This incentive argument for inequality applies analogously to economic growth, where another argument enters the picture. Until recently, many economists considered inequalities of wealth and income necessary to generate the savings vital to growth. Poor people have the distressing habit of spending all their income, and all of any additional income: their marginal propensity to consume is disappointingly near one, sometimes higher. Yet saving, which by definition is the act of refraining from present consumption, is necessary to finance the net investment instrumental to growth. I will examine each point in turn.

That redistribution would mean little absolute change in the income of the poor is a moot point. It hinges on what is thought to be little; small absolute increases in income might seem large to those whose incomes are small, and for whom small absolute increases are large percentage increases, especially if the increase put them over the line below which living decently is difficult or impossible. Also, we should take care to think of mean, not median income: the latter is considerably below the former precisely because the distribution is skewed.[11]

As for the second point, some research suggests that disincentive effects, both statically and dynamically, both on the top and the bottom of the income distribution, might be surprisingly low. The question is neither simple nor settled, and would depend crucially on how much redistribution we contemplate and on the difference between transitional and long-run effects.[12] The long-run effects can only be matters of speculation, but the practice of moonlighting among lower-middle-class heads of households and the obviously driven quality of the work and dedication of those executives who already have more money than they can dispose of, certainly suggest that the disincentive effects could easily be overestimated.

The third point, justifying inequalities as necessary to the financing of growth, has lost considerable weight since Keynes. We know now that compensatory fiscal and monetary policies can be used to promote growth and redistribution simultaneously. Paul Samuelsen adds employment to this list, and bluntly argues that "a community can have full employment, can at the same time have the rate of capital formation it wants, and can accomplish all this compatibly with the degree of income redistribution it ethically desires."[13] Samuelsen's implied optimism concerning the requisite political will and economic expertise to prevent inflation and to redistribute, no doubt strikes us as a bit overdone in light of recent experience. But his essential point holds. In the post-Keynesian context the continued advocacy of inequalities in order to promote growth cloaks, in the language of bogus economics, a political choice on behalf of inequality.

But the question of whether growth is worthwhile is logically prior to whether we need inequality to promote it. So turn to growth itself—irrespective of how it is financed—and its supposed contribution to welfare and redistribution. Two common rationales for growth are that its gains are widespread, or at least trickle down; and second, insofar as they are not, the haves will be more prone to share with the have-nots in an expanding economy. The latter is the "not yet" approach to redistribution: we are not rich enough, not yet. There are few economists who will not offer these arguments once the subject of the disadvantaged is broached. Sometimes a weaker form of them is offered: growth is Pareto-optimal, improving the lot of at least one and worsening the fortunes of no one. Yet the news from the redistribution front is mixed and its interpretation is unclear.

And there are reasons for believing that the contribution of growth per se to redistribution may be negligible, or increasingly slim.[14] The economy from which generally impoverished minorities now demand their fair share has changed radically from that which faced the waves of immigrants who arrived in the nineteenth and early twentieth century: it has been suggested that ours is a nation that built all its pyramids before fully freeing its slaves. The corporate industrial sector, the great provider in the past of relatively unskilled but good-paying jobs with hope of advancing part way up the socioeconomic ladder (if only in the next generation) seems to be giving way to a sector of the economy for which highly advanced training is a prerequisite. "Training" and "education" barely hint at the growing cultural distance involved. Given the persistence of high levels of both inflation and unemployment, surely the edge must be granted to those economists who argue that much of our unemployment is not due to a deficiency in aggregate demand.[15]

That the black middle class made considerable progress during the 1960s does not necessarily contradict this argument. There is evidence that these gains had as much to do with political pressures and measures, eventually with deliberate governmental anti-discriminatory and social welfare measures, than with the natural course of an expanding economy. Central to these measures was the recognition that ascripted social disadvantages must be deliberately combated, and that discrimination in favor of certain skills and levels of educational attainment is discrimination against the human beings who lack them. Growth may have indirectly facilitated this heightened consciousness of the plight of the poor, but it did not foreordain it. It was initiated and carried through, as Martin Luther King, Jr. was fond of saying, by those who were sick and tired of being sick and tired. And many have never arrived.[16] Habermas has stressed that the issue facing the Left in advanced industrial societies is not so much the plight of the exploited as that of the excluded. Truth may still be seen in the eyes of the new poor, but it is harder and harder to see the new poor as the embodiment of socialist logic in history.

Notwithstanding the glaring exceptions, there has been a sizable increase in the real income of most groups in this economy's postwar years. Are we better off?

Crucial to the case for economic growth is the proposition that wants exist independently of the goods that satisfy them. Otherwise it is fair to ask, with Galbraith, why we would not be as well off without the additional wants and the additional goods. Or better off, considering the additional pains it takes to acquire them. The half-serious joke among economists is that happiness equals consumption divided by the desire for consumption. But few make jokes about the necessity of increasing the numerator: holding down the denominator is a dated strategy, however sound theoretically. What is apparently happening is neither of these: desires seem to be expanding apace with consumption.

Consider a simple thought-experiment. Think of the level of desire for consumption twenty-five years ago. Make the plausible assumption that, in each income class, the desire for consumption items exceeded consumption by about 10 percent. That is, we were about nine-tenths happy. Had desire remained unchanged from then until now, we should be deliriously happy at least. We should now be drowning in uninvested savings rather than in rising prices. Or reverse the experiment. If desire were as high then as now, then frustration must have been unimaginably, unbearably high. The nostalgia craze serves as a symbolic reminder that there is no such evidence.[17]

Desire for consumption seems to be holding its own vis à vis what is available. It is probably a causal relationship, not a mere correlation. After all, there is a multibillion dollar per year industry whose primary goal is to see that it is no accident. And we must not let our justifiable skepticism concerning the efficacy of any one advertising appeal affect our judgment on the overall contribution of advertising to our anxiety and dissatisfaction with what we have and who we are.

Of course our comparisons are not only with how much we used to have but also with what others have now. That this is also by design, and designed by some of the same architects, can be ascertained from the most random and cursory sampling of television commercials, together with the majority of the programs they sponsor. Most Americans might prefer a 5 percent increase in their own income, holding the incomes of others constant, to a 20 percent increase in everyone's income, theirs included. If so, it would be a good measure of the low-synergetic nature of our success goals. This form of the proposition sounds extreme, and certainly we would not expect it to hold for those who need the 20 percent increase just to get by. But there is reason to believe that a milder version of this relative income hypothesis does hold, and there is no reason at all to think that the scarcity mentality necessary to growth makes it any less likely. Growth and the emphasis on it make major contributions to the human knack of imagining and thus creating scarcity – the same scarcity whose elimination serves as a rationale for growth.

To summarize: the distribution of income and wealth in a free market reflects relative scarcities of supply of labor and resources in conjunction with relative intensities of demand for final products. Looking at the factors affecting supply and demand leads us back to the initial distribution of income and wealth, a prime determinant of both. Since the given distribution cannot justify itself by reference to itself, there is nothing necessarily optimal nor just about it. Approaching the same question from the consumption standpoint, either we assume that utility is a meaningful concept, in which case utility theory has strong egalitarian implications; or we deny that utilities can be compared among individuals, and we are left with no defense of any distribution, including the given one. A third alternative of great historical and theoretical importance in attempting to finesse the questions of inequality and redistribution is to shift the emphasis to aggregate production and economic growth. But similar conclusions obtain here. It is questionable whether significant redistribution would so adversely affect the aggregate production through disincentive effects that the poorest would thereby be worse off. Nor does it seem necessary, not since Keynes, to rationalize gross inequalities as a means of financing growth. Moreover, the contribution of growth to redistribution is uncertain. This is partly because the new poor, the excluded no longer are automatically included in the fruits of economic expansion. It is also because growth seems to be predicated on increasing the very dissatisfaction and envy it is supposed to alleviate, tending to make welfare and distributive justice matters of relative shares alone. Everyone cannot win, yet the emphasis is on winning: hence another rationale for growth undercuts itself.

Having said all this, we need to be clear on what has not been said. That we cannot avoid the question of redistribution by means of economic growth is not necessarily an argument against growth. Growth may be needed to prevent increasing inequality – a proposition for which there is logical and some empirical support, beginning with the compelling fact that should the size of the pie ever be fixed, then the absolute shares of the richer must decrease if the lot of the poorer is improved. The conclusion is a negative one: neither market principles nor economic growth can dispose of the question of inequality. Distributive justice is, as was always, a collective problem.

This should come as no great surprise. The ground I have covered is familiar, and the distributive criteria I have criticized have an air of nineteenth-century innocence or escapism about them. By now many of us have faced up to the fact that a just distribution is no more given in economics texts than in the stars. Certainly this is not news to those who have had the political wherewithal to affect the parameters and conditions under which economic activity has proceeded, and thereby the results which have obtained. Socialism for the rich; free enterprise for the poor, who do not have the choice of whether to honor laissez-faire or breach it. But I believe we can go further, to state good reasons for recognizing the situation of the excluded as a collective concern. In part this is because that loss of innocence may be spreading to the excluded; reducing inequalities may become a matter of enlightened self-interest on the part of the haves, as President Kennedy suggested. But also because there has always been a genuinely egalitarian streak in American character—however escapist or ineffectual, however little the feeling of social equality has been reflected in the distribution (and redistribution) of wealth and income; and however innocent we may be of the way the economy not only produces but also demands losers. Faced with competition, Americans are competitors. But we must not do ourselves the disservice of assuming that our rational individual adaptations within the given legal and social context necessarily coincide with our best thought and sentiments concerning what would be a better society. Nor can we ignore the egalitarian trajectory of American history. In any event the question of whether we are better off as a result of economic activity and growth is larger than the question of whether per capita income, or indeed every single income, has risen. The notion that society must accept that distribution of the goods and services generated by the economy is but one important facet of our rulelessness, of the ignoble idea that society is necessarily sort of a by-product or residual of (largely profit-propelled) economic activity. Surely the home of the free can do better. Taking temporary leave of the question of inequality, let us turn to a wider consideration of the effects of economic activity. For even if the question of distributive justice could somehow be resolved by growth—and surely it cannot—growth would remain problematic in its own right.

The Collective Control of Spillovers

Whether or not we focus on distributive justice, welfare cannot be reduced to economics. One important qualification to the proposition that welfare increases with per capita income is that we must take account of any side effects of economic activity, whether in production or consumption. A final, most modern and liberal argument upholding the positive connection between growth and welfare will introduce the problem of the spillovers of economic activity.

This argument is as simple as it is appealing: higher incomes mean increased options, and this in itself is a good thing. In economic discourse the argument is associated with a modern child of utility theory, the theory of revealed preferences, which purports to take the value judgment out of utility. Utility, in this view, does not exist apart from observed choices; individuals simply prefer what they are observed to prefer.

But this takes the utility out of utility theory, not the value judgment. Utility that does not exist apart from actual choices and which cannot be compared from person to person is barely intelligible, much less useful. As for the value judgment, it involves two assumptions. First, the general expansion of choice is desirable. Second, certainly but more subtly a value judgment: higher incomes make this possible. As Mishan has remarked, this approach substitutes a theory of freedom for a theory of satisfaction. The older focus on satisfaction was troublesome anyway. It tempts us to discriminate among and meddle with the individual's choices, and to wonder whether more net satisfaction might be obtained by transferring dollars to the poor. Instead: more choice is better, period. In the final analysis what matters is not the goods delivered by the economy, but the choices.

Therefore we should judge this rationale for economic growth, the doctrine of increased choices, as a theory of freedom, and as such it is objectionable on two grounds. The first is that even if higher incomes did expand options, the implied view of freedom is shallow, as my preceding arguments concerning human ambivalence have suggested. The multiplication of choice can frighten, bewilder, or bore us. It may exhilarate us, however temporarily. Under certain circumstances it may contribute to the enhancement of freedom. Why it should make us free, or in itself constitute freedom, or progress, is not clear. Whatever else human freedom involves, it must include reasoned choice among identifiable alternatives by reference to criteria that are more or less understood by the chooser. We are not so instinctually blessed as to avoid contradicting ourselves and making a mockery of our freedom when we release our choosing from all constraints. Choices are like questions posed to us, and questioning everything leaves us no standards by which to evaluate the answers. Standards and guidelines, however temporary their authority, are even necessary for us to know what it is we are overcoming or transcending, and when. An appeal to instinct or to basic human needs will not do, unless by basic human needs we mean some humanly created conception of human nature by which we structure our preferences. This is one reason the mindless multiplication of choice would be a species of subjection.

The theory is likewise shallow in not recognizing that our interest in freedom is ambivalent, as I suggested in discussing the rise of the supposedly therapeutic culture. Chaos would be deeply disturbing even if it did not mean we kept contradicting ourselves, failed to plan ahead, and generally made a mess of things. Part of the motivation in expanding options is to find that better, more secure, more comforting, more lasting option. The option to end all options, perhaps, to be done with the proliferation of choices by which the underlying malady is more aggravated than soothed. The very speed and frenzy with which we drop each new choice for another, the lack of attention we show it, are rough indexes of powerful conservative needs. Of course we are culturally trained (witness this theory of freedom) to misinterpret the resulting frustration as being due to a deficiency in the number of our options. So we redouble our efforts to double them. But the stress on expanding options can not only undercut the intelligibility or validity of criteria by which options hold significance for us; it can also rob us of the emotional tolerance and the fascination necessary to appreciate them. Among the costs connected with too many choices and too few criteria is the inability to notice when significant choices are passed over or even destroyed forever. The multiplication of choice can decrease our tolerance for real variety. It can blind us to genuine variety, and to the destruction of variety. What it cannot do is make us satisfied with such results. After all: freedom is the goal, and alienation is to be overcome. Who wants his options destroyed?

Not only is the doctrine of increased choice emotionally untenable when carried to excess, it may also be literally untrue. It is probably impossible to expand choices in general. All growth is change, destroying as well as creating options. By some crude quantity theory of freedom, it might be argued that there are more choices once incomes are higher. But sooner or later such a theory must confront the questions of what is a choice, and what are significant choices—not to mention the question of more choices for whom. Once these questions are raised it will be obvious that the theory gives preference to certain kinds of choices over others, and then we are entitled to ignore its claim to be value-free.

Higher incomes probably do mean that we have more consumption options as a result, though even this is a proposition requiring considerable qualification. This "more" is rarely inclusive of the previous consumption options. Even if consumption options were expanded in the inclusive as well as quantitative sense, the proposition that things are thereby better, or even that choices have generally expanded, remains dubious. Not only do new consumption menus typically involve the destruction of the old alternatives— nothing so dated, so unavailable, as last year's fashions—but also they are stressed at the expense of choices in different spheres of our lives.

As Mishan has suggested, it can be argued that the more relevant and significant choices relate to the possibility of alternative social and cultural environments, even by reference to the sheer magnitude and pervasiveness of consequences, or the quantity-of-choice criterion. The most dedicated, privatistic, sophisticated-hedonist-of-a-consumer should be among the first, not last, to agree. In any event, consumption choices and frenzy can be promoted at the expense of the choice of environments necessary to their enjoyment: the contribution of the automobile to the destruction of the integrity of local communities is a notorious case in point. And growth or change-induced deterioration in conditions of the work setting must further qualify our advocacy of growth and change.

Thus we come to the question of the spillovers of economic activity in its full generality. Any negative or positive effects of growth, whether these occur in connection with consumption or production, must be tallied in assessing the contribution of growth to welfare: "All the measurable effects on other people or firms arising in the production and use of any good—other than those effects which already register in the market mechanism in the form of alterations in product and factor prices—must be brought into the cost calculus."[18]

According to the economist's overcompensation principle, the price charged and fetched in any transaction should be greater or equal to the total social costs involved in the production or use of the object of the transaction. Economically speaking, the winners should compensate the losers. It is an impeccably liberal principle, respectful of the wishes of everyone who is affected, not just the immediate parties to the transaction. It may be regarded as a relaxation of the principle of Pareto-optimal change. Pareto-optimal change benefits someone without harming anyone, and if taken seriously would probably allow for no change whatsoever. The overcompensation principle allows change so long as those harmed are compensated; otherwise it has a strong element of moral neutrality. Birthrights may be sold if there is no coercion and the price is right.

The conditions under which price exceeds or falls short of total social costs ought therefore to be matters of great interest even to liberals. In economic parlance the divergences between private costs (which enter the reckoning of individuals and groups, the accounts of

business firms, and so forth) and total social costs (which may or
may not) are called externalities. The explicit reference is to the
internal cost accounting of private firms, with respect to which
externalities are external. In this way we are reminded of what is
perhaps the most important source of violations of the overcompensation principle.

Less technically (following Mishan), these divergences may be
called spillovers. Spillovers can be positive or negative; they can
range from effects easily calculated in dollars to those whose very
nature, much less magnitude, is unknown. There is no necessary
agreement on what in fact are costs, or who suffers them. Nor is
there necessary agreement on just how far we should go in assessing
spillovers. As Mishan has pointed out, the very idea of your having
purchased a new car may distress the rest of us mightily; but forcing
you either to compensate us for the psychic damage or else return it
may open Pandora's box, out of which might spring all manner of
illiberal meddling.

But we need not limit ourselves to examples involving psychic
costs, however interesting or important these might be to ponder.
A good case can be made that our interdependency and interactions,
though not our sense of relatedness, are growing. While not denying
that perceptions of what is a spillover cost, how much is tolerable,
and what is private and public can change, the tangible social consequences of nominally private decisions and actions have actually
increased. Unlike the psychic distress your owning a new car causes
me, these costs are not in my head. They may be in my lungs: your
car may contribute to my eventual asphyxiation. Or it may crash
into me. In and out of our cars, the bumping together is physical,
demonstrable, indisputable: it is the evidence of our senses. We may
be running out of space, quiet, privacy, nonrenewable resources,
energy, and time. In the broadest possible sense, we are becoming
increasingly congested.[19]

The factors behind the upswing in externalities include the closing
of our frontiers, a relentless growth in population, and increased
urbanization (if we include the suburbs). Also contributing were
increased occupational and geographical mobility; improvements in
automobile and jet transportation and associated increased interest

in travel; and improvements in communications, especially television but also bugging devices. We have seen the growth of huge institutions—government, corporations, unions—whose actions involve larger and larger numbers and affect still more. Undergirding all this has been economic growth and change, propelled by the implementation of new technologies, particularly those employed in the service of private profit. What we now enjoy might therefore be called, as Lewis Mumford has suggested, the unearned excrement of profit-propelled economic growth and technological innovation.[20]

This proposition is considerably less controversial now than, say, fifteen years ago. But the exact identity of even the nature of the difficulties, not to mention remedies, is considerably more controversial. A simple exercise will be helpful in dispensing with simplistic answers.

Whatever else we know about congestion, we know it begins at home. The decision to make or not make a baby is paradigmatic as well as basic.[21] Even the fact that it is sometimes a nondecision can be instructive. Assuming it is not accidental, what enters into the decision? The benefits parents derive from an additional child can be among the most intense, profound, and personal. (Increasingly, children are more likely to be consumption items, rather than additional means of production in helping, say, with farm work.) Direct costs to the parents are by no means negligible (through college, easily $50,000), but then little of this expense is incurred at the outset. More important, in such matters of the heart many consider such calculations distasteful.

If this underestimation of costs is true where direct costs to parents are concerned, it is doubly true of the additional social costs of an additional child. Even with the best of intentions and techniques, it is hard to imagine parents making such an estimate with much precision. Both intentions and techniques are largely absent partly because we have little by way of ideology to make such calculations a matter of moral concern. Nor are we coerced into paying some approximation of the total social costs of this most intimately private act. The child's contribution to social costs is negligible with respect to total spillovers, and will be scattered about in countless contexts. The same congestion that makes his contribution problematic makes it inconsequential compared to the total. One child does not overcrowd the world.

Were we to follow this hypothetical child through his imaginary life we would undoubtedly observe his making countless decisions, weighty and trivial, involving many of the same considerations as the decision, or nondecision, that put him here in the first place. The same kind of disparity between rational, self-interested individual adaptations and desirable collective results—many of which he too desires—would obtain. In part this may be because he does not give a damn. In larger part it will be due to not thinking, or being encouraged or forced to think of the external costs attendant to his decisions, much less to pay for them. At least not until the collective results are in, at which time we may all pay.

It is tempting to blame all this on the bourgeoisie, their direct and indirect influence over the media and the attitudes and behavior-patterns they foster among all of us. Certainly, one of the outstanding if not defining characteristics of bourgeois institutions and attitudes is that they encourage us in the Smithian belief that, as Schelling said, a benevolent teleology relates our individual adaptations to collective results; and then they encourage behavior for which the opposite relationship obtains. The direct and indirect contribution of identifiably bourgeois institutions and attitudes to spillovers is in little danger of being overestimated, certainly not in this culture. But the problem of such disparities, as we follow the child around, can be seen as a broader one. Admittedly, as a producer he will typically be involved in institutions whose livelihood depends on being seductively Philistine about the total social impact of their economic activity: the circumstances under which the search for profit coincides with the overcompensation principle have little to do with the success or failure of the search. Similarly, as a consumer his Lockean attitudes toward the use and disposal of his private property often do not help matters. He may dirty up the landscape or disturb its serenity with a ridiculously clean conscience.

But again, more important, the prices affixed to many things he buys and does will not cover the costs—of the noise he can make, the pedestrians he can tyrannize, and the traffic jams and fouled air to which his purchase entitles him to contribute. Moreover, growth and change per se, and his attitudes toward them, play independent roles, independent of specifically bourgeois attitudes and institutions on the one hand and the inevitable dictates of technology on the other.[22] His restlessness, his penchant for mobility or newness or bigness, are not bourgeois in themselves (though we would be remiss in not recognizing in the background the Cheshire smile of the manufacturer of this year's new and bigger model as our child motors by). In many cases an old-fashioned, serious, lasting concern with one's private possessions, whether automobiles or farm land, can be more socially responsible than the temporary attitudes appropriate to a temporary society.

Similarly with technology, whose pernicious effects cannot all be ascribed to bourgeois greed or to its inevitable applications. Technology can blow things up; it can also prevent things from happening—the child himself is a prime example. In general, but especially in the farthest reaches of the biological sciences, science and technology are asking us to make our definition of humanity more explicit and binding, lest we relegate ourselves to the status of by-products of whatever technological advances are made and implemented.[23] That is, our attitudes toward technology, whether it manifests itself as the bomb or the pill, are independently important and deeply embedded in our attitudes toward what is human. After a certain point indicting greedy capitalists and the pursuit of profit obscures as much as it reveals; and the notion that the effects of technology are pernicious and inevitable must be a combination of selective perception and the fact that the development and implementation of technology have often combined the inappropriate with the unprincipled.[24] At the same time, it is clear that we cannot afford to have the development and marketing of the bomb, or any of literally hundreds of new technological capabilities, guided solely by the principle of profit or the attitude that we must do it because we are capable of it. Under these circumstances it would be only accidental if prices covered total social costs, and both bomb and pill remind us that there are some accidents we cannot afford.

Finally there is a most important and often neglected complication involving the extent to which the gains of growth are widely distributed, and new technologies are marketed on a mass basis. More of us have the wherewithal to spread our spillovers over more of the countryside, and recently there has been a mass revival of interest in the great outdoors. So part of our failure to adequately consider the social costs of our private decisions is a failure to calculate these increasing costs by reference to an egalitarian context in which everyone is deciding to do, and increasingly has the means to do, roughly the same things.[25] We imagine ourselves escaping, pulling away from that light, alone. But we *all* do, and that is why the light may change several times before we can move these days, by which time we may all have run out of gas, along with the oil companies.

This is to say, then, that in important ways we are all in this together, all implicated in the generation of spillovers. Yet the *prima facie* case that our hypothetical child delights in polluting, chooses to participate in traffic jams, and does not care about the consequences of his activities is not altogether convincing. Choices, whether these concern spillovers or inequalities, are skewed when prices (construing the term broadly) do not reflect total social costs. This means that acquiescence, as Schelling has argued, is not necessarily a sign that things are well. The problem is that "virtue may be its own reward, but the reward is too often a collective good, shared only minutely by the virtuous individual."[26] Thus, as in our attitudes and actions toward the less fortunate, our contributions to spillovers do not tell the whole story of the collective outcomes and the kind of society we desire. Social responsibility must be in large part a product of social institutions and public policies which define responsibilities and then enforce the definition.

There is a free marketing answer to the problem of spillovers and congestion, of course: make sure that prices are free to move so as to accurately reflect scarcities. But such arguments sometimes suggest a lack of understanding of what a market is. It is one thing to discuss those conditions under which certain activities are best handled by markets, and quite another to suggest that markets are not themselves embedded in a cultural and political matrix. The so-called free market operates within parameters of law and politics and custom, and it is naive or escapist to suppose that these do not effect the structure of relative prices, what economic activity occurs in what way at what pace, not to mention to whose benefit.

So the free market solution reveals a curious asymmetry in its attitude toward coercion, as Mishan has pointed out:

> preventing a person from acquiring a good is, in economics, on all fours with compelling him to receive a bad. In either case he is constrained to accept a situation different from that which he would otherwise have chosen, and his welfare is reduced accordingly. . . . yet it can be observed that the liberal economist reacts sharply to the first form of coercion and remains comparatively unmoved by the second. . . .[27]

Accordingly, we call goods "goods," not "bads," which is why we seem to have a plethora of both goods and bads. But goods are scarce, too, or believed to be. How else could we have managed to produce so much?

This does not imply a wholesale condemnation of Western activism, which in any event would be futile, nor a mindless preference for desisting over doing. Nor is it an attack on economics and economizing, for what the new Malthusianism suggests above all is the need for a better price system. Even for activity which can be handled most simply and efficiently by decentralized decision-making in the form of markets and prices, collective decisions must provide the framework in which the system works. Depending on that framework, and the degree of institutionalized concern for affected parties, the prices charged and fetched by economic activity may or may not reflect total social costs.

The principle applies to the failure to produce collective goods as well as to not refraining from producing collective bads. As suggested in connection with Olson's critique of pluralism, the logic of collective action is such that the rational individual may refrain from helping provide collective goods for the same reasons he refuses to refrain from helping produce collective bads. In both cases the virtuous individual seems to lose more than he gains. Collective bads may be produced whether or not *I* desist, and in any case my contribution is negligible. Collective goods may be produced, and I can

enjoy them whether or not I made a contribution, which in any event
would be negligible and not crucial to their provision. Why bother?
To do so is irrational. So both forms of rationality—the private doing
and the public inaction—contribute to the irrationality of the collective results.

But there are reasons for believing that Americans are bothered.
Few commentators could write today with the confidence expressed
by Partridge in 1960. Referring to the consensus that supposedly
destroyed political philosophy, he posed the following question:

> Is there not an all but universal acceptance of the belief that
> continuous technological and economic innovation, uninterrupted
> expansion of economic resources, a continuously rising stream of
> "material welfare" are the main purposes of social life and political
> action, and also the main criteria for judging the success and
> validity of social order?[28]

That these remarks sound dated, despite the present preoccupation
with short-run, guns-and-butter economic issues, suggests that a
change in thinking has occurred. Part of the explanation for this
change is that spillovers have probably worsened. But this can only
be a beginning, as we can see from the disputes over whether any
single measure (of pollution, for example) indicates improvement
or deterioration, often even in cases where there is no dispute over
the data. Perhaps economic men are being slowed down and steadily
replaced by psychological men, as Rieff describes them, and the latter
are less likely to confuse economics with welfare, or the consumer's
paradise with unrestrained growth and consumption. Or the recognition is dawning that spillovers in an egalitarian culture produce situations in which, whatever our moral sentiments or our stage of moral
reasoning, we may all have to consider more carefully what principles
of behavior are generalizable, what goals we can pursue together, and
what freedoms, from this point of view, are privileges. Or maybe
welfare is irreducible to economics for reasons more fundamental
than the existence of spillovers, and the concern with spillovers is
really a symbolic stand-in for other communal concerns and needs
we have difficulty expressing directly.

Be this as it may, the analysis of spillovers, as with the question of inequality and the excluded, suggests another sense in which the notion that society should be a by-product of the economy is ignoble, outmoded, escapist, and unbecoming, another sense in which we suffer from rulelessness. It might prove a disastrous notion as well. In the long run, no doubt prices (again construing the term broadly) will respond to cover more of total social costs, though in the meantime new messes and crises will have been created. But of course in the long run—to use that well-worn remark of Keynes's without which any discussion of economics is incomplete—we are all dead.

The Excluded and the Congested

The question of distributive shares led us to a concern with the excluded, and the question of externalities led us to a concern with spillovers. Both concerns, I would argue, are basic elements of a potential, sorely needed communal ethic. A brief discussion of the relationship and possible conflicts between the two kinds of concerns is therefore in order.

Spillovers have distributional effects: external costs that do not cost someone are not costs. These problems are inseparable, whether or not they are amenable to simultaneous solution. Moreover, it is likely that these costs are skewed in the direction of even more inequality: that is, as a result of spillovers, welfare is distributed even more unequally than income and wealth. Those who are better off have better means by which to spread the external costs of their activity, the mobility to leave behind their waste material (as well as that of the poorer neighbors), and the financial and political resources to press their advantages and redress their grievances. Paradoxically, it is the "excluded" who cannot escape so readily: we must not automatically assume that those who can afford to be agitated and can pay handsomely to be heard are those who are affected most.

Yet the skepticism with which the excluded, or those with egalitarian sympathies, may greet the environmental movement, for example, cannot be dismissed so easily. For one thing, there is the spectacle of corporations cleaning up the mess they themselves have made at a profit, and then charging higher prices on their products to finance advertising campaigns in which they pat themselves on the back for their ecology-mindedness. This should make us wonder who will eventually pay the costs. In addition, it is likely that the industries employing the economically disadvantaged would be hit the hardest by a thoroughgoing attack on the sources of pollution.[29] Whether or not the readjustments and relocations are rendered less costly and painful, the opportunity costs of a too-narrow focus on the environment would be considerable. Or they would be for a too-narrow notion of environment, one that does not consider that the relevant environment for millions of poor and working-class Americans has more to do with working conditions, housing shortages, and safety on the streets than with overcrowding in Yellowstone and Yosemite. Unless we assume some miraculous change in what makes Americans go—as naive as the opposite assumption that we can go on indefinitely the way we have been—then the poor would have little chance in a stagnant economy.

The passionate concern for posterity, as Beckerman has suggested, is typically a middle-class concern, conveniently dealing with their guilt at being relatively affluent, leaving their own positions largely untouched while ignoring the pressing needs of members of other social strata. Stopping or slowing down the race is more likely to be favored by those who have arrived or are nearing the finish line. No doubt this often represents a genuine change of heart and values, as if the hierarchy of our needs is such that affluence allows us to feel and express the need to belong to a great natural scheme of things, to achieve some serenity, a place of rest. But also, many environmental problems and crises—from highway congestion to wilderness protection to urban sprawl to pollution to overcrowded resorts to energy shortages—result from the entry of the previously unwashed, uncultured, unobtrusive masses to the middle class. This threatens the traditional provinces and prerogatives of the already-arrived. Those with egalitarian sympathies are well advised to wonder what will be left of traditional leftist concerns once they are taken over by moralistic middle-class ecologists.[30]

This implies that we should try to take seriously both the environmental and the distributional impact of economic growth and technology, both the necessity of including the less fortunate and caring better for the environment of which we are all interdependent parts. Egalitarian measures and goals may well aggravate the problem of congestion, but surely this depends in large measure on how we define growth and on what it is we try to share. In theory, the question of who pays is separable from whether spillovers are controlled. Aside from the initial incidence, it is the overall impact of taxation and the uses to which governmental monies are put that will determine whether the cause of greater equality has been served. In the meantime it should be noted that we are actually paying for externalities anyway, and only our national income statistics, which tend to ignore the "bads" or count them as "goods," prevent us from seeing this.

So what is required is the redirection and redefinition of growth and dynamism, not their elimination, in order to hasten that day when we are

> free, therefore, to return to some of the most sure and certain principles of religion and traditional virtue—that avarice is a vice, that the exaction of usury is a misdemeanor, and the love of money is detestable, that those walk most truly in the paths of virtue and sane wisdom who take least thought for the morrow. We shall once more value ends above means and prefer the good to the useful. We shall honor those who can teach us how to pluck the hour and the day virtuously and well, the delightful people who are capable of taking direct enjoyment in things, the lilies of the field who toil not, neither do they spin.[31]

Though these remarks are reminiscent of that famous passage in the *German Ideology*, their author is not Marx but Keynes, the reputed rescuer of capitalism. And our grandchildren may occupy good Keynesian time, frolicking in those fields. Of course Keynes suggested that we must continue to pretend that "fair is foul and foul is fair" for at least another hundred years. One hundred years: the ghost of Adam Smith dies hard indeed. The way to exorcise it is to treat *all* versions of the notion that private greed rebounds to public good, those relating to spillovers as well as to distributive shares, as dubious empirical propositions and not unquestionable articles of faith.

The Anomic, the Excluded, and the Congested

I have suggested that anomie involves the frustration of personal communal or conservative-communal needs for acceptance, related-ness, dependence, affection, security, as well as the success goals stressed by Merton. I assume that anomie also underlies a variety of emergent, inchoate, and often inarticulate concerns: with loneliness, the quality of interpersonal relationships, regaining our moral bear-ings, the quality of life, and indeed the often ambiguous notion of participation on which our democratic critics place such emphasis. As our vague and awkward language suggests, the separate concerns involved and the people who are differentially affected are typically fused and confused. In particular this is true of the relationship of anomie to the question of distributive justice and the control of spillovers, concerns that are basic to an adequate conception of community and threats to community. Here I wish to explore in a tentative way the relationship of these different communal concerns.

I will begin with a caricature of the argument I am making, one provided by a group of social critics of a sociological or psycho-analytic-sociological persuasion.[32] It is to their credit that they have sought to comprehend the common significance and sources of these concerns, which are typically treated either separately or as irreconcilably opposed. But in the process they have indulged in what might be called promiscuous syncretism. Freely paraphrased, their analysis goes something like this: we are ruthless or callous toward minorities and the poor because we are rootless and anomic. We spoil each others' nests for the same reason. It is as if the successful are frustrated and lonely, they suffer in some personal way, because they have little contact with ghetto blacks.

Similarly, certain critics speak as if the same basic human needs are violated by polluted streams as they are by personal relationships and interactions polluted by competitive struggles and anxieties. (Slater, for example, virtually equates "psychic pollution" with real pollution.) The pursuit of individualistic success is a lonely affair, so they argue, which simultaneously despoils the environment and excludes the less fortunate. All such criticisms are blended into an indiscriminate indictment of the quality of life under advanced capitalism. Apparently we all are lonely, excluded, congested to about the same extent, and our difficulties have a common capitalist source and a common, vaguely socialist, solution. In these ways the psychological aspects of anomie get confused with the problems of inequality and environmental despoilation. And what is unsatisfactory about cultural goals gets confused with what is unfair, or unworkable.

Let us attempt to avoid these difficulties by discussing in pairwise fashion the relationship of anomie, first to questions of distributive justice and the plight of the excluded; and then to the problem of externalities and the spillovers of economic growth and technology.

Victimization of the excluded comes about in the first instance from the nature of a game that demands losers, and in some measure requires that we ignore them, or treat them as obstacles or pawns. Seeing this aspect of anomie does not require fancy pscyhoanalytic spectacles, and has nothing directly to do with whether our goals are satisfying if attained. But I have tried to suggest how our ambivalence toward individualistic success and its pursuit helps explain its exaggerated, exclusionary character; how that pursuit, speaking to one side of our ambivalence, is itself pursued. This suggests why our inattention to the less fortunate is sometimes pronounced and willful, and our attention is sometimes hostile and vindictive. The real people apart in this society, as Merton points out correctly but explains inadequately, are those who drop out, who just stop trying. Anyone who fails is suspect—a suspicion by which, as Nietzsche would say, we betray ourselves. To stop trying, or to be suspected of it, is even a more serious and threatening mutation than being the wrong color, though there are overlapping projections involved, overdetermined defense mechanisms.

As to whom is affected by what: seeing the problem of distributive justice and the plight of the excluded in light of the anomie which underlies and aggravates it is a separate matter from suggesting that

people in different socioeconomic circumstances are equally concerned with each problem. The less fortunate are understandably less
inclined to speak of the quality of life than the quantity of their
income; generally their discontents are much less elusive. To preach
of the bitter fruits of success to those who have not yet tasted
for themselves is to show a serious lack of sensitivity. But it is a mistake to assume that they have no concern with what the competitive
struggle does to the quality of their lives and to the ties among
human beings merely because they have neither time nor energy
nor freedom nor vocabulary with which to criticize the pollution of
interpersonal relationships, or to point out how the culture speaks
inadequately and misleadingly to their human ambivalence toward
success and striving. Any analysis of those who fail or deviate should
reveal the implied protest involved, and the resulting difficulties in
distinguishing "can't" from "don't want to," in distinguishing the
truly incompetent from those who may be too sensitive, tasteful,
different, or scrupulous to ever go very far. To suppose that the poor
are so simple as to not be subject to the same ambivalence toward
success and upward mobility is another case of viewing them as
people apart, as if only the jaded upper middle and upper classes
were concerned with the finer things and the meaningful maladies.

As for the relatively successful, no doubt many find neither real
nor intelligible the alleged problem of the lonely success, the painfully private accomplishment. Social critics should be willing to
entertain the possibility that success and egoistic striving might be
quite satisfying, and might even gain for you friends and acceptance.
And that success might just happen to be at the expense of others,
or be ecologically unsound and socially irresponsible. We must avoid
automatically assuming that only the righteous are rewarded or
happy. Nevertheless, there is little doubt that motivations in
pursuing success are mixed, and that for this reason success is not
exactly what it promises to be. It is not at all fanciful to imagine our
individualistic pursuit of success itself being pursued by assorted
communal demons—needs for love, relatedness, affection, acceptance,
inclusion—which are being continually frustrated.

But what should be emphasized is that the demons can be
released and satisfied in various ways and contexts. Some can be

satisfied at the expense of the less fortunate in the community; that is, the resulting community excludes the less fortunate. If we believe Freud, the cohesiveness of any community depends on leaving out at least one person (or race, class, nation): nothing welds a group together like a common object of hatred.[33] Alternatively, we may limit ourselves to pious and gratifying expressions of ineffectual egalitarian sentiments, which are heartfelt yet conveniently, suspiciously difficult to operationalize. Affection for distant others, as Lane has put it, is often combined with shutting out real people. We should at least be willing to consider that something more or different from an interest in equality can often be found wrapped in its banner.[34]

What I suggest is that human interests in community and in redressing inequalities may coexist, but do not necessarily: again, it depends on the kind of community. I would argue against those who, with Freud, suggest that they cannot coexist, as a matter of logic or psychology. For some, mere mention of community (or consensus) conjures up ascripted advantages, hierarchy, stagnation, provincialism, racism, intolerance, and a host of "barriers such that under them modern men cannot breathe"—as Simmel said in reference to life in small towns. It is a point of view consistent with the history of past communities and tragically underlined by the experience of Nazi Germany, after which the concept of political community should never again be used carelessly or lightly. Robert Lane writes: "It is the very absence of community that makes a democracy possible. It is the failure to see the difference between a nation-state and a city state that has given plausibility to the argument for community."[35] Indeed, he continues, "in the nation-state some identity diffusion and a touch of anomie are necessary for democracy to survive."[36] And finally: ". . . those seeking 'intimacy' seek totalitarianism." In this view, it is not the rootless who are ruthless. On the contrary: the predicate of social harmony, stability, and even progress may be universal and benign indifference, not unmixed with a touch of confusion and a general lack of passion and heroism, at least in connection with collective ideals and goals. It is a vision similar in many respects to Rieff's therapeutic culture.

Yet it is possible to wholeheartedly endorse Lane's prescription, and with it his underlying concern for what community can imply and has meant, while denying his implicit diagnosis of the state of the patient, and denying this is what community necessarily means. The diagnostic spectacles I have fashioned here reveal a chronic case of acute anomia, not just a touch. And our alienation is equally acute: the two are not so much opposite maladies as they are mutual breeding grounds for each other. From chaos and confusion and uncertainty it is a short and natural step to the notion that this, that, or the other is just the way things are. One does the following in situations of this kind. The national interest requires it. Wartime rallies around the flag, any war. I'm only doing my job. The President, or the CIA, knows best. (Certainly we already have a national political community of sorts.)[37] We must accommodate ourselves to the economy, to technology, to progress. We even hear that it is human nature to play the game, to compete—and particularly relevant here—to accept the pattern of rewards meted out by the market, to ignore those who are shortchanged. Stuck with an immutable human nature, here in the home of the free!

I suggest that recognizing our common and human ambivalence toward striving and success—all Americans want success and distinction, in some sense and measure, and all want something different—is an important prerequisite to a fuller understanding of our treatment of the less fortunate, and thus their plight. To observe that black economic progress is a major source of the feeling of loss and dispossession among the white lower middle class should be the beginning, not the conclusion of analysis—especially in light of the modesty of black demands and black progress. Why is more equality so feared, even in small doses? Why is our (genuine) egalitarianism so escapist and ineffectual? Of course our fear is inflamed by commercial interests, by relentless and omnipresent corporate propaganda and advertising, by the few whose interests lie in dividing the many. But surely there must be more to it.

Part of the problem of justice is simply inattention to the problem, to the humanity of the excluded. And in a cultural context that has so effectively exploited our human capacity to distinguish ourselves, to falsely believe we can opt out of the human race, all those people apart, but particularly the poor, threaten us with what, in part, we are—or might, or could be. The blurring of these rigid but brittle boundaries can be profoundly disturbing. What may actually be an integration of lost repressed parts of the self can seem like disintegration: *our* coming closer together can seem like *my* falling apart.

So a concern with anomie and community is potentially separable from the passion to exclude, to keep the poor and the black in their places—separable from the advocacy of ascripted social advantage, hierarchy, intolerance—and may be of crucial help in explaining our sometimes spirited indifference in the face of unjustified inequalities.

Turn next to the relationship of anomie to spillovers, which is in some respects similar. Contrary to what many critics imply, assessing the collective results of our individualistic pursuits, reflecting on the exigencies of social interaction in an egalitarian context, and asking whether we can continue to go on this way have no immediate connection with human nature. Nor is there an immediate connection with the question of whether enjoyable individual activity can have pernicious social consequences. However, as in the relationship of anomie to distributive justice, the question of what is unsatisfactory about our goals does shed light on the frantic production of negative spillovers, and the failure to adequately consider what private behavior is socially possible.

This, then, is the kind of connection to emphasize. But we should not carry it too far. As in the relationship of the anomie to the excluded, there are various, more and less preferable ways of satisfying needs for fellowship and belonging and inclusion—again, the category of what is human or satisfying may be larger than the category of what is socially satisfiable. Some of these ways exclude or ignore the less fortunate; others are ecologically unsound or socially disruptive.

Both Thomas Schelling and Philip Slater have written pieces which mark them as sociologically-minded critics.[38] Schelling is concerned with the "new Malthusianism," and with the persistence of archaic attitudes and institutions held over from a time when the problem was a "scarcity of goods, not a plethora of bads." Slater is likewise concerned with spillovers, to a lesser extent with inequality, but most of all with the *loneliness* or anomia which he believes underlies both. At one point both critics use the example of a traffic light to illustrate their arguments.[39] Here the similarities end.

Schelling praises the traffic light unabashedly: what a splendid use of technology! A paradigmatic example of *decentralized* control contributing to a desirable collective goal—that is, the smooth flow of traffic. A perfect illustration of his contention that the crucial element in meshing individual adaptations with desired collective results is often coordination, not coercion. By means of the ingeniously simple arbitrariness of the red and the green, the chaos of the four-way stop sign or the no-stop intersection is largely eliminated. Who dares call this coercion?

Slater almost does. For him it represents, albeit on a small scale, a kind of *centralized* control—arbitrary, and what is worse, mechanical. It metes out a certain formal justice, but this is coupled with an inconsiderate hardness and impersonality (just as Simmel described the trade-offs in establishing the rule of law). Better to resolve differences over who should proceed (after all, some may be in more of a hurry or have more urgent business, and so on) in a spirit of mutual respect, indentification, co-performance. And spontaneous and holistic affection toward the unique individual whom, in your judgment, you have just beaten to the intersection. Smiles and gestures will do: the human, personal touch.

Surely Schelling has the better argument here. Anyone with much driving experience can confirm the fact that at a busy four-way stop, gestures tend to the obscene. And a bunch of well-meaning individuals at such an intersection might really muck up the works. Where the smooth flow of traffic is concerned, human nature is apparently less relevant than social institutions—and Schelling contends this is generally the case. But my purpose here is not to suggest the universal superiority of Schelling's approach, but to illustrate the common confusion of community in these distinct senses—the one concerning workable patterns of social interaction, the other concerning personal communal needs—and thus the widespread tendency among social critics to ignore the fact that there are more and less workable ways to take seriously and accommodate such needs.

As the example of Slater suggests,[40] it is clear that the dramatic rise in concern over spillovers cannot be adequately explained in purely physical terms—such as the sheer frequency of our arriving simultaneously at four-way stop signs, our bumping together, the magnitude of social costs external to private consumption and production, or passing those critical points in pollution and congestion and technological wherewithal beyond which we can no longer choose to ignore the costs. No doubt many social critics and many of the rest of us are projecting the anarchy and frustration of our personal lives onto the social canvas, thereby confusing two different (if equally important) aspects of community.[41] But this confusion of personal needs with the problems of social-institutional interaction, of what is satisfying with what is workable or satisfiable, is at least understandable and surely significant. Moreover, an analogous criticism applies to the critics' confusion of the personal concern with being accepted and included with the issue of inequality and the problem of including those who are economically excluded.

What these paired discussions suggest, then, is that the caricature that blurs the distinctions among the unsatisfactory, the unfair, the unworkable—and thus among related aspects of community—must be rejected. But the discussions also suggest that to blur such distinctions may be helpful in combating the more usual error of segregating problems that are intimately related and have common sources. The argument implies the need for an explicitly communal ethic which explores the potential complementarity of such concerns, and it views the fact that we have failed to do so as itself a basic manifestation of anomie. To radical critics and many liberals it suggests that their all-too-general exhortations to expand freedoms, their refusal to explicitly treat communal concerns and needs, must be supplemented with a concern with human ambivalence, with anomie as well as alienation, and with a relatively explicit image of community and its fundamental dimensions. And to democratic theorists of all persuasions, the argument suggests that the failure to treat these concerns is, in more than one sense, escapist.

PART 4
Democracy, Anomie, and the
Liberal Democratic Community

I began this study with some representative democratic critics of democratic pluralism, and argued, with the assistance of recent contributions in axiomatic political theory, that something was amiss in our conception of democracy. Put crudely, that conception is that we are more democratic to the extent that we enable more people to get more of what they want, more of the time, through the political process. It is entertained in large measure by pluralists, their democratic critics, and axiomatic theorists alike. I questioned whether the competing claims and ideals impinging upon the political system could possibly be reconciled by this notion of democracy, even in an abstract theoretical fashion. I therefore suggested that how we should conceive of democracy, what we can expect from it, and how it can be explained and justified are matters of considerable confusion.

At that point I turned to more radical critics, radical in the sense of trying to rethink the human basis of the polity; to question, from this point of reference, the wants impinging upon the political system; and to reorient social and democratic theory on the basis of this supposedly better conception of the nature of human nature. By means of an analysis of some typical representatives of the left literature of freedom, I suggested that their explanation for the alienation they see is not convincing because of their neglect of human ambivalence, and that this underlies their neglect of anomie and their frequent failure to make clear the sense in which appeals to human nature underpin their critiques.

Thus I suggested a reinterpretation of anomie emphasizing the notion of ambivalence, the close relationship of anomie and alienation, and the distinction between goals that are inherently unsatisfactory and those that are simply not satisfiable or shareable when all are free to pursue them. I considered the problems of distributive justice and the control of spillovers in the context of anomie, and suggested the need for an explicitly communal ethic simultaneously concerned with community in these three senses.

Where, then, does this leave democracy? It is democracy, Robert Paul Wolff recently asserted, that offers the only possible chance of reconciling individual liberty with necessary collective authority. My argument has been concerned with the desirability and the share-ability of the dominant cultural consensus of demands and goals with which the political system must deal. It implicitly suggests that state-ments such as Wolff's involve those grandiose expectations which lead to rapid disillusionment with, and thus to unwarranted depre-cation of democracy. (Indeed, I will consider an example of this from Wolff's own work.) This is the more likely to the extent that such statements are accompanied by excessively abstract attempts to perform the reconciliation of these demands, and when unaccom-panied by a critical analysis of the wants themselves, and the way freedoms are defined and used.

The axiomatic theorists I initially considered, and by means of whom I introduced the "quiet crisis in democratic theory," do not ordinarily claim to be doing philosophy. Indeed, it is the supposed absence of normative considerations in their "positive" theory that is a source of pride as well as self-definition. Yet clearly they intend their conception of man and what motivates him, and their models of interactions in specific institutional settings to apply to the explanation and defense of the whole democratic system. I will therefore treat them as if they were attempting to justify democracy, together with theorists who, working with similar root-assumptions, have directly addressed the question of democracy on this more philosophical level. I will suggest, in short, that the question of whether democracy can be reconciled with individual autonomy, whether democracy can speak adequately to the demands placed on it, cannot be dissociated from the analysis of anomie and concern with community. Thus I will suggest that liberal democracies, to the extent that they exist, survive, and prosper, can only be liberal democratic communities.

9 Justifying Democracy Before and After the Revolution

Our initial discussion of pluralism and its democratic critics raised serious questions concerning how to conceive and what to expect of liberal democracy. In large measure this was accomplished with the help of the axiomatic or economic approach to democratic theory, a literature whose virtue is to make explicit, to take consistently, to explore systematically the basic assumptions shared by most pluralists and many of their democratic critics. That discussion ended on the question of whether this economic approach to democracy amounts to an implicit denigration of democracy, as some have wondered and suggested, or instead is tantamount to an indictment of its *own* conception of democracy. Here, in light of the intervening discussion of ambivalence, anomie, and community, I argue that the latter is more nearly the case. I do so by looking first at the implicit justification of the democratic system as a whole found in these analyses; and then by looking briefly at the more explicit attempts to justify democracy which are grounded in similar neoutilitarian assumptions.

Debunking the Debunkers

Not surprisingly, the flavor of the economic approach to democratic theory is distinctly utilitarian. The very tendency to ignore their intellectual lineage, the exaggerated sense of starting anew with new-found rigor and precision, powerful tools, and more realistic assumptions—all these suggest their parentage. As Plamenatz reminds us, in 1956 Robert Dahl half-mockingly suggested that it had become fashionable in some academic quarters to think that everything believed about democratic politics prior to World War II had been nonsense. The classical ghosts have been exorcised. But some ghosts have been dealt with far more effectively than others: compare the fate of Rousseau and the idea of political community, for example, to that of Bentham and the image of man as a sophisticated schemer and pleasure machine.

It is true that neoutilitarians (the label is Plamenatz's) do not speak of pains and pleasures. The same reluctance was encountered in considering modern defenses of distribution based on market criteria. We want what we want and prefer what we choose: hang the reasons, which in any event are too difficult to disentangle from the choices themselves. Only the Englishman desires utility, or mere pleasure, but everyone wants his wants. Neither do the theorists presume to add my utility to yours: interpersonal comparisons of utility are passé. It is understood that Bentham's basic rule—act so as maximize the net sum of the happiness you create minus the misery you spread—may involve such comparisons, and in any event is not easily operationalized. They know, too, that elementary logic suffices to explode the dream of the greatest number enjoying the greatest happiness. We may be able to speak intelligibly of distributing a given amount of happiness among the greatest possible number, or of maximizing the happiness of a given number, but not of both at once. It is further recognized that there are spheres of our lives in which the focus on utility and Bentham's self-preference principle does not seem particularly relevant or enlightening.

Yet I suggest that ghosts of just such principles as the greatest-happiness-greatest-number are loose and at large in the work of these axiomatic theorists and the many pluralists and critics who share their basic assumptions.[1] One is tempted to call them guiding fantasies. Certainly notions like maximizing goal-attainment and joint optimizations are not-so-distant relatives of Bentham's principles.[2] Similarly, the exaggerated importance ascribed to Arrow's impossibility theorem suggests the fantasy that if only the theorem had some logical flaw, if only this cosmic joke were not planted in the process of aggregating preferences, then perhaps we could all have our way, and find and save our democratic soul. Then we could achieve economic and social justice without explicitly concerning ourselves with justice. Despite their careful (and valuable) analyses of just how and why we cannot joint-optimize, much less all have our own way, it is as though they believed that if only we could find the proper set of instrumental institutions and decision-rules, then somehow we might all win, or at least enjoy a truly equal weighting of preferences.[3] We might never have to ask ourselves what kind of society we want. In short, I suggest that there is a kind of escapism, or escapist egalitarianism at work here.

We have already seen this escapism at work in similar contexts: in connection with ignoring the logical implications and empirical consequences of our cultural success goals; and with the pluralist's notion that pressure groups should be allowed an equal chance to unequally influence political outcomes. In discussing the rationale for accepting the distribution of rewards meted out by the market, I suggested that the question of inequality and the plight of the excluded is political before it is economic. But a conception of politics that involves nothing more than transferring the competitive struggle from the market place to bids for governmental favors and reparations no more justifies the resulting distribution than do market principles or the ideology of growth, and for analogous reasons. The pluralist-democratic solution to the problem of distributive justice, expressed crudely, is that those who are hurting most will presumably squeal loudest, will be listened to and helped. Or will help themselves, should they discover no one is listening. We do not have to bother, therefore, with explicit shared conceptions of distributional criteria; nor with our fear of equality, our neglect of the excluded, and what these conceal and reveal. The question is whether this solution reflects the same naiveté as the market rationale for distribution—particularly if we believe that distributive justice would involve reducing inequality and better including the excluded. That is, it is not clear that we have faced up to the full significance of this absence of shared conceptions of what is just. We have concealed this aspect of rulelessness from ourselves, both in our economic and political theory.

There are additional places to observe these guiding fantasies at work. Consider Dahl and Lindblom's notion that political equality and majority rule are instrumental to everyone's pursuit of prime goals, which are personal in nature. "The important prime goals of human beings in Western societies include existence or survival, physiological gratifications (through food, sex, sleep, and comfort), love and affection, respect, self-respect, power or control, skill, enlightenment, prestige, aesthetic satisfaction, excitement, novelty, and many others."[4] Democracy, of which political equality and majority rule are the basic elements, is the most important of "seven goals that govern both the degree to which these prime goals of individuals are attained and the manner of deciding who is to attain his goals when individuals conflict in their goal seeking."[5] This is an ambiguous formulation, as if they wished to suggest that political equality and majority rule facilitate the attainment of everyone's personal goals without taking the risks involved in saying so outright. If we interpret it in this way, then it is easy to see that the qualifications to the proposition that democracy is instrumental to the pursuit of personal, prime goals are numerous and telling: the details of their own analyses contribute many of them. Political equality does not necessarily imply majority rule, and neither implies an equal weighting of preferences even in the simplest of cases. But supposing this were intelligible and possible, it is a giant step to the idea that political equality is an instrumental goal. Of course Dahl and Lindblom can justifiably complain that all they actually claimed is that democracy governs "the degree to which these prime goals of individuals are attained." If so, they have claimed very little, far less than they apparently wish to. Totalitarian states also govern the degree to which individual goals are attained.

Or consider the self-regarding assumption that Downs and Olson make about the individual voter and political participant. Their idea of his conception of good representation and good leadership is that these exist to fulfill his personal wants in the order that he lists them. Leadership and representation are thought of in terms of responsiveness to demands, particularly his demands. And democracy is thought of as the attempt to give as many as possible as much as possible, as a search for those conditions and institutions under which the possibilities are maximized. Of course then the question becomes: when, if ever, can we say the *system* is democratic, or becoming more or less so? The question cannot be answered, even theoretically, so in practice the neoutilitarians revert back to a consideration of which liberal democratic procedures and institutions are present or absent, as in Dahl's famous seven-point checklist for polyarchies.[6] But as a rule this is done without dropping the assumption that these are instrumental, or else it is dropped quietly.

Let us reconsider voting and political participation with the same questions in mind. A brief attempt to look at the matter through the citizen's eyes suffices to start us to wondering whether Downs's paradox of voting may be a mere artifact of an excessively utilitarian view, and whether it is but one of many such examples. Even if the citizen is a genuine philistine about what's in-it-for-him, he typically understands that he cannot win them all, however richly he deserves to. He cannot foresee all the turns events will take, nor does he have the time nor expertise nor interest to order all his preferences, even if he could foresee the issues that would arise. He cannot even expect to always know when he is winning, not without social supports for his intuitions, and leaders to guide and to articulate them. "Alternative expected streams of utility," though sometimes offered in the name of realism, are peculiarly bloodless abstractions.

As Plamenatz suggests, no doubt the voter often has an intuitive understanding of the difference between representatives that are *responsive* to him and those that are *responsible* to him. He may even think, however preconsciously, that the latter kind of representation is preferable, if only to insure the greater long-run responsiveness of the system to what he really wants, as opposed to his day-to-day impulses and half-baked preferences. This is a major source of our considerable ambivalence toward the politician, the one who bows to political pressures. This is still a telling charge to level at political opponents in American politics, or so politicians seem to think. And we miss something if we focus on the self-seeking and hypocrisy often involved in these charges and countercharges, instead of focusing on the virtues that are being complimented, appealed to, and asked for in this way. For there is a latent but widespread understanding that bowing to all political pressures at once is impossible, that the representative needs some conception of his tasks and his responsibilities to help him resist simply doing favors for whatever interests come along. And it is not only the rabid populist who understands that in practice the politician with nothing more in his head than the wish to service the interests of his constituency often winds up serving the "interests," those who already have the wealth and power, are organized, and have access to the legislature. It is the mark of the man of character that he does not give himself just anything he wants. Nor does he try to do so for us. Somehow, perhaps over the long run, we find ourselves attracted to him, applauding, perhaps voting for him. Especially if we are convinced that he really did listen to us and took our case seriously, even when his decision went against us. His leadership, if it is "instrumental" to our purposes, is instrumental in a human as well as material sense.

It has been objected that to argue in this way is to view the American citizen as a child: perhaps what I have suggested roughly reflects the actual state of affairs, but it is an ignoble and childish ideal. Without denying that in this large nation-state we have only begun to tap the possibilities of political participation, I must nevertheless suggest that there is something odd about this objection. For the view of the citizen I am suggesting assumes that in many cases he is mature enough to recognize that in politics, even democratic politics, we must discriminate among wants, and that often this means favoring those who want certain things and curbing those who want others. It is the child who often forgets, or has yet to learn, where his ego stops and the world begins. It is the child who demands to win them all. By comparison, the average citizen is potentially mature enough to expect that his interests be listened to, taken account of, but not necessarily mechanically translated into the votes of his representative. He may be mature enough to demand that he have a share in the decision to elect or reject his representatives. He may be concerned that there be regularized, institutionalized procedures and channels, and independent media and countervailing institutions, to facilitate the expression and hearing of his interests on issues that come up between election periods. But another mark of his maturity is that he recognizes that the function of even democratic leadership is, after all, to lead. He may also understand that leadership can have its symbolic as well as instrumental functions, and he may feel the need to have alternatives delineated, purposes defined, and his aspirations and ideals embodied. And if he understands none of this, if he is not nearly so mature, then one must ask whether being brought up on vulgarized versions of neo-utilitarian doctrine has played a significant part in rendering him immature. Insofar as childishness has something to do with egoism and selfishness: who is taking a childish view of the citizen?

The citizen's evaluation of the general drift of political affairs may not be selfish, but it certainly does not follow from the assumption that he is self-regarding. Yet Olson's and Downs's self-regarding individuals (and Dahl and Lindblom's individuals, with their prime, personal goals), are certainly supposed to be selfish, biased toward personal (or familial) payoffs and avoiding costs, typically quantifiable in dollar terms. To repeat: even if the individual sees or imagines a strong personal stake in some general course the community should take, Downs or Olson do not predict his voting or his participation in significant numbers, certainly not in the numbers he does. Once again: you can rationally desire a certain outcome of the voting, even desire that the institution of elections continue to function, and still rationally refuse to take action in its behalf. Formally, the Downsian, Olsonian answer to the failure of their assumptions to explain voting and participation seems to be this: their theories do not apply to those situations in which the costs of voting or participation are not viewed as costs. It is rather strange: participation costs are not costs when they are not *viewed* as costs. The vocabulary of self-interest, one fears, begins to obscure more than it reveals.

Is it possible that, of all people, economists and their pluralist fellow travelers, even in this most bourgeois and utilitarian of cultures, misunderstand the citizen? Is not the beauty of economic man that he knows what he wants, and the beauty of economics that it knows economic man? Whether their model distorts reality is not the point. The question is whether it is a shrewd distortion, illuminating the topics on which it focuses and convincing us of their significance. And some of their crucial assumptions do serve to obfuscate more than enlighten, whether we consider analyses of voting, political participation, majority rule, representation, constitutional choice, or democracy itself. Moreover, the balance shifts significantly toward obfuscation as we move closer to the attempt to explain or justify the democratic system as a whole. There is an unmistakable air of unreality that surrounds and renders confusing the defenses of democracy ostensibly based on their assumptions. Where are shared democratic ideas and ideals in all this? Where are beliefs about democratic forms, apart from their efficiency or efficacy, about personal and political liberties, rights and responsibilities? How can democracy be defined, much less justified, apart from the ideas and beliefs and images of democracy that people entertain of democracy? (On the face of it, such attempts would seem to be themselves "undemocratic.") And where, in all these analyses, is patriotism, in this country of all countries?

One place, apparently, is voting, in that large residue of votes which for Downs constitutes a paradox. Apparently some people vote because they think it is only right. Similarly, civic-mindedness and unselfish devotion to a cause or candidate are found in political participation, and those participants for whom the costs of participation are not considered costs. And such ideals are also found in the wants themselves. It is not simply that we may corrode our ideals in the powerful acid of falsely imputed usefulness, though this is a serious objection indeed. It is also that we cannot separate what we want from what we value so easily. Both are products of a certain kind of society, with a particular history, and both occur at a particular point in time. And their co-incidence is not entirely coincidental. Note that neither burning nor raping nor pillaging are ever listed among the prime, personal goals. That is, there may be liberal-democratic wants as well as ideals, because the latter, and the institutions which embody them, determine and channel and delimit the former to a great degree, and thus in large measure determine their own usefulness. Means that determine ends begin to look remarkably like ends.

I can truthfully say that I do not want to rob banks, neither as a profession nor as a hobby. Have you thereby learned more about my ideals or about my interests? You might have difficulty separating the two; and implicitly these theorists admit as much. Closely observe the hypothetical individual who wanders through their analyses. Of course from all we can glean from their references to the source of his wants, these could have been brought along by the stork. But if we think about those wants, and the kind of individual who has them, he soon becomes familiar. His utilitarian orientation, especially at the outset of analysis, is decidedly crude and unqualified, and we must wonder whether he cheats a little when it serves his purposes. But fortunately it turns out that he keeps promises and bargains and does not make a habit of breaking laws. He may even vote, does not cheat much on his taxes, and certainly does not rob banks. He just seems to want things such that he has a reasonable prospect of obtaining them without consistently running afoul of those liberal-democratic instrumental procedures and institutions. Perhaps he can even use them.

In this country in many ways so idealistic, it does not serve the cause of realism to fail to take account of the ubiquity and importance of ideals; to fail to see their interpenetration with our wants; and to fail to see that in many respects both are products of this particular society. Admittedly, for some explanatory tasks, those that refer and are confined to specific institutional contents, this may be unnecessary. But it is crucial when we try to bring our utilitarian guns to the defense of a whole conception of democracy, of the whole system. Then we should see the difficulty in asserting, in effect, the universal instrumentality or efficacy of liberal-democratic forms—which we may just happen, as products of this society, to value in themselves, as well as for their generally over-estimated usefulness in meeting private demands.

It is only realistic, then, to recognize the role of ideals, and the fact that we value our institutions as well as use them. But the point here is not to applaud idealism and boo cynicism. To do so is to take part in a fake and sterile controversy, one to which the neoutilitarians have inadvertently contributed. Their contribution is embedded in their assumptions that individuals are self-regarding and that personal goals are prime. For the equating of self-regarding actions with actions that are selfish is without justification. Selfishness, social destructiveness and irresponsibility vary independently of whether actions are self-regarding.[7] *Shareability*, as it relates to *satisfaction* is the key question, and in light of this question the neoutilitarians (and they are by no means alone) exhibit an escapist egalitarianism. In spite of all the careful analysis of what the heterogeneity of wants means and how it precludes everyone having his way, the crucial question of their shareability somehow gets shortchanged.[8] Or if it is not shortchanged, then what is neglected is the extent to which their model of the democratic process has called itself into question. One significant example is the assumption that individuals are self-regarding, which has nothing intrinsically to do with whether and to what extent their wants conflict with the wants of others. It is likewise reflected in the lack of emphasis on the simple problem of the outvoted standing minority—as opposed, say, to the intensive search for the weakest conditions under which the transitivity of majority rule is not violated.

In light of this it is fair to ask, with Plamenatz, just how important Arrow's intransitivity problem is. How relevant is it to democratic theory?[9] Arrow's impossibility theorem does not even apply when there are only two positions and two parties.[10] But under these conditions the problem of the outvoted standing minority can nevertheless obtain. The excluded are in a minority in this society, if they had no other disadvantages with which to contend. If among the wants of the majority is not the desire to help, the impossibility of the situation of the disadvantaged and excluded does not require exotic logic to fathom. If the majority does want to help, no doubt the solution to the plight of the excluded is complicated and extremely difficult, and opinions as to how to proceed will differ. But then we have seen reasons—for example, in discussing Condorcet's jury theorem and in Rae's rationale for majority rule—why, given a rough consensus on objectives, the instrumentality of democratic forms starts to come into its own, and is at least ahead of whatever's in second place.[11]

Of course one problem is that beyond this there is little that is particularly new or clever to say about consistently outvoted or underrepresented minorities, certainly little that requires specialized, high-powered tools and powers of abstraction. To dwell on such problems, someone has suggested, is to display ineffectual outrage: odd that we demand of outrage that it be effective, and then display truly touching tolerance for the ingenious impotence of analyses whose passions are more sublimated. Of course to dwell on these simpler matters is to make more obvious the fact that we are discriminating among different kinds of wants, among the wants of different people, and giving unequal weight to some. Unequal weight: that is the crux. To concern ourselves explicitly with reducing inequality is, in the final analysis, not egalitarian enough.[12]

It is as if, in the real world, personal and political, democratic or otherwise, we did not have to discriminate among wants and to treat people unequally in the interests of equality. Surely the idea or ideal—implicit in most of these analyses—of giving everyone more of what they want is not altogether unworthy. It is in itself a "want"— a prime want perhaps, for many of us. Why then the general lack of critical attention to the pattern of wants and ideals, the cultural consensus, that works against the realization of this want, this ideal? Why the lack of attention to the question of what wants we can reasonably pursue together?

There is something charming about this attempt to begin again, to provide a more precise, tough-minded, no-nonsense utilitarian rationale for our liberal democratic institutions and ideals, and thus to avoid talking explicitly about political community. It is quaintly modern. But what my arguments have suggested is that we cannot do without notions of the political community, replete with institutions that, if at all instrumental, are so only or primarily to certain kinds of wants, wants which those institutions have a large hand in creating and molding, which we have been encouraged and taught to want. The notion that the political community is nothing more than a community of communities, or an arena for the clash of interests (and the notion this often degenerates into that society, not excluding the political system, is necessarily a by-product of the private corporate economy)—these too are conceptions of community, though problematic ones indeed. Maybe what has happened is that the news is leaking out now—a loss of innocence analogous to our loss of innocence concerning the rewards and results of a laissez-faire economy—the news that now there are obviously competitive conceptions of what the community is or should be all about.

If what I am saying is true, the democratic critics with whom we began do little to relieve this unhappy situation of not having or using the proper words to describe what is happening to us. Instead, they flirt with and are often seduced by the tough-minded pitch of the neoutilitarians. As Tocqueville aptly observed, it is as if we Americans were embarrassed by our beliefs, our idealism, our altruism, and have to redescribe everything we believe and do in terms of egoistic self-interest. Thus, as Plamenatz observes, there is a phony air surrounding the whole debate between the pluralists (who to a large degree share this economic, neoutilitarian orientation) and their democratic critics (who often do, too), and we need not impugn motives in saying so. Similarly for the more radical critics of pluralism. Surely, as Plamenatz complains, democracy is not being defended nor criticized on the basis of maximizing or not maximizing goal attainment, expected streams of utility, or overall responsiveness. The real thrust of the criticisms and defenses points to competing conceptions of a political community that deserves to be called democratic. If we desire a better reconciliation of the claims of liberty and equality—and a better record of reconciling democratic promises and performance—then we have little choice but to deal more explicitly with what such a community is all about. It is not for democracy, as such, to promise these things. We must begin by recognizing that the ruleless gap between promises and deliveries is our own creation. Then we can focus on deliveries.

Democracy: What's in It for Me?

I wish to use a brief comparison of Robert Dahl's *After the Revolution?* and Robert Paul Wolff's *In Defense of Anarchism* to sum up and bring home the implications of my argument. Dahl is concerned with the conditions under which democratic authority is justified and acceptable; Wolff is concerned with demonstrating that there is no justification for democratic authority. Neither Dahl nor Wolff are content to describe or defend democracy as that which self-proclaimed democrats do. Despite their political differences, both apparently affirm the notion that democracy consists of giving as many people as possible as much of what they want as possible (though in Wolff's case this is not without some ambivalence and ambiguity). I will suggest that the cogency of their analyses suffers from the absence of an explicit and articulate conception of the community, both liberal and democratic, that the two theorists seem to have in mind. In the process I will suggest that the solution to the question of legitimate democratic authority, and the threats to it, is more likely to be found along the sociological, or psychoanalytic-sociological lines I have conveyed.

Let us begin with some surprising similarities. Both Dahl and Wolff put us in the shoes of a shrewd and unsentimental individual, one who looks at the question of democracy with a cool and calculating eye and asks: what is in it for me? What else can you show me?[13] There is no place here for preconceived notions of democracy or shared democratic ideals. Both discussions are thoroughly divorced from a consideration of what kinds of things their individual and other individuals want or need or demand from democracy or democratic participation, and whether these wants can be reasonably pursued together with the rest of the policy. Similarly, the individuals have no beliefs or prejudices concerning the intrinsic value of democracy. The assumption seems to be that if democracy cannot be justified in this highly general, abstract, universalistic and instrumentalist way, then it cannot be justified at all. We are not to inquire about the nature of his attitudes and demands, nor their relationship to the society of which he is a part, nor the social basis of his very identity. We are not to ask whether he is of the proletariat or the bourgeoisie. Or if "he" is a he or a she. Nor are we to question what his being human portends for democracy.

Nevertheless, the individuals to whom they address their arguments do have, on closer glance, specific qualities; and these are not entirely unfamiliar. Wolff's hypothetical individual seems to be rather cranky and uncompromising, almost surly. He is fiercely independent, obsessed with maintaining his autonomy. Autonomy is apparently an all-or-nothing affair with him, like virginity: either he has it or he has been violated. Furthermore, he apparently knows precisely what he wants, and he expects to be satisfied. Otherwise, one senses, he might just take his marbles and leave. And as he begins his quest for the reasons he should submit to democratic authority, he exhibits a flair for drama: in this age of clay-footed idols, "the belief in all forms of traditional authority is as weak as the arguments which can be given for it. There is only one form of political community which offers any hope of resolving the conflict between authority and autonomy, and that is democracy."[14] Given his uncompromising view of autonomy, we should not be surprised that Wolff's book is thin, and that its conclusions are basically negative.

It is important to recall that in a book published two years earlier Wolff was vigorously and carelessly advocating a most extensive and radical democratization of the American policy, as we saw earlier.[15] He suggested then that the society must become more rational by making more and more previously chaotic situations, particularly those resulting from countless uncoordinated individual choices, the "objects of social decision." We can only speculate as to why, two years later, he is defending individual choice and autonomy—and anarchism—in a most uncompromising way.

Again the sense of drama:

> When I first became deeply interested in the subject, I was quite confident that I could find a satisfactory justification for the traditional democratic doctrine to which I rather unthinkingly gave my allegiance. Indeed, during my first year . . . I taught a course on political philosophy in which I boldly announced that I would formulate and then solve the fundamental problem of political philosophy. I had no trouble formulating the problem— roughly speaking, how the moral autonomy of the individual can be made compatible with the legitimate authority of the state. I also had no trouble refuting a number of proposed solutions which had been put forward by various theorists of the democratic state. But midway through the semester, I was forced to go before my class, crestfallen and very embarrassed, to announce that I had failed to discover the grand solution.[16]

Whatever the specific reasons for this dramatic failure, the trajectory of his thought is a clear illustration of what Dahl and others have contended: to entertain grandiose expectations of democracy is to flirt with unwarranted, excessive disillusionment with it.

To make a short story shorter: Wolff's hypothetical individual must severely compromise his autonomy under any form of democratic authority except direct unanimous democracy, a form which is thoroughly unworkable in this large and heterogeneous country. Direct democracy per se, in the absence of the requirement of unanimity, will not do for obvious reasons. Representative democracy, even at its very best, is still worse. As we have seen, if the issues the representative must decide upon number more than one or two, and similarly for the possible positions on the issues, then the odds are astronomical that this individual will not even be able to find his candidate in the race, much less elect him. To imagine that we are free just because we choose our representatives is to deceive ourselves, just like the Englishmen Rousseau satirized, "who, by the use they make of their brief moments of liberty, deserve to lose it."

Of course majority rule, whether or not compounded by representation, discriminates against minorities and Wolff tacitly assumes his individual will not always be in the majority. Arrow's problem, the possible intransitivity of majority rule, makes matters worse, or so Wolff thinks: "it is perfectly possible for a group of rational individuals with consistent preferences to arrive, by majority rule, at a completely inconsistent order of group preferences!"[17] Thus "it turns out that majority rule is fatally flawed by an internal inconsistency which ought to disqualify it from consideration in any political community whatsoever."[18] Given that for Wolff, autonomy does not admit to degrees of attainment, it is not clear how more autonomy is violated as a result of this internal inconsistency than by the simpler and less subtle intrusions of majority tyranny. Nor does Wolff observe that Arrow's problem applies to minority rule as well. But no matter. Both are disqualifiable on other grounds, along with any other possible form of democratic authority.

Logically speaking, Wolff's individual has reached the end of the road, and we would expect his story to end with it. And yet: "I confess myself unhappy with the conclusion that I must simply leave off the search for legitimate collective authority."[19] Why is Wolff not delighted at no longer being deceived? Why this reluctance to leave off the search? Because, he argues, everyone wants, in true Hegelian fashion, to overcome the utter "otherness" of the world. The world of nature, he contends, is irremediably "other." But how can it be so with society—which is, after all, only a human product?

Men come to imagine themselves more completely enslaved by society than they ever were by nature. Yet their conviction is fundamentally wrong, for while the natural world really does exist independently of man's beliefs or desires ... the social world is nothing in itself, and consists merely of the totality of the habits, expectations, beliefs, and behavior patterns of all the individuals who live in it. ... .[20]

What is required, then, is that we banish ignorance and bad will. And, lo and behold, private interest!

But since each man's unfreedom is entirely a result either of ignorance or of a conflict of interests, it ought to be in principle possible for a society of rational men of *good will* [my emphasis] to eliminate the domination of society and subdue it to their wills in a manner that is impossible in the case of nature. ... when rational men, in full knowledge of the proximate and distant consequences of their actions, *determine to set private interest aside and pursue the general good* [my emphasis], it *must* be possible for them to create a form of association which accomplishes that end without depriving them of their moral autonomy.[21]

Thus in the end we are left with a solution which, shed of its Hegelian mystique, amounts to little more than an advocacy of righteous behavior, as heartwarming as it is unenlightening. And unconvincing. For where has Wolff left his original cranky, uncompromising individualist—who after all had *free*, not necessarily *good* will?

Turn now to the kind of individual Dahl's analysis appears to address. One gathers he is a more reasonable chap. Although his orientation toward democratic institutions is apparently equally instrumental (again there are few clues concerning just what he wants or values, or where he got his cravings or ideals), his whole approach, Dahl implies, is more shrewd and sophisticated. And for this reason, more compromising. Equally interested in having his own way, he realizes that he must be willing to give up a little autonomy here in order to have a little more there, or in exchange for a favorable decision in which he took no part whatsoever. He might even view both kinds of exchanges as means of enhancing his autonomy, not encroachments upon it. Or perhaps he would simply assert that autonomy is not everything. Even in this instrumentalist view of authority—apart from whether he might enjoy or crave submission to authority, or need its guidance in formulating his preferences—Dahl's individual is sensitive to the fact that liberty and and authority do not always work at cross-purposes.

As a result his possible strategies and options are much more sophisticated and ingenious than anything Wolff's individual imagines. Because of his calm demeanor and his enlightened opportunism, because he is not so obsessed with autonomy, it cannot be assumed that he will summarily reject democratic authority. After all, there are so many possible forms and layers of democratic authority, so many opportunities for exploiting the ambiguities, looseness, and indeterminateness of the democratic system. Or at least this can be readily imagined to be the case, so long as we are kept ignorant of what he and the others want, and whether these wants are compatible.

One of the interesting ironies of this comparison, then, is that Dahl has a more balanced picture of the different potential threats to individual autonomy. His concern with individual autonomy is the more effective for being the more compromising, for recognizing that liberty and authority are not always opposites, or that autonomy is not everything an individual desires. A crucial aspect of this irony is that it is entirely consistent with Dahl's approach to recognize that one of the most important potential and historical functions of state authority, and one of the reasons for relinquishing some of our autonomy to it, has been to curb *private* violations of our autonomy, especially that of various minorities. And this is from Dahl, the reputed archpluralist. But in *Defense of Anarchism* Wolff is so obsessed with the possibility of state infringement of autonomy (strange, for a once radical democrat) that what he winds up advocating does not maximize autonomy, much less the other things his individual might value. Keeping in mind Wolff's earlier publications, we can easily imagine his pursuing an alternative analysis, one in which his hypothetical individual, never having heard of the idea of the state, democratic or otherwise, has a similarly paranoid fixation on the surrounding *private* threats to autonomy:

giant corporate conglomerates, labor unions, churches, local customs for which he does not care, individuals who step on his toes or just get on his nerves . . . the list is endless. These infringements can occur even if individuals or groups are not out to get him, though many probably are. Perhaps the outcome of this alternative analysis would be Wolff's advocacy of a strong state to curb these illegitimate, autonomy-infringing private powers, with virtually unlimited powers to insure that it can do so. Given its power to infringe on personal autonomy, it might not matter whether this state was formally democratic or not, and chances are that Wolff the anarchist would be among the first and loudest to complain.

But let us return to Dahl's individual. We follow him through a deceptively simple and lucid exploration of the complications of pluralist democracy. Why should he accept the whole system? How can he have his way, yet submit to democratic authority? At the outset, his possibilities and opportunities are many. The system may leave matters of special interest to him in the domain of personal choice. If he is lucky his ideas about what choices should be so designated will largely coincide with the ideas of others. Or he may choose to withdraw into consensual associations, regional or functional, outside the scope of democratic or other private authority, if this is permitted. To do so he may have to be willing to be a party to a system of mutual guarantees by which different consensual associations agree to limit their interference in one another's affairs. If he is a reasonable sort, and if they are, and if there is a measure of agreement on when interference with each other is legitimate and when it is not, this may work. On matters in which he can agree with others about the necessity of public jurisdiction, he will probably agree to majority rule once he recognizes them as political equals, so long as he does not expect to be in the minority too often. On some matters he will recognize he has little competence to make the decisions, nor does a majority, and will readily yield to someone with the appropriate expertise. It is hoped that others will agree on this principle, and on where it applies and where it does not. He does not care to democratize open-heart surgery, for example, neither as participant-doctor nor participant-victim. Perhaps most of us will agree, even in those cases where political judgments are obviously involved in deciding who has the expertise. On occasion Dahl's individual will yield to someone with more time to participate and to lead: he applies the criterion of economy as well as that of competence. In all of these cases he is keen in knowing when to submit to the authority of others. If he is lucky, the others will be equally, similarly keen. Maybe none of this requires that we know the identity and origin of his or anyone else's wants, that he have affective ties with his countrymen, that he values his liberal democratic heritage, or that we investigate the human and cultural obstacles to achieving such fellow feeling and shared values.

Maybe. Dahl does succeed in suggesting the many potential uses of democratic authority, and uses of limits on democratic authority, democratically agreed upon. He strongly suggests the possibility that others will find similar authority and limits useful, too. He points to the flaws in any simplistic view of the sources, aids, impediments, and threats to individual autonomy. He suggests many reasons we might accept a system of decision-making in which we have little or even no part in many decisions, and in which many decisions go against us. There is no denying the force of this *ex post facto* explanation or demonstration. After all, democracy, or something widely believed to be democracy, does exist in this country, and is reasonably stable. Wolff certainly cannot explain it, except by invoking coercion or inertia.

But somehow it is unconvincing, unless we think of it all as a sophisticated (and most valuable) "reiteration of the arrangements"— to recall Tussman's characterization of pluralism. Dahl makes no serious attempt to demonstrate that the present arrangements that have evolved are instrumental even to *his* individual's goals, much less the goals of others—just as we saw no serious attempt to show that political equality and majority rule contribute to the achievement of prime personal goals in this society. There is no consideration of how their instrumentality might vary among different economic strata, regions, races, sexes. He simply suggests the possibility that, depending on what I want in relation to what others want, these procedures may be instrumental to this or that extent in this or that situation. Their instrumental quality is therefore questionable. The test to check their instrumentality would be hopelessly complicated to contemplate, much less perform, even in an individual case. And this raises the additional question of why they survive.

Moreover, apart from insuperable difficulties in assessing the evidence, and even determining what would serve as evidence, any attempt to measure the usefulness of our institutions in satisfying wants has a serious flaw. If political equality, for example, happens to be instrumental to an individual's goal achievement—in this or that way on such and such occasions given certain assumptions concerning what the other people involved want—how can we maintain that what he wants is independent of what he believes about the rightness (or efficacy) of political equality? Plamenatz has pointed out, in reference to the instrumental goals discussed by Dahl and Lindblom in *Politics, Economics, and Welfare,* that:

> most of Dahl and Lindblom's instrumental goals are either moral or political principles. What do they want us to understand? That people in the West come to value these principles because their general observance helps them to achieve their personal aims (to get what they want for themselves or for other persons they care about)? Or would they admit that even personal aims are determined, at least to a considerable extent, by the principles (not excluding these instrumental goals) that people accept?[22]

For all we learn from Dahl's account—assuming we interpret it as an explanation and a defense of the entire pluralist democratic system— the validity and efficacy of liberal democratic forms is universal. But in other contexts Dahl himself has been among the most knowledge-able and incisive analysts of the peculiar, historically unique constellation of social preconditions that are necessary to recognizing these moral and political principles and establishing and maintaining the liberal and democratic institutions which embody them.

So in a limited sense Wolff has the better of it here: by carrying the radically individualistic, instrumentalist approach to justifying liberal democracy to its logical and absurd extreme, he inadvertently shows that its justification must lie elsewhere, and that an explicit image of a community which is liberal and democratic is necessary to his project of reconciling autonomy and authority. A community composed of liberal democratic people, whose wants as well as attitudes are not corrosive or destructive of liberal democratic institutions. Conceivably, we could interpret his patently doomed quest for legitimate democratic authority (totally respectful of individual autonomy) as an elaborate and subtle parody of any attempt to justify democracy in a way that is too crudely economic or utilitarian, or as a melodrama contrived at the expense of the whole economic approach to democracy. Or as a sly critique of our liberal tendency to see liberty and authority, individual and community as irremediably distinct and opposed; and of the liberal culture that encourages us to think this way. Or as a disguised appeal to rethink these cultural premises, because a reconciliation of individual and community is obviously impossible unless we change our ways.

But we must not read my arguments into his work. This would represent excessive subtlety on my part, just as it would to interpret the economic debunking of democracy as a sly critique of its own constrictive and unrealistic conception of democracy. Of course Wolff and these other theorists expect their models to be disproved in this or that respect, and as good scientists may chalk it up, if it should happen, to progress. But surely our models, especially their basic assumptions, tell more about us than what we expect to see proved or disproved. They speak eloquently of what we expect of ourselves and others. They speak of who we are, where we live, and how we were brought up and educated.

But if Wolff's negative conclusion, freely interpreted in this manner, is sound, then his positive solution is a nonsolution indeed. There is no articulate or plausible account of the community that he eventually realizes is desirable or necessary, except for a vague network of voluntary private associations presupposing levels of cooperation and goodwill which his original individual (the one who existed prior to the revolution) would find inexplicably and unacceptably selfless. Instead, we have a magical change in the willingness of that individual to cooperate and compromise. Wolff does not enlighten us as to why, in the face of his previous compelling arguments, he continues to believe in that reconciliation of liberty and authority he has demonstrated to be impossible. All he knows is that it "must" be possible to reconcile legitimate authority with everyone's perfect autonomy, and everyone's desire to get whatever one wants. Nor does he explain, even in the most general terms, what the best interests of that political community are, except to observe that ignorance and bad will do not serve them.

To summarize briefly and bluntly: whether Dahl or Wolff has justified democracy, before or after the revolution, is questionable. The comparison illustrates that both critics and defenders of democracy cannot and do not dispense with an underlying conception of the political community they think of as democratic or liberal democratic, and that there are sound reasons for this. Nor can they avoid making assumptions about human nature and the cultural context of their democracy, as these influence the "content" and social consequences of individual self-interest—not to mention the attitude with which disputes are approached. For images of community and assumptions concerning its members are crucial to whether any social order can be achieved, much less one which is liberal democratic. About these conceptions and assumptions we can argue fair or foul, but as to their necessity, their crucial importance, and the desirability of making them more explicit, I suggest that there need be little argument.

Democracy: How Much of It is in Us?

The approach of both Dahl and Wolff, and that of the many axiomatic theorists, pluralists, and democratic critics who share it, differs significantly from a sociological or psychoanalytic-sociological understanding of liberal democracy and its supposed crisis. For Dahl's proffered solution to work, he must build in a host of assumptions about his individual's attitudes and wants; the wants of others, and of the society and culture which nurtured him and helped make him what he is. Wolff, rather more realistically, leaves out the rosy assumptions, and the resulting blatant egoism precludes any solution at all. In the process both exhibit what Braybrooke has referred to as individualism-in-epistemology, arguing as if in principle the whole of human knowledge, including a viable conception of democracy, could be constructed by such lone wolves as they pretend to depict and address. The sociological vacuum their individual finds himself in is as unreal as Locke's state of nature; and of course the resemblance is not accidental. And their utilitarian-contractarian approach is subject to the same basic objection: even if its terms could somehow be agreed upon, the social contract is itself a collective good. Thus rational self-interest may lead me to recognize my interest in everyone else's observance of its terms, but it may also lead me to cheat when I can. Until we learn more about me—my attitudes, wants, values—we must assume this is an ever-present possibility. Anomie, as Gouldner has put it, is the normal pathology of utilitarian culture.

Yet their approach is quite common, even typical. The same kind of difficulties plague the much-discussed work of John Rawls, for example, despite his concern with developing an alternative to utilitarian conceptions of justice and democracy.[23] Rawls's theory of justice can be viewed as a contractarian attempt, grounded in Kant and a Kantian reading of Rousseau, to overcome the shortcomings of utilitarianism in social ethics and political theory. He attempts to articulate and defend the crucial features of a just political community in self-conscious contrast to the image of politics as an arena in which self-interest is mitigated solely by instrumental rules and institutions. Rawls's difference principle, the most substantial and controversial of his results, suggests that only those income differences that leave the least well-off better off than they would be in a condition of less inequality can be considered just. He arrives at that principle by means of the now-famous device of the veil of ignorance. Behind this veil, his abstract rational self-interested men, and presumably women, bargain and scheme, attempting to reach agreement on the basic provisions of the just society in supposed ignorance of the social and genetic advantages or handicaps they will enjoy or labor under in that society. In this way he attempts to find a solution that, given this original position, everyone will find to his advantage. This is his ingenious attempt to validate that "sweet assumption" of the liberal faith, as Kaufmann puts it, "that there is no reason why society should not be able to make everybody happy."[24]

Unhappily, given this way of formulating the problem, it has no solution. Or rather: there are two alternatives, one providing an unpalatable solution, the other providing no solution at all. As for the first, it is undoubtedly possible, and Rawls appears to flirt with this alternative, to equip his nakedly egoistic schemers with sufficient sociological clothing and ethical baggage to lead them smartly to his difference principle, or at least to something resembling it; to build in numerous problematic assumptions concerning their moral constraints, personality quirks and traits (notably, risk-avoidance and the absence of envy), and the nature of their wants and how these connect and collide with the wants of others. This of course is the kind of thing I accuse Dahl of doing, though by and large he does it between the lines. And this is what Wolff must do, if he is to make plausible his abstract anarchistic reconciliation of autonomy and authority. But to the extent that Rawls (or anyone else) resorts to such assumptions, it begins to look as though he knows more about his players than they do about themselves. This, I submit, is odd. What's more, these are precisely the sorts of sociological and psycho-sociological particulars that he, along with Dahl and Wolff, strives mightily to avoid.[25]

However, to the extent that he manages to avoid attributing such sociological and moral "identity" to his subjects, his rational men will reach no such agreement as he envisions. This is rather easy to demonstrate on the basis of elementary game-theory. And ironically, the Rawlsian critic who has most effectively pinpointed and documented this dilemma, in a careful and incisive reconstruction and critique of the Rawlsian theory of justice, is Robert Paul Wolff.[26] Wolff points out that in Rawls's original formulations of justice as fairness he seems to regard the difference principle as a potentially demonstrable theorem in game theory. As the difficulties of such a proof become increasingly apparent, there began a series of sociological and psychosociological amendments to the game, added assumptions about its players and what kind of people they are, in an effort to rescue his substantive conclusions. Not only are these additional assumptions excessively optimistic, especially in light of the cultural setting in which he writes, but making any such assumptions calls into question the eternal quality of his "viewpoint of eternity." Because that Archimedian point from which his rational beings were to view and settle these matters is purportedly outside both history and culture.[27]

The path Rawls takes is parallel to the one Wolff follows in considering whether democracy is philosophically tenable. But Wolff's odyssey is considerably shorter. His own doomed attempt (after rejecting all others) to reconcile autonomy and authority in a similarly abstract vein—abstracted from questions of human nature and the cultural setting, what his individuals want and what will satisfy them—ended with a forthright admission of failure (even to his students!). That admission or demonstration of failure is much more convincing than his belated and halfhearted anarchistic attempt to save both autonomy and authority. For Wolff's vague solution, not to mention the more specific and controversial contours Rawls suggests for his good society, can easily be leveled by the same guns Wolff trains on the various democratic solutions.

While I agree with Wolff that there is no such Rawlsian theorem in game theory, not until we learn much more about the gamesters, my argument suggests that there is a sense in which Rawls has not been ambitious enough. In effect I have suggested that the Rawlsian-Kantian argument must be extended to question the reasonableness and workability of cultural goals and social institutions not merely from the standpoint of distributive justice. On the other hand, his elusive Archimedian point is not, and probably cannot be, so far outside or above the culture or subculture that nourished the very idea of such a viewpoint. It is for this reason that his overly Kantian view of human nature does not effectively call attention to the human and cultural obstacles to the reconciliation of equality and freedom posited by his theory, nor to the intimately related question of what else we want from and mean by community. It must be supplemented by the notion of human ambivalence and a psychoanalytic-sociological critique based on it.

What I offer is less of a solution than the basis of my conviction as to the direction in which the solution must be sought. I have argued that the crucial questions concerning the cultural setting of democracy revolve around human satisfaction, social shareability, and their interaction. It is therefore crucial to inquire, with these issues in mind, whether there are in fact liberal democratic wants, and liberal-democratic people—and to ask what they are like, and what obstacles lie in their path.

The obstacles, I contend, are human as well as cultural and institutional. Our culture taps, exploits and reflects a basic human propensity to make distinctions, exaggerate them, and then be tyrannized by them. On close examination that propensity reveals apparently opposite dispositions and needs. For this reason our intellectual life tends to be plagued by continual oscillation between apparent opposite poles: we oscillate between submerging and suffocating the individual in the community, and radically separating him from of the communal context necessary to his very existence and meaning. This seems particularly true of the left and the liberal-left. Indeed, in roughly two years, Wolff himself moves from radical majoritarian centralist democracy to uncompromising anarchism, from a close identification of the individual and the social to a radical and unrealistic schism between the two. Extremes beget extremes. Sometimes it all happens inside an individual's head, one man's thought being driven from one extreme, and by that extreme, to the other, and so on. In some cases we depend on others to express and advocate the other extremes, the ones which are most emphatically not us. Moderating the extremes, dampening the excesses of the intellectual and political cycles, depends critically on our recognizing that inside each of us lurks a little extremist for every one we see or conjure up outside. That is why the ones out there sometimes seem so large, so threatening, and so attractive.

I suspect that there is something about the liberal democratic idea which attempts to face up to a fundamentally human, humanly general ambivalence. On the one hand is the wish to distinguish ourselves, to be our own person, to realize our productive, creative potential, to have and go our own way, to have our differences appreciated or respected or at least tolerated. Autonomy is the goal, and alienation is to be deplored and avoided. On the other hand we wish to be accepted and to accept, to be included and to include, to make and be equal; we need community and fear anomie. This, too, is a fundamental human truth, as if deep down we did not believe our separations and distinctions really made a difference. Of course they do make a difference, for we have no other way to conceive of ourselves and our difficulties. Both kinds of truths are true, then, and apparently opposed. But sufficiently opposed, segregated, and compartmentalized, neither is as likely to be realized or sustained.

The liberal democratic community would seek to simultaneously affirm and do justice to these apparently opposite and contradictory needs and aspirations, to overcome these oppositions as if they were not really opposite and contradictory. If in so doing such a community manages to speak to needs and aspirations which are universally human—if this sociological approach proves to be not culture bound, after all—why then, is this not a nice, and most appropriate irony!

10 Conclusion: The Liberal Democratic Community

Some fifteen years ago Daniel Bell, a most distinguished representative of the point of view I have labeled sociologically-minded pluralism, was busily engaged in applauding pluralistic American stability and its contribution to the supposed end of ideology.[1] Ten years later he argues convincingly that America must move toward an explicitly communal ethic, something far beyond the pluralist conception of a community of communities.[2] I agree with his more recent view, and I think or hope we know more about that community, its bases and its characteristics, than we have yet told. I have tried to tell a little of it by means of a critical look at our cultural goals, from the standpoint of their human desirability, their social shareability, and the connection between the two.

This suggests a view of democracy as a residual affair, dealing with those minor disputes left over after we reach agreement on essentials and change our ways. There is some truth to this. But to admit this is so is not so much a denigration of democracy as an argument that we must respect democracy by enlarging our conception of it and the threats to it. Moreover, the argument leaves a great deal with which liberal democratic institutions must contend, and suggests that, given a rough consensus on what the political community is all about, some of the instrumentalist rationales for those institutions and processes begin to come into their own. If it is utopian, then it is not obviously more so than some of the guiding fantasies of the pluralists and the neoutilitarians; nor the escapist egalitarianism, the head-in-sand quality of the liberal culture in which such fantasies are embedded and from which they unquestionably derive. The irony I have underlined is that such a perspective takes wants more seriously than those who try to deal with wants, with joint-optimization of goals and so on, by dealing abstractly with the nature of those wants, by removing them from the cultural setting and by immunizing them and the culture from criticism. To take seriously the genuinely egalitarian thrust of this culture—as reflected in the concern for freedoms which can be shared and the idea of satisfying everyone's wants as fully as possible—to take seriously as yet inchoate and less articulate concerns with other aspects of community—is to focus more carefully and consistently on the nature of the wants and goals, their shareability, how this relates to what we really want, and what we are really like. As Brian Barry has said, the attempt to allow as many as possible to obtain as much of what they want as possible may not be a particularly heroic conception of democracy, but neither is it altogether ignoble. In order to enjoy our liberties and our democratic forms, however, we need a conception of political community that values them enough to relieve them of intolerable strains and burdens. Ultimately it is only the community-minded who can afford to be self-regarding, those in basic agreement who can afford to disagree, and those affirming a fundamental kinship who can respect and appreciate differences.

Though the more radical critics I have considered are sensitive to such criticisms, at least as they apply to the pluralists and neo-utilitarians, they are less sensitive to the implications for their own critical projects and prescriptions. Their own escapism is reflected in their failure to articulate a convincing model of man to replace the Marxist and liberal images; to respond adequately to the political experience of this century and to various intellectual challenges, particularly depth psychology and the sociological tradition; and to clearly articulate the connection between their view of human nature and their social critique. I have found most of their accounts of human needs misleading, their treatment of the question of shareability inadequate, and their exploration of the relationship of these concerns both misleading and inadequate. And their persistent attempt to see in capitalist and bureaucratic institutions the sole source of our alienation gives us no assurance that these questions would be adequately addressed, as Dahl puts it, after the revolution.

Nevertheless, it is on the left and liberal-left that both the sense of loss and the desire for reconstruction is most keen, and I have therefore spent a great deal of time poking among the ruins, now-shattered or badly battered ideals and images of man, liberal and left. There is much to be learned from a close study of the pieces themselves and our shared reaction to fragmentation—personal, social, intellectual. Mere agreement on the fact of fragmentation, of rulelessness—and that the alienation to which we are subjected is intimately bound up with the species of subjection which is anomie— would represent an important beginning. Thus I have sought to put both dissenters and defenders in the context of such concerns, the better to distinguish what really concerns us, as Rieff puts it, from what is being railed against; to distinguish what really divides us from that exaggerated posturing whereby we reveal our fear that the other man's truth may be true for us as well. On the basis of such considerations I have tried to suggest, in a tentative and limited fashion, some of the crucial aspects of an explicit communal ethic.

Whoever demands more of freedom than freedom itself, Tocqueville warned, is born for tyranny: "they call for equality in freedom; and if they cannot obtain that, they call for equality in tyranny." The protests of the critics, together with the contributions of recent democratic theorists, help us to see with increasing clarity that neither equality nor liberty, much less fraternity, necessarily result from liberal democratic procedures and institutions. The purported pluralistic reconciliation of liberty, equality, and fraternity with which we began is not convincing. Not unless we make, either explicitly or inadvertently, some additional and unjustifiably rosy assumptions about the cultural context of these institutions, the wants encouraged by the culture and the demands that impinge on the institutions. Otherwise, liberal democracy and playing by the liberal democratic rules are not antidotes to anomie, but major symptoms and manifestations of that rulelessness; not ways of settling disputes so as to bring us together, but ways of reflecting and even aggravating our separation, and with it the gap between what is expected of our institutions and what they provide. Those who are most free will be those who apprise themselves of the limits that freedom must set for itself, both with reference to human nature and to social interaction.

For all of us do, in fact, demand more than freedom from freedom, and more than democracy from democracy. These demands have to do with belonging and being included as well as with distinguishing and asserting ourselves. Even free men require a home, and freedom requires a willingness to share it. That is why we must concern ourselves with the liberal democratic community, if we value liberal democracy. And that is the sense in which we need to bring what is left back home.

Notes

Introduction to Part 1

1. John Schaar, "Legitimacy in the Modern State," in *Power and Community*, ed. Philip Green and Sanford Levinson (New York: Randon House, Vintage, 1970), p. 288.

2. At this point I exclude those democratic theorists who emphasize and explicitly rely on their view of what it means to be more fully human; these theorists are treated in Part Two. I also exclude the more philosophical works which attempt to explain and justify democracy. Most of the critics I consider here tend to assume the acceptance, legitimacy, and intelligibility of democratic ideals and standards. Part Four will deal with some of the more philosophical treatments of democracy.

3. Most of the following examples receive some attention in the text: Peter Bachrach, *The Theory of Democratic Elitism: A Critique* (Boston: Little, Brown, 1967); Peter Bachrach and Morton Baratz, *Power and Poverty: Theory and Practice* (New York: Oxford University Press, 1970); various pieces in Charles McCoy and John Playford, eds., *Apolitical Politics* (New York: Crowell, 1967); Henry Kariel, ed., *Frontiers of Democratic Theory* (New York: Random House, 1970); Theodore Lowi, *The End of Liberalism* (New York: Norton, 1969); Michael Rogin, *The Intellectuals and McCarthy: The Radical Specter* (Cambridge, Mass.: M.I.T. Press, 1966), especially chap. 1 and chap. 2; Mancur Olson, *The Logic of Collective Action* (New York: Schocken, 1968); Henry Kariel, *The Promise of Politics* (Englewood Cliffs, N.J.: Prentice-Hall, 1966); also Kariel, "Pluralism," in *International Encyclopedia of the Social Sciences* (New York: MacMillan Co., The Free Press, 1968), vol. 12, pp. 164–68; Robert Paul Wolff, *The Poverty of Liberalism* (Boston: Beacon, 1968) and *In Defense of Anarchism* (New York: Harper & Row, 1970); Joseph Tussman, *Obligation and the Body Politic* (New York: Oxford University Press, 1960); (Tussman's *Government and the Mind* [New York: Oxford University Press, 1977], is not nearly as vulnerable to most of the criticisms of the earlier work I voice here.) John Schaar, "Equality of Opportunity, and Beyond,"

in *Nomos IX: Equality,* ed. J. R. Pennock and J. W. Chapman (New York: Atherton Press, 1967); P. H. Partridge, "Politics, Philosophy, and Ideology," in *Political Philosophy*, ed. Anthony Quinton (Oxford: Oxford University Press, 1967); E. E. Schattschneider, *The Semi-Sovereign People* (New York: Holt, Rinehart & Winston, 1960); Sheldon Wolin, "Political Theory as a Vocation," *American Political Science Review,* vol. 53, no. 4 (December 1959); and Grant McConnell, *Private Power and American Democracy* (New York: Random House, 1966). Related works by these and other authors are mentioned along the way.

This work parallels but largely postdates the controversy surrounding C. Wright Mills's thesis concerning the power elite. For a summary of this debate, and selections from liberal, radical, and highbrow critics of Mills, see G. William Domhoff and Hoyt B. Ballard, eds., *C. Wright Mills and the Power Elite* (Boston: Beacon, 1968), especially the pieces by Dahl, Parsons, and Sweezy. The ways in which the critics discussed here are indebted to Marx are usually clear and sometimes considerable, though, like Mills, they tend to speak with populist, not Marxist accents.

Chapter 1

1. Among the sociologically-minded I would include Robert Nisbet, *Community and Power* (New York: Oxford University Press, 1953), and *Tradition and Revolt* (New York: Random House, 1970); William Kornhauser, *The Politics of Mass Society* (New York: Free Press, 1959); Daniel Bell, *The End of Ideology* (Glencoe, Ill.: Free Press, 1961), especially "America as a Mass Society: A Critique"; Seymour Lipset, *Political Man* (Garden City, N.Y.: Doubleday, 1953); Edward Shils, various articles, including "Ideology and Civility: The Politics of the Intellectuals," in *Sewanee Review,* July–September 1968; Harry Eckstein, *A Theory of Stable Democracy* (Princeton, N.J.: Center of International Studies, 1961); Ralf Dahrendorf, *Class and Class Conflict in Industrial Societies* (Stanford, Calif.: Stanford University Press, 1959); Talcott Parsons, in many of his essays. This is essentially the group of theorists discussed and assessed in Michael Rogin's *The Intellectuals and McCarthy: The Radical Specter* (Cambridge, Mass.: M.I.T. Press, 1966), and Rogin provides a helpful bibliography. I have also found Robert Paul Wolff's account of pluralism, which stresses sociological as well

as liberal influences on pluralistic theory, most helpful. (*The Poverty of Liberalism*, chaps. 3 and 4.)

2. Much of the discussion of the preceding two paragraphs parallels the argument of Robert Nisbet in *Community and Power*. As indicated, I have also drawn on Michael Rogin's excellent discussion of pluralism in *The Intellectuals and McCarthy: The Radical Specter*, chaps. 1 and 2.

3. Certainly it is possible to make too much of distinctions among pluralists, between sociologically-minded pluralists and those of other stripes. Sociological pluralism relates closely to a more traditional and philosophical pluralism: the political philosophy which argues that the power of the state over private associations should be limited, which fears the omnipotent state but also fears the extremes of individualism and anarchism, and thus lends its support to a pluralistic society. Representative of this variety of pluralism is A. D. Lindsey, *The Modern Democratic State* (New York: Oxford University Press, 1943).

Both of these varieties, in turn, lend support to what has been called the group approach to politics, or analytical pluralism, the literature which emphasizes the significance and often the benign qualities of interest or pressure groups in the political process. Three works particularly important in the literature of group politics are Arthur Bentley's *The Process of Government* (Chicago: University of Chicago Press, 1908); Earl Latham's *The Group Basis of Politics* (Ithaca, N.Y.: Cornell University Press, 1952); and David Truman's *The Governmental Process* (New York: Knopf, 1958).

There are significant disagreements as well as different emphases, even among those who might be willing to call themselves pluralists. This is important to bear in mind in considering the critics of pluralism, some of whom conjure up straw men and nonexistent schools of thought to criticize. One such disagreement concerns the extent to which the pluralist model is actually descriptive of the distribution of power in this country. Another concerns the extent to which the pluralist model is supposed to provide for a just, or liberal, or democratic order, as well as a stable one. Some tend to argue that the pluralistic equilibrium provides the best or safest way of approximating the public interest; others contend that there is no such thing as the public interest apart from the existing state of competition among groups—and that, moreover, politics is rational precisely to the extent that no one concerns himself with the public interest. The latter is Bentley's view: "usually we shall find, on testing the 'social whole' that it is merely the group or tendency represented by the man who talks of it, erected into the pretense of a universal demand of society." (Quoted in Mancur Olson, *The Logic of Collective Action* [New York: Schocken, 1968], p. 120.) Shils flirts with this position, too, and Lipset's somewhat ambiguous contention that democracy is the "good society itself in operation" is in this vein.

Similarly, some argue that a certain rough justice emerges from the tendency of group power to generate powerful countervailing groups; others deny this, and see some role for the state in promoting countervailing powers. (Some seem to change their position on this matter over time—notably Galbraith.) There are those, like Kornhauser, who apparently believe that a viable social pluralism will automatically and effectively promote a stable and free social order, while others, Nisbet and de Jouvenel for example, argue that deliberate governmental policy should encourage (but may sabotage) this social pluralism, and with it a free social order. Finally, still others argue that in addition to a vigorous pluralistic pursuit of group interests, the maintenance of a pluralistic and free society requires an elite which shares and defends a consensus on the rules of the liberal democratic game. (See for example V. O. Key, Jr., *Public Opinion and American Democracy* [New York: Knopf, 1961].) This view has also been expressed by Talcott Parsons.

In making many of these distinctions among pluralists, I am indebted to Mancur Olson's stimulating discussion in chap. 5 ("Orthodox Theories of Pressure Groups") of *The Logic of Collective Action*.

4. Often their targets are not distinguished with sufficient precision, and sometimes the targets are not even named. But Robert Dahl's work is often taken as the best representative of the general orientation (in the case of Wolff, Bachrach and Baratz, Kariel, Schaar, among numerous other critics); or (less accurately) as representative of the "whole tribe of pressure group analysts" (Partridge). Dahl himself has on several occasions probed the weaknesses of the pluralist persuasion as well or better than many of his critics, though this is typically not acknowledged.

Works of his often singled out for special attention include the following: *Who Governs?* (New Haven and London: Yale University Press, 1961); *A Preface to Democratic Theory* (Chicago: University of Chicago Press, 1956), with its precedent-setting rigor in conceptualizing different models of democracy; and "A Critique of the Ruling Elite Model," in G. William Domhoff and Hoyt B. Ballard, eds., *C. Wright Mills and the Power Elite* (Boston: Beacon, 1968). A popularized account of his general point of view, but one which sacrifices little sophistication or rigor, is *After the Revolution?* (New Haven and London: Yale University Press, 1970); see especially parts 1 and 2. This is treated in chapter 9, as a relatively explicit philosophical attempt to explain and justify pluralism.

5. E. E. Schattschneider, *The Semi-Sovereign People* (New York: Holt, Rinehart & Winston, 1960), pp. 30-31. See also V. O. Key, *Politics, Parties, and Pressure Groups* (New York: Crowell, 1952), p. 83.

6. Robert Paul Wolff, *The Poverty of Liberalism* (Boston: Beacon, 1968), p. 153.

7. Bachrach and Baratz, *Power and Poverty: Theory and Practice* (New York: Oxford University Press, 1970), p. 44.

8. Economists have long used this simple idea in a number of contexts, for example, to explain the inevitable element of coercion involved in taxing to finance public goods.

9. Olson, *The Logic of Collective Action*, p. 127.

10. Ibid., p. 167.

11. Henry Kariel, *The Promise of Politics* (Englewood Cliffs, N.J.: Prentice-Hall, 1966), p. 8.

12. The phrase is Sheldon Wolin's. See his list of problems in "Political Theory as a Vocation," *American Political Science Review*, December 1959, p. 1082.

13. Robert Dahl, *After the Revolution?*, p. 64.

14. See Dahl's discussion of this point in *After the Revolution?*, pp. 98-101.

15. Of course it is possible to overdo things in the opposite direction, as perhaps this country has done. Dahl points out that even the citizens of Fridley, Minnesota, labor under eleven distinct layers of government. In this connection, see his discussion of the "Chinese boxes," pp. 88-99, in *After the Revolution?*. The problem is actually more complicated, since in addition to being imbedded like Chinese boxes, one in another, political jurisdictions overlap one another as well.

16. See Peter Bachrach, *The Theory of Democratic Elitism: A Critique* (Boston: Little, Brown, 1967), chap. 7, "An Alternative Approach."

17. Robert Dahl, *Political Oppositions in Western Democracies* (New Haven and London: Yale University Press, 1966), p. 396.

18. Joseph Tussman, *Obligation and the Body Politic* (New York: Oxford University Press, 1960), p. 83.
    19. Wolff, *The Poverty of Liberalism*, p. 90.
    20. Ibid., p. 121.

Chapter 2

1. *Axiomatic* is perhaps the more common designation, but *economic* has the virtue of calling attention to the principal disciplinary source of their tools and assumptions. Two works regarded as forerunners in this area are Joseph Schumpeter's *Capitalism, Socialism, and Democracy* (New York: Harper & Row, 1942) in which democracy is redefined as a competitive struggle among elites for the people's votes; and Robert Dahl's *A Preface to Democratic Theory* (Chicago: University of Chicago Press, 1956), which attempts to delineate axiomatic models of Madisonian, populistic, and polyarchical conceptions of democracy. Other basic points of reference include Anthony Downs, *An Economic Theory of Democracy* (New York: Harper & Row, 1957); Mancur Olson, *The Logic of Collective Action* (New York: Schocken, 1968); James Buchanan and Gordon Tulloch, *The Calculus of Consent* (Ann Arbor: University of Michigan Press, 1962); Kenneth Arrow, *Social Choice and Individual Values* (New Haven: Yale University Press, 1951); Duncan Black, *The Theory of Committees and Elections* (London: Cambridge University Press, 1958). William Riker and Peter Ordeshook, *An Introduction to Positive Political Theory* (Englewood Cliffs, N.J.: Prentice-Hall, 1973) provides a helpful overview of the public choice literature. Of particular interest here is the literature of constitutional choice: in addition to Buchanan and Tulloch, see also James Buchanan, *The Limits of Liberty* (Chicago: University of Chicago Press, 1975); Douglas Rae, "The Limits of Consensual Decision," *American Political Science Review*, vol. 69, no. 4 (December 1975), and his "Decision-Rules and Individual Values in Constitutional Choice," *American Political Science Review*, vol. 63, no. 1 (March 1969); Robert E. Goodin, *The Politics of Rational Man* (London: John Wiley & Sons, 1976). Works in political science and increasingly in political theory which employ the tools and assumptions of liberal economics—or related perspectives of game theory, welfare economics, and analytic philosophy—are too numerous to document. One notable contribution to the literature of constitutional choice which attempts to use game-theory and economic perspectives in the service of a nonutilitarian theory of justice is John

Rawls's *A Theory of Justice* (Cambridge, Mass.: Harvard University Press, 1971). Brian Barry's *Sociologists, Economists, and Democracy* (London: Collier-MacMillan, 1970) is a trenchant analysis of the comparative strengths of the economic and the sociological approaches to democratic theory, and I have found it most helpful in organizing my argument in chaps. 1 and 9.

2. John Plamenatz, *Democracy and Illusion* (London: Longmans, 1973). Though I came across Plamenatz's analysis after most of my reflections on recent American democratic theory had crystallized, the points of our agreement are several and significant, as I shall indicate. The major shortcoming of his excellent critique of the neoutilitarians is that he does not attempt to develop in any detail the alternative he has in mind, to spell out those "best interests of the community" on which his critique would appear to hinge. To some extent this criticism also applies to what is perhaps the most mature statement of his political outlook: *Karl Marx's Philosophy of Man* (Oxford: Clarendon Press, 1975); and to *The English Utilitarians* (Oxford: Basil Blackwell, 1949) as well, in which the elements of his own alternative are typically buried in careful, close critique of others. Nevertheless, these works, together with his two-volume *Man and Society* (London: Longmans, 1963) constitute a sustained and noteworthy effort to steer a middle course somewhere between Bentham on the one hand and Marx and Rousseau on the other.

3. John Schaar, "Legitimacy in the Modern State," in *Power and Community*, ed. Philip Green and Sanford Levinson (New York: Random House, Vintage, 1970), p. 288. Compare with H. L. Mencken's suggestion that "democracy is grounded upon so childish a complex of fallacies that they must be protected by a rigid system of taboos, else even half-wits would argue it to pieces" (*In Defense of Women* [New York: Knopf, 1928], p. xi).

4. Schumpeter, *Capitalism, Socialism, and Democracy*, especially pp. 250–73.

5. Downs, *Economic Theory of Democracy*, p. 246.

6. Meaningless in instrumentalist terms, that is. As Riker and Ordeshook (*An Introduction to Positive Political Theory*) point out, what I have labeled *costs* here might well include benefits—the good feeling associated with being a good citizen, and so on—which are also independent of the presumed benefits of the preferred outcome. Indeed, this might make the term positive, in which case the act of voting is only irrational, they suggest, to the extent to which we consider such symbolic behavior, and the socialization process from which such behavior derives, irrational. Though they

stop short of labeling it irrational, they turn to a closer analysis of
the voting act clearly in search of an alternative explanation which
demonstrates instrumental rationality—clearly their preferred definition of rationality. In their resulting formulation, the probability
that the citizen will affect the outcome is seen to depend on the size
of the electorate, the closeness of the election, and the state of the
citizen's information. Their treatment of the last two factors is particularly interesting, in that relatively little interest is shown in the
question of whether such complicated calculations are even approximated by more than a few voters, and because they seem considerably more tolerant toward possibly grossly irrational and inflated
estimates by the citizen of the impact of his vote than toward the
irrationality of his voting, say, because he thought it was the right
and patriotic thing to do. This seems especially curious in light of
their own estimate ("A Theory of the Calculus of Voting," *American Political Science Review* 62 [March 1968]) that the probability
of one citizen actually determining who becomes president is approximately 10^{-8}, and that therefore, as Ferejohn and Fiorina have
put it, "all the action is in the D term," the term which represents
the direct utility from the voting. For an analysis in the same instrumentalist vein, but which employs an alternative rationality criterion of "maximum" regret, see John A. Ferejohn and Morris P.
Fiorina, "The Paradox of Not Voting: A Decision Theoretic Analysis," *American Political Science Review* 63 (June 1974). Closer to
my view is the argument of Paul Meehl in "The Selfish Voter Paradox and the Thrown-Away Vote Argument," *American Political
Science Review* 62 (March 1977): "all economic theories of voter
participation are radically incoherent, because such participation is
irrational as an instrumental action toward an egocentric end."

7. Brian Barry makes much the same point in *Sociologists, Economists, and Democracy*, chap. 2. My discussion here, particularly of
the Downsian paradox, has benefitted greatly from his critique of
both the economic and the sociological approaches to democratic
theory.

8. Downs, *Economic Theory of Democracy*, p. 261; also see
Barry, *Sociologists, Economists, and Democracy*, chap. 2, especially
pp. 13–23.

9. See Barry's discussion *Sociologists, Economists, and Democracy*, pp. 23–40. Nor does Olson's other solution, the use of coercive devices to insure participation in large groups, account for all of
the remainder.

10. R. E. Wagner, "Pressure Groups and Political Entrepreneurs,"

Papers on Non-Market Decision-Making; see also Barry, *Sociologists, Economists, and Democracy*, pp. 37–40. His discussion called my attention to Wagner's article, as well as Coleman's.

11. J. S. Coleman, "Individual Interests and Collective Action," *Papers on Non-Market Decision-Making*, p. 1.

12. Barry, *Sociologists, Economists, and Democracy*, p. 46.

13. Robert Dahl and Charles Lindblom, *Politics, Economics, and Welfare* (New York: Harper & Row, 1953), p. 41.

14. Downs, *Economic Theory of Democracy*, p. 257.

15. Dahl, *Preface to Democratic Theory*, pp. 60–62.

16. Dahl, *After the Revolution?* (New Haven and London: Yale University Press, 1970), p. 14.

17. See Plamenatz, *Democracy and Illusion*, p. 171.

18. In discussing the relationship of political equality to majority rule I am indebted to a stimulating class discussion of some of these points led by Douglas Rae.

19. Rae, "Decision-Rules and Individual Values in Constitutional Choice."

20. Ibid., p. 54.

21. Ibid., pp. 54–55.

22. See Plamenatz, *Democracy and Illusion*, pp. 170–71.

23. Similarly for the question of whether the solution is fair. Walter Kaufmann points out in a related context that "even if everybody should be pleased, it would not follow that each got what he deserved; it might mean merely that the selfish were rewarded while the unselfish, who take delight in the good fortune of others, were not" (*Without Guilt and Justice*, [New York: Dell Publishing Co., 1973], p. 93).

24. Noteworthy exceptions are Buchanan and Tullock, *Calculus of Consent*, and Buchanan, *Limits of Liberty*. For an effective critique of their alternative principle, unanimity, see Rae, "Limits of Consensual Decision." Rae shows how their analytical models neglect the costs of not changing (which is the only way to make the requirement of unanimity seem reasonable). Buchanan and Tullock have tradition on their side, in the sense that basic features of the social contract are traditionally conceived as being unanimously acceptable and accepted. In this light, the problem is not so much their emphasis on consensus, but rather the nature of the consensus they postulate, and the starting point or baseline we are supposed to accept. For Buchanan the baseline distribution seems to be determined by what if anything each individual manages to grab and hold onto in the war of each against all, before civilization and the social

contract arrive to legitimate and protect such possessions. (See *Limits of Liberty*, especially the discussion of the "natural" distribution, pp. 23–31.) It is not clear why even a majority, much less a consensus, would ever voluntarily acquiesce in such a state of affairs, and it is even less clear why such a Spencerian struggle lends any legitimacy to the resulting distribution.

25. It should be repeated that, despite considerable ambivalence as to whether democracy is a means or an end in itself, the democratic critics of pluralism have nevertheless been instrumental in questioning a strictly instrumental view of democratic institutions. See for example Peter Bachrach's *The Theory of Democratic Elitism: A Critique* (Boston: Little, Brown, 1967), pp. 1–9.

26. Arrow, *Social Choice and Individual Values,* especially chaps. 3, 5, and 7. See also Black, *Theory of Committees and Elections*; and Riker and Ordeshook, *Introduction to Positive Political Theory*, chaps. 2 and 4.

27. Arrow, *Social Choice and Individual Values,* p. 59.

Introduction to Part 2

1. Particularly relevant here are the writings of the young Marx, including *The Economic and Philosophic Manuscripts of 1844* (1844, reprinted ed., London: Lawrence and Wishart, 1959); *Karl Marx: Selected Writings in Sociology and Social Philosophy*, trans. T. B. Bottomore, foreword by Erich Fromm (New York: McGraw-Hill, 1956); Karl Marx and Friedrich Engels, *The German Ideology*, ed., with introduction by C. J. Arthur (New York: International Publishers, 1947). In this connection also see *Alienation*, by Richard Schacht, introduction by Walter Kaufmann (Garden City, N.Y.: Doubleday, Anchor, 1970), especially pp. 73–160; and Peter Berger and Stanley Pullberg, "Reification and the Sociological Critique of Consciousness," *New Left Review* 35 (January–February 1966): 56–75.

2. In addition to "Reification and the Sociological Critique of Consciousness," see Berger and Thomas Luckmann, *The Social Construction of Reality* (Garden City, N.Y.: Doubleday, Anchor, 1966); and *The Sacred Canopy* (Garden City, N.Y.: Doubleday, Anchor, 1969), especially chap. 1.

3. Henri Lefebrve, *The Sociology of Marx* (New York: Random House, Vintage, 1969), p. 54.

4. Fred Weinstein and Gerald M. Platt, *The Wish to Be Free* (Berkeley: University of California Press, 1969), p. 2.

5. Whether to be left or radical is to be for anything other than change itself, expanded freedoms, or options in general, has been answered in the negative with surprising and increasing frequency in recent times. C. Wright Mills suggested a redefinition of the left in this vein, and Thomas Thorson offers a similar definition in *The Logic of Democracy* (New York: Holt, Rinehart & Winston, 1962). Stuart Hampshire apparently considers the general expansion of freedoms to be the essence of radicalism ("In Defense of Radicalism," *Encounter* 5 [1955]: 36–41.) See also Warren Bennis and Philip Slater, *The Temporary Society* (New York: Harper & Row, 1968). On leftism as undistorted, unrestricted communication, see Jürgen Habermas's *Knowledge and Interest*, trans. Jeremy Shapiro (Boston: Beacon, 1968), and Trent Schroyer's account of Habermas's work in *Recent Sociology No. 2*, ed. Hans Peter Dreitzel (London: Macmillan & Co., 1970).

Such a loose conception of radicalism is also implicit in the perspectives of many critics who have naively adopted some of the most romantic and least precise formulations of the young Marx, who have applied his remarks on the alienation syndrome to practically everything in sight, to the point of making alienation practically synonymous with any and everything the critic doesn't like and wishes were otherwise. This, Kaufmann suggests, is about as informative as calling everything you like "groovy." Erich Fromm, who has played fast and loose with the notion of alienation, is typical of this numerous tribe, though I consider other representatives in chaps. 3 and 4.

General, too-general challenges to transcend the given order, to expose and develop whatever is latent and repressed by present institutional realities, are likewise too numerous and commonplace to document: Henry Kariel, whom I briefly consider in this chapter, may be taken as representative. In Part Three I suggest the affinity of such views with the sophisticated liberal economist's defense of economic growth–that growth expands options, and more options are better than less–a resemblance which should be disconcerting to the above authors, but apparently is not.

6. In this century the dilemma is perhaps epitomized by Sartre, and the distance he must travel from the "phenomenological ontology" of *Being and Nothingness*, trans. Hazel Barnes (New York: Simon & Schuster, Washington Square Press, 1966), to the super-Kantianism of "Existentialism is a Humanism" (translated by Walter Kaufmann, in Kaufmann's *Existentialism from Dostoevsky to Sartre* [New York: World Publishing, 1956], pp. 267–311) and the

rather pronounced Marxism of his *Search for a Method* (translated by Hazel Barnes (New York: Random House, 1968), in which existentialism is described as a rather short-lived moment in the Marxist dialectic.

7. See Ben Brewster's comments in response to Berger and Pullberg's "Reification and the Sociological Critique of Consciousness." Berger himself is among those who have been most adamant in rejecting any conception of essential human qualities ("humanness is socially variable"), except for anthropological constants like world-openness and instinctual plasticity—though, like Sartre, he seems to build in more assumptions about humanness than he lets on. This radically sociologistic view distorts his analysis of Marx, in that Marx attributes more "density" or specifically human qualities to the human subject than Berger is willing to recognize. This in turn is related to his unqualified contention that any kind of rapprochement, much less synthesis, of Marx and Freud is impossible. (See for example *The Social Construction of Reality*, pp. 193–205.)

Chapter 3

1. Philip Rieff speculates in this vein in his *Freud: The Mind of a Moralist* (Garden City, N.Y.: Doubleday, 1959), especially chap. 10: "The Emergence of Psychological Man"; and *The Triumph of the Therapeutic: The Uses of Faith Since Freud* (New York: Harper & Row, 1968), chaps. 1–4. Rieff's perspective will be treated in more detail in chapter 6. Two other conceptions of the crisis of special interest are Daniel Bell's *The Cultural Contradictions of Capitalism* (New York: Basic Books, 1976); and Hannah Arendt's discussion of how "the modern age not only challenged one or another form of authority . . . but caused the whole concept of authority to lose its validity altogether," in *Between Past and Future* (New York: Viking, 1968), "What is Authority?", pp. 91–141.

2. T. S. Eliot is associated with the argument that a viable culture must be based on shared religious belief. He offers this thesis in *Notes Towards the Definition of Culture* (New York: Harcourt Brace and Co., 1949).

> I do not overlook the possibility that Britain, if it consummated its apostasy by reforming itself according to the prescriptions of some inferior or materialistic religion, might blossom into a culture more brilliant than we can show today. That would not be

evidence that the new religion was true, and that Christianity was false. It would merely prove that any religion, while it lasts, and on its own level, gives an apparent meaning to life, provides the framework for a culture, and protects the mass of humanity from boredom and despair (p. 32).

3. The critics I will discuss—and I emphasize that I do not intend to offer an overall assessment of their work—are representative of what I will call the leftist literature of freedom, a designation to be further explained and explored in chaps. 3 and 4. The designation excludes those who have no apparent concern for collective goals and ideals, those whose perspective on the society is less critical, and those who exhibit less of a gap between their metapsychological premises and their social critique, between their liberalism and leftism. Two familiar figures in this literature who do not receive explicit attention here are Erich Fromm and Paul Goodman; the main thrust of my comments applies to both. In particular, see Fromm's *Man for Himself* (Greenwich, Conn.: Fawcett, 1947), and Goodman's *Growing Up Absurd* (New York: Random House, 1960), especially chap. 1. John Schaar's fine critique of Fromm's work (*Escape from Authority* [New York: Harper & Row, 1961]) bears important similarities to some of the criticisms I offer here. In a loose way the critics I examine are representative of a voluminous literature. Approaches to social criticism which are grounded in psychology are legion; and the adoption of psychological jargon, whatever the critical perspective or approach, is even more prevalent. Most of the following analyses share the problematic aspects of those I have singled out.

Among those analyses which exhibit and acknowledge a debt to Freud is Daniel Yankelovitch and William Barrett, *Ego and Instinct* (New York: Random House, 1970). See also Norman O. Brown, *Life Against Death* (New York: Random House, Vintage, 1959). Paul Robinson provides a study of the Freudian left in his book by that name, *The Freudian Left* (New York: Harper & Row, 1969). Philip Slater has drawn on Freudian perspectives in *The Pursuit of Loneliness* (Boston: Beacon, 1970), and "The Social Bases of Personality," in *Sociology*, ed. Neil Smelser (New York: John Wiley & Sons, 1967), though in important ways his perspective is more sociological (see Part Three). The vast literature on identity is best represented by Erik Erikson and his unique blending of psychoanalytic and sociological emphases: see "The Problem of Ego Identity," in *Identity and Anxiety*, ed. Maurice Stein, Arthur J. Vidich, and David Manning White (New York: Free Press, 1960).

Humanistic, or "third force psychology"—that is, an alternative both to psychoanalysis and behaviorism—is associated with Abraham Maslow, Gordon Allport, and Erich Fromm, among others. See Maslow's discussion of the hierarchy of human needs, "A Theory of Human Motivation," *Psychological Review* 50 (1943): 370–96; and the collection entitled *New Knowledge in Human Values*, ed. Abraham Maslow (Chicago: Henry Regnery, 1970). Jeanne Knutson, in *The Human Basis of the Polity* (Chicago: Aldine, 1972), argues that Maslow's hierarchy of needs is the central armature around which most recent social-psychological research can be wound. Loosely related to these perspectives is existential psychology: see R. D. Laing, *The Divided Self* (Middlesex, Eng.: Penguin, 1965), and Jean-Paul Sartre, *Existential Psychoanalysis*, trans. Hazel Barnes (Chicago: Henry Regnery, 1953). A different perspective, but one which some social theorists and critics have used in similar ways, is that afforded by cognitive developmental psychology: see Jean Piaget and Bärbel Inhelder, *The Psychology of the Child*, trans. Helen Weaver (New York: Basic Books, 1969), a summary of Piaget's work; and Piaget, *The Moral Judgment of the Child*, trans. Majorie Gabain (New York: Free Press, 1965), to which Lawrence Kohlberg's work (see chapter 6) is indebted. Scarcely restrained enthusiasm for humanistic psychology is found in *Radical Man*, Charles Hampden-Turner (Cambridge, Mass.: Schenkman, 1970).

Three somewhat different representatives of the leftist literature of freedom deserve special mention: Marshall Berman, *The Politics of Authenticity* (New York: Atheneum, 1970), which draws on Montesquieu and Rousseau as well as R. D. Laing; C. B. Macpherson, *Democratic Theory: Essays in Retrieval* (Oxford: Clarendon Press, 1971), which bases its quasi-Marxist case for the reorientation of liberal democratic theory on a largely undeveloped notion of essential human powers; and Ellen Meiksens Woods, *Mind and Politics* (Berkeley: University of California Press, 1971), which draws on Kant and Rousseau as well as Piaget. My criticisms of Bay, Marcuse, Kariel, and Etzioni apply in large measure to the work of Berman and Macpherson as well, especially to Berman.

4. Friedrich Nietzsche, *Beyond Good and Evil*, trans. with commentary by Walter Kaufmann (1886; reprinted ed. New York: Random House, 1966), p. 145.

5. People were actually beside themselves with delight over this new faculty, and the jubilation reached its climax when Kant further discovered a moral faculty in man . . . the honeymoon of German philosophy arrived. All the young theologians of the

Tübingen seminary went into the bushes—all looking for "faculties." And what they did not find—in that innocent, rich, and still youthful period of the German spirit, in which romanticism, the malignant fairy, piped and sang, when one could not yet distinguish between "finding" and "inventing." (Nietzsche, *Beyond Good and Evil*, p. 18).

6. Peter Berger, *The Sacred Canopy* (Garden City, N.Y.: Doubleday, Anchor, 1969), p. 153. See also Berger's review essay of Lionel Trilling's *Sincerity and Authenticity* (Cambridge, Mass.: Harvard University Press, 1972): "Sincerity and Authenticity in Modern Society," *The Public Interest* 31 (Spring 1973): 81-90. Berger has been influenced by the German sociologist Arnold Gehlen's theory of the increasing "underinstitutionalization" of individuals in Western societies, and gives a short account of Gehlen's work in "Arnold Gehlen and the Theory of Institutions," *Social Research*, vol. 1, no. 32 (1965), pp. 110-15.

7. Amitai Etzioni, *The Active Society* (New York: Free Press, 1968); especially the epilogue, chap. 21: "Alienation, Inauthenticity, and Their Reduction." The significance of the chapter is confirmed by Etzioni's choice of it to appear simultaneously with a review symposium on *The Active Society*. See "Basic Human Needs, Alienation, and Inauthenticity," *American Sociological Review*, vol. 33, no. 6 (December 1968), pp. 870-75.

8. See p. 634, *Active Society*: "Unless otherwise specified, the following statements refer to democracies."

9. Ibid., p. 622.

10. Ibid., pp. 622-26. This might be called the Adelphi method (that is, polling the experts) were there any experts in this area. He does issue this disclaimer: ". . . nor should we focus on the specific items on the list [of basic needs] at the present state of our knowledge": the "key proposition" is that the "flexibility of basic human needs is limited in that they can be more readily and full satisfied in some social structures than others." See also his note 11, p. 657.

11. Ibid., pp. 625-26.

12. Ibid., p. 626. In general, the left literature of freedom is not known for its tragic view of life.

13. Ibid., p. 653.

14. Ibid., p. 617.

15. Ibid., p. 638.

16. Ibid., p. 641.

17. Ibid.

18. Ibid., p. 644.

19. Most of the specific references here are to "Behavioral Research and the Theory of Democracy," *Berkeley Journal of Sociology* 14 (1969): 18–34; and *The Structure of Freedom* (Stanford, Calif.: Stanford University Press, 1958). Also relevant are "Politics and Pseudopolitics: A Critical Evaluation of Some Behavioral Literature," *American Political Science Review*, vol. 49, no. 1 (March 1965), pp. 39–51; and "Political and Apolitical Students: Facts in Search of a Theory," *Journal of Social Issues*, vol. 23, no. 3 (1967), pp. 76–92. A more recent article is "Freedom as a Tool of Oppression," in *The Case for Participatory Democracy*, ed. C. George Benello and Dimitrios Roussopoulos (New York: Viking, 1971), pp. 251–69. Bay sees this article as an extension of the argument of *Structure of Freedom*, but its emphasis is significantly different and bears some resemblance to the criticisms of his earlier pieces which I offer here.

20. *Structure of Freedom*, p. xvi.

21. "Behavioral Research and the Theory of Democracy," p. 26. Compare with Fromm, *Man for Himself*, especially chap. 1 and chap. 2, section 3, pp. 30–33.

22. "Behavioral Research and the Theory of Democracy," p. 24. He does vacillate on this point, by castigating pluralist democracy for the apparently opposite sin of *frustrating* majority rule. See pp. 20–22.

23. *Structure of Freedom*, p. 379.

24. This is what is called a lexicographical ordering of principles, or lexical, to use John Rawls's term: ". . . an order which requires us to satisfy the first principle in the ordering before we can move on to the second. . . . a principle does not come into play until those previous to it are . . . fully met." John Rawls, *A Theory of Justice* (Cambridge, Mass.: Harvard University Press, 1971), pp. 42–43.

25. *Structure of Freedom*, pp. 130–31.

26. Ibid., p. 13.

27. Ibid., p. 125.

28. Macpherson's parallel argument (in *Democratic Theory: Essays in Retrieval*) exhibits similar ambiguities. He contends that modern liberal democratic theory is grounded in the claim that, in conjunction with the market, liberal democratic institutions maximize total utility, and in the corresponding view of man as an infinite appropriator and consumer of utilities. This Benthamite view of man is "perverse, artificial, and temporary," and democracy should instead seek to maximize "essentially human powers," a view he attributes to "traditional" democratic theorists, primarily Mill and

and Marx. "Human attributes . . . may be taken to include the capacity for rational understanding, for moral judgment and action, for aesthetic creation or contemplation, for the emotional activities of friendship and love, and, sometimes, for religious experience. Whatever the uniquely human attributes are taken to be, in this view of man their exertion and development are seen as ends in themselves . . . not simply a means to consumer satisfactions" (p. 4). The preoccupation with power over others must be supplanted by the concept of power as the "ability to use and develop essentially human capacities," in order for men to "live as fully as they wish." In one view, this list of human attributes is not long enough: less attractive human qualities, which would make trouble for his eventual claim that socialist democracy could promote and allow everyone to "live as fully as they wish," are absent. But from another point of view the list is already too long, as well as excessively vague concerning the specific directions in which such general attributes might lead us. Even dedicated consumers might qualify on several of these vague dimensions, and many might now be living as fully as they wish, if their incomes were only 10 percent higher. In the same spirit, one might also ask whether these attributes form any kind of hierarchy, and whether the exercise and maximization of my specifically human powers might ever thwart your effort to exercise and maximize yours. Macpherson anticipates and answers both these questions—and with them, Bay's vexing problem concerning the relationship between his view of human nature and his emphasis on the shareability of various freedom demands—in one fell swoop.

> When capacities are postulated in a democratic theory, the postulate must include a further assumption which incidentally makes a hierarchical order unnecessary. The further assumption, which at first sight is a staggering one, is . . . that the essentially human capacities may all be used and developed without hindering the use and development of all the rest. . . . for what would be the use of trying to provide that everyone should be able to make the most of himself, which is the idea of a democratic society, if that were bound to lead to more destructive contention?

Therefore, the "human capacities are taken to be only . . . the nondestructive ones," which "are taken to be enough to enable him to be fully human." Compared to Bay's inconclusive struggle with these questions, Macpherson's "staggering" formulation or solution wins high marks for tidiness.

But this answer is of the peculiar sort that annihilates the questions themselves, that makes you wonder why anyone ever asked such questions in the first place.

29. Maslow's original discussion of the supposed hierarchy of needs is in "A Theory of Human Motivation," *Psychological Review* 50 (1943): 370–96. Jeanne Knutson's *The Human Basis of the Polity* focuses more consistently on Maslow's work than Bay does, though her study is concerned primarily with the psychological obstacles to appropriate or full participation in given liberal democratic institutions, rather than the reorientation of democratic institutions and theory.

30. See M. Brewster Smith, Jerome S. Bruner, and Robert W. White, *Opinions and Personality* (New York: John Wiley & Sons, 1956), especially chap. 3.

31. "Political and Apolitical Students," pp. 83–90.

32. "Politics and Pseudopolitics," p. 42.

33. "Behavioral Research and the Theory of Democracy," p. 29. Here again there is some circularity, and it is not altogether clear whether Bay means that blocking the pursuit of basic needs is pathological, or leads to pathology. See also *Structure of Freedom*, p. 112:

> Do I assume that every person's basic motives are humanistically inclined? Yes, in a very broad sense of the term I do. . . . loyalty to anti-humanistic principles in general, apart from the perceived necessity of protection against other men, is invariably, I believe, a symptom of deficiencies in *somebody*'s psychological freedom. A high degree of psychological freedom insures the access to consciousness of man's basic sympathy for other men, or, more strictly, it largely consists in this access to consciousness.

34. "Political and Apolitical Students," p. 91.

35. See "Behavioral Research and the Theory of Democracy," pp. 24, 27.

36. "Political and Apolitical Students," p. 89.

37. My emphasis here is on those publications which give Freud or the Freudian vocabulary some precedence. *Eros and Civilization* (New York: Random House, Vintage, 1955), is therefore of central interest. Written at a time when leftist dissent was a low ebb in this country, this book is alive with Freudian perspectives, though there is some hedging on whether some of these (the hypothesis of the primal crime, for example) should be understood metaphorically or literally. Marx is not even mentioned, which is strange, given that

the thrust of his argument, and many of the concepts ("surplus repression," for example) are at least as inspired by Marx as by Freud. The epilogue of this book consists of a blistering attack on the neo-Freudians, particularly Erich Fromm, for de-emphasizing the instintual and for exhibiting a penchant for theoretical eclecticism.

Elsewhere, more recently, his use of Freud has been more relaxed and tentative, as if he did not need the added artillery. In some contexts—for example *One Dimensional Man* (Boston: Beacon, 1964)—it has been virtually absent. Especially relevant to the present discussion are the following: *Five Lectures* (Boston: Beacon, 1970), particularly the first three chapters; *Negations* (Boston: Beacon, 1968), chap. 7 (a critique of Norman O. Brown) and chap. 8; *An Essay on Liberation* (Boston: Beacon, 1968), especially "A Biological Basis for Socialism?" and "The New Sensibility"; and *Counter-revolution and Revolt* (Boston: Beacon, 1972), chap. 2, "Nature and Revolution." Paul Robinson (*The Freudian Left*) senses a mild disenchantment with psychoanalysis in Marcuse's recent thought, and this is probably the case. But recent publications do suggest that Marcuse continues to find Freudian concepts quite useful.

38. Marcuse, *Negations*, p. 251.

39. Jürgen Habermas, *Toward a Rational Society*, trans. Jeremy Shapiro (Boston: Beacon, 1970), p. 113.

40. *Essay on Liberation*, p. 13.

41. Introduced by Freud in a tentative way in *Beyond the Pleasure Principle*, trans. James Strachey (1928; reprinted ed. New York: Bantam, 1959). His speculations about the conservative nature of the instincts were set in motion by the obsessional neuroses, and the peculiar compulsion to repeat. The hypothesis is less timid and tentative in *Civilization and Its Discontents*, trans. and ed. James Strachey (1930; reprinted ed. New York: Norton, 1961), and *The Ego and the Id*, trans. Jean Riviere, rev. and ed. James Strachey (1923; reprinted ed. New York: Norton, 1962), the last major theoretical description of the psychical structure of the mind. See especially chap. 4, "The Two Classes of the Instincts."

42. *Civilization and Its Discontents*, especially chap. 3. Marcuse has a tendency to confuse actual guilt (in connection with destructive, aggressive behavior) with a sense of guilt (which is what Freud means by guilt).

43. Fromm also receives no mention here. Marcuse's argument is that the death instinct actually yearns for the tranquillity of inorganic matter ("Nirvana"): the conflict between life and death is reduced by a life which obtains more gratification. This closely resembles Fromm's

contention that "destructiveness is the outcome of an unlived life."

44. Saul Bellow, *Herzog* (New York: Viking, 1964), p. 206.

45. *Essay on Liberation*, p. 10.

46. *Essay on Liberation*, pp. 10–11, especially note 1.

47. *Counter-revolution and Revolt*, p. 71. See also *Essay on Liberation*, pp. 16–17, and p. 5.

48. *Negations*, p. 254.

49. *Counter-revolution and Revolt*, p. 71.

50. I have tried to separate the component parts of this argument, whereas Marcuse typically lumps them together. For example: "Socialist solidarity is autonomy: self-determination begins at home—and that is with every I, and the We whom the I chooses" (*Essay on Liberation*, p. 88).

51. These preferences are both political and esthetic, as Lionel Trilling has pointed out; Marcuse tends to confuse the two criteria with one another, and both with the moral. See Lionel Trilling, "Authenticity and the Modern Unconscious," *Commentary*, vol. 52, no. 3 (September 1971), pp. 39–51; and also Leon Bramson, *The Political Context of Sociology* (Princeton, N.J.: Princeton University Press, 1961), especially chap. 5. Passages affirming the desirability of discipline, reason, character and socialist order appear with increasing frequency in his more recent works. See for example chap. 4, "Solidarity," in *Essay on Liberation*.

52. Small surprise that in one of the very few passages dealing with what liberated sexuality will amount to, we are told that we probably will not actually do as much, we will just do more of it in meadows and the like, away from the untidiness and clamor that Marcuse finds characteristic of America.

53. *Counter-revolution and Revolt*, p. 80.

54. *Counter-revolution and Revolt*, p. 129.

55. *Essay on Liberation*, p. 12. But see "Industrialization and Capitalism in the Work of Max Weber," in *Negations*. Possibly the comment is in response to a highly effective critique of his notion of a new technology by Jürgen Habermas in "Technology and Science as 'Ideology'," *Toward a Rational Society*.

56. *Toward a Rational Society*, p. 107. Marcuse offers a similar argument in "The Obsolescence of the Freudian Concept of Man," *Five Lectures*, chap. 3.

57. My discussion refers primarily to "Expanding the Political Present," *American Political Science Review*, vol. 63, no. 3 (September 1969), pp. 768–77; and to *The Promise of Politics* (Englewood Cliffs, N.J.: Prentice-Hall, 1966), especially pp. 26–40, "Man in

Process" and "The Implementation of Scepticism." See also "The Political Relevance of Behavioral and Existential Psychology," *American Political Science Review*, vol. 61, no. 2 (June 1967), pp. 334–42.

58. See above, Introduction to Part Two, note 6.

59. Kariel does not distinguish between alienation and reification; he seems to prefer the latter concept. Peter Berger and Stanley Pullberg distinguish alienation (as forgetfulness, or a rupture between producer and product) and reification ("the moment in the process of alienation in which the characteristic of thinghood becomes the standard of reality") in "Reification and the Sociological Critique of Consciousness," *New Left Review*, 35 (January–February 1966): 56–75. The analysis of reification owes a great deal to George Luckacs's *History and Class Consciousness*, trans. Rodney Livingstone (1923; Cambridge, Mass.: M.I.T. Press, 1971), and his generalization of Marx's analysis of economic fetishism.

60. In effect he imagines a society of artists, who will function much like Wilde's artist, to "express everything." See Oscar Wilde, *The Soul of Man under Socialism, and Other Essays*, intro. Philip Rieff (1906; New York: Harper & Row, 1968).

61. "Expanding the Political Present," p. 771.

62. Ibid., p. 773.

63. See above, introduction to Part Two, note 4. A similar point applies to the ideal of "authenticity" in Berman's *Politics of Authenticity*. In his discussion of eighteenth-century Paris he is aware of the way modern society harnesses change in the interest of not changing, the way it simultaneously makes relatively unique identities ("being oneself," as he ambiguously puts it) both possible and difficult to achieve. Yet, like Kariel, he seems unaware of the conservative or even reactionary possibilities of his spongy concept of authenticity. His crude opposition of the individual and the social is reminiscent of those familiar first essays in an introductory course in political philosophy or sociology—whose authors speak of rejecting social roles and categories, doing their own thing, and so forth, and thereby think they have said something radical and progressive. Thus he compares society and social roles to clothing, but—missing half the point of Burke's metaphor—implies we should discard them entirely. Inauthenticity is just about total in modern societies, one gathers, and must be totally abolished by a "radical liberalism" which might put Spencer to shame, for all we learn of its objectives. One sees and senses here the inexorable movement from one simplistic notion to its equally simplistic opposite (to paraphrase

Kaufmann's characterization of the Marxist dialectic)—from total alienation to total submersion in community and creed—much as in Sartre. (In subsequent chapters I will argue that this movement involves and is propelled by opposed basic dispositions as well as the dialectic of ideas and concepts.) While he sympathetically criticizes such oscillation between polar extremes in Rousseau's life and thought, while he recognizes and deplores the "constant alternation of enchantment and disenchantment, hope and despair" which "has made the search for authenticity almost unbearable," he fails to ask whether his unbearable notion of authenticity might not contribute its part to that most sterile dialectic which he deplores. Therefore it is with considerable unintended irony that he quotes Trotsky with such enthusiasm: "you may not be interested in the dialectic, but the dialectic is interested in you."

64. Compare with "Every absolute is a mask justifying man's exploitation of man." Henri Lefebrve, *The Sociology of Marx* (New York: Random House, Vintage, 1969), p. 31.

65. Berman, much like Kariel and Etzioni, has a more specific conception of authentic behavior and who exhibits it than one would gather from his general recommendations to discard our social role, become ourselves, and do our thing. Thus an occasional revealing passage, as in Etzioni's treatment of alienation and inauthenticity, suggests in a more substantive way what and whom he has in mind: "Our society is filled with people who are ardently yearning and consciously striving for authenticity: moral philosophers who are exploring the idea of 'self-realization'; psychiatrists and their patients who are working to develop and strengthen 'ego-identity'; artists and writers who gave the word 'authenticity' the cultural force it has today [sic] . . ." (*Politics of Authenticity*, p. 325). If we rely solely on the vague and ambiguous conception of authenticity that pervades his analysis, it is not clear why these groups and their behavior are more authentic, say, than the middle-class taxpayers and their current revolt, or white parents' efforts to stop the busing of their children. Presumably such activities do not qualify as authentic in Berman's view, or so their absence from his list and analysis suggests.

66. "Expanding the Political Present," p. 769.

67. Ibid.

68. Ibid., p. 772.

69. Ibid., p. 768.

70. Ibid., p. 769.

Chapter 4

1. See B. F. Skinner, *Beyond Freedom and Dignity* (New York: Random House, Vintage, 1971); chap. 2, "Freedom."

2. *Beyond Good and Evil*, trans. with commentary by Walter Kaufmann (1886; reprinted ed. New York: Random House, 1966), p. 54.

3. Lionel Trilling, *Beyond Culture* (New York: Viking, 1968), p. 113.

4. One explicit statement to this effect is by C. J. Arthur, introduction to *The German Ideology*, Karl Marx and Friedrich Engels (1846; reprint ed. New York: International Publishers, 1970), p. 21. Another is the reply of Ben Brewster to Peter Berger and Stanley Pullberg's "Reification and the Sociological Critique of Consciousness," *New Left Review* 35 (January–February 1966): 72–74. As to what may underlie this apparent fear of discovering any density to the human species at all, Nietzsche wrote that "it is almost always a symptom of what is lacking in himself when a thinker senses in every 'causal connection' and 'psychological necessity' something of constraint, need, compulsion to obey, pressure and unfreedom; it is suspicious to have such feelings—the person betrays himself" (*Beyond Good and Evil*, p. 29).

5. Compare with *The Economic and Philosophic Manuscripts of 1844* (1844; reprinted ed. London: Lawrence and Wishart, 1959), p. 196: "All these consequences are contained in the definition that the worker is related to the product of his labor as to an *alien* object. . . ."

6. Christian Bay is a partial exception, but his treatment of anomie, borrowed from Merton, is vitiated by the resulting tendency to associate anomie primarily with deviance. See *The Structure of Freedom* (Stanford: Stanford University Press, 1958), chaps. 3 and 4; and below, chap. 7.

7. To label all four of these critics "leftist" might seem decidedly idiosyncratic or simply erroneous, particularly in the case of Etzioni and Bay, particularly if by "left" we automatically connote "socialist." Perhaps "leftish" of "left-leaning" would be better characterizations, if these terms were not so awkward. Instead, I have tried to take advantage of confusion (in most circles) over what being on the left means, and have tried to specify a loose sense in which they could meaningfully be labeled leftist.

8. This assumption is implicit in much of Talcott Parsons's "grand

theory," though the level at which this consensus is supposed to obtain is not always clear. It is an assumption he shares with some of his critics: see for example Ralf Dahrendorf, *Essays in the Theory of Society* (Stanford, Calif.: Stanford University Press, 1968), especially chap. 4 ("Out of Utopia") and chap. 5 ("In Praise of Thrasymachus"). Also see Lewis Coser's contrary argument, based on the sociology of Georg Simmel, in *The Functions of Social Conflict* (New York: Free Press, 1956).

9. Conceptually speaking, the economist is better equipped to spot the error in equating lack of consensus with social conflict. Stressing the gains from trade, from specialization of task and taste—from the lowliest of exchanges to comparative advantage in international trade—he is more likely to see and stress the advantages of our wanting different things in a world of scarce resources. His thinking is conditioned by a kind of Jack Sprat model of social harmony. But when scarcity enters the picture, the problem may no longer consist of getting Sprat's platter clean, but keeping it filled. See Mancur Olson's "Economics and the Social Sciences," in *Politics and the Social Sciences*, ed. Seymour Lipset (London: Oxford University Press, 1969). Olson's example of how it pays to differ is that congestion and conflict are reduced when some prefer the seashore and some prefer mountains. But this effect can be rendered negligible by a gasoline shortage, in which case the consensus on going, to one place or another, appears to be the source of conflict. Thus the important questions relate less to consensus or pluralism of wants than to shareability, and whether the expectation that they can all be satisfied simultaneously is reasonable.

10. Abraham Maslow, "Synergy in the Society and in the Individual," *Journal of Individual Psychology*, vol. 20, no. 156 (1964); also, Philip Slater's discussion of synergy in "The Social Bases of Personality," in *Sociology*, ed. Neil Smelser (New York: John Wiley & Sons, 1967), pp. 566-70.

11. *An Essay on Liberation* (Boston: Beacon, 1964), p. 17: "It is precisely this excessive adaptability of the human organism which propels the perpetuation and extension of the commodity form and, with it, the perpetuation and extension of the social controls over behavior and satisfaction."

12. See Maslow's contribution to *New Knowledge in Human Values*, ed. Abraham Maslow (Chicago: Henry Regnery, 1970). One of his examples involves observing the kinds of choices made by unusually healthy chickens so as to learn more about what health

in chickens means and requires. Applied to humans, however, where the question of what is healthy development or what is most human is precisely what is at stake, the procedure quickly becomes circular, and amounts to a normative statement on behalf of certain values and goals, dressed up as humanistic psychology.

13. Philip Rieff, introduction to George Horton Cooley's *Human Nature and the Social Order* (New York: Schocken, 1964), p. xvii.

14. Marcuse's close relationship to New Left dissent is well known. Etzioni teaches at Columbia, his book was published in 1968, and many of the examples to which he appeals make it clear that "the active ones" are typified for him by student protesters. (His dedication makes this explicit: "For the Active Ones/In particular, my students at Columbia and Berkeley.") Kariel's examples and implicit models are similar. And Bay's interest in humanistic psychology and psychological development was apparently spurred by a study of the correlation of leftist views and student protest with higher grades and intelligence. See "Political and Apolitical Students: Facts in Search of a Theory," *Journal of Social Issues*, vol. 23, no. 3 (1967), pp. 76–92. However, with the possible partial exception of Etzioni, none of these interests are strikingly discontinuous with their previous research concerns.

15. Perhaps this is what Etzioni has in mind with his program of adding up the costs of frustrating basic human needs, though he does tend to confuse what is efficient with what is moral. The costs (of social control, for example) are themselves determined in large part by values, and implicitly he admits, if only by writing such a book, that we disagree on what we value.

Two opponents of such a search for human universals are Fromm and Geertz. Fromm bluntly asserts that what is valuable about individuals is unique to them, and Geertz argues that "even if substantive connections could be found, the question still remains whether such universals should be taken as the central elements in the definition of man."

16. This is what Arnold Brecht refers to as "factual, not logical links between Is and Ought." See his *Political Theory* (Princeton, N.J.: Princeton University Press, 1959), chap. 9.

17. My position here accords with that of Marvin Zetterbaum, cogently expressed in his article "Human Nature and History":

in the final analysis, we cannot abandon the search for human nature . . . Whatever else may be true of our nature, this search, this

seeking for understanding of ourselves is constitutive of our being. . . . we are not simply free to decide either that the medley of
human projects is man's nature, that man is his history, or that
this history is but an epiphenomenon thrown up by some ultimate
we know not what. (Marvin Zetterbaum, "Human Nature and History," in *Human Nature in Politics*, ed. J. Roland Pennock and John
W. Chapman [New York: New York University Press, 1977].

Chapter 5

1. Durkheim discusses anomie in connection with his analysis of
anomic suicide in *Suicide* (1897; reprinted ed. New York: Free
Press, 1952), pp. 241–76, especially pp. 246–54; see also *The Division of Labor in Society* (1893; reprinted ed. New York: Free
Press, 1964), Book 3, chap. 1: "The Anomic Division of Labor."
For Marx on alienation, see the reference in note 1, Introduction
to Part Two.
2. Nietzsche considered the faith in opposite values the "fundamental faith of the metaphysicians," and this is one sense of the
question with which he begins *Beyond Good and Evil*: "supposing
truth is a woman—what then?". See especially Part One ("On the
Prejudices of Philosophers").
3. Nietzsche suggests that the belief in distinct things is a pre-
condition of our logic, and writes of the law of contradiction as
follows:

We are unable to affirm and to deny one and the same thing:
this is a subjective empirical law, not the expression of any "necessity" but only of an inability. If, according to Aristotle, the
law of contradiction is the most certain of all principles, if it is
the ultimate and most basic, upon which every demonstrative
proof rests, if the principle of every axiom lies in it; then one
should consider all the more rigorously what presuppositions
already lie at the bottom of it. (Nietzsche, *Will to Power*, trans.
Walter Kaufmann, ed. R. J. Hollingdale and Walter Kaufmann
[New York: Random House, 1967], p. 279.)

See especially his epistemological speculations in Book 3, "Principles of a New Evaluation." Many of these remarks, unlike the
better part of *Will to Power*, did not find their way into his more
polished works.
4. *Twilight of the Idols*, in *The Portable Nietzsche*, ed. and trans.
Walter Kaufmann (New York: Viking, 1954), p. 482.

5. Nietzsche, *Will to Power*, p. 277.

6. "We search for things in order to explain why something has changed. . . . Even the atom is this kind of super-added 'thing' and 'primitive subject'" (*Will to Power*, p. 296). "There is no such thing as a sense of causality, as Kant thinks. One is surprised, one is disturbed, one desires something familiar to hold onto—As soon as we are shown something old in the new, we are calmed. The supposed instinct for causality is only fear of the unfamiliar and the attempt to discover something familiar in it—a search, not for causes, but for the familiar" (Ibid., p. 297).

7. On the subject of necessary, but necessarily painful distinctions, there is no finer commentary than a great old hymn, white Southern Appalachian in origin, probably from the 1920s, titled "There'll Be No Distinctions There," that is, in heaven. Though no doubt it was sung in segregated churches, there is nevertheless something deeply felt in its expressed wish that the "colored and the white folks, the Gentiles and the Jews" will all be there, and equal there. That the author of the hymn did not quite overcome his earthly prejudices is revealed in the chorus, however: "for the Lord is just and the Lord is right, and we'll all be white in that heavenly light, there'll be no distinction there. . . ."

8. The perennial claims that the law of contradiction has been successfully defied by this person or that culture must be examined skeptically. On closer examination it appears that it is the old oppositions and categories (or oppositions salient in other cultures) which are being denied or overcome, not oppositions in general. This is not to deny that some conceptual schemes blur distinctions which are troublesome or crucial to other schemes, nor that some languages and modes of thought are generally more syncretic or change-conscious than others. Whether they are thereby more "primitive" or more sophisticated is not easy to determine, given that clarity and what constitutes it are questions of value.

9. "Situated with regard to another or to each other so that the greater part of their location is between the two." (*Random House Dictionary, College Edition* 1st ed. [New York: Random House, 1968]). This definition of opposites may be more mysterious than opposites themselves, as if we knew more than we can tell.

10. The oppositions I introduce here are in some respects similar to David Bakan's distinction between agency and communion:

Agency manifests itself in self-protection, self-assertion, and self-expansion, communion manifests itself in the sense of being at

one with other organisms. Agency manifests itself in the formation of separations; communion in the lack of separations. Agency
manifests itself in isolation, alienation, and aloneness; communion
in contact, openness, and union. Agency manifests itself in the
urge to master; communion in noncontractual cooperation. Agency manifests itself in the repression of thought, feeling, and impulse; communion in lack and removal of repression. (*The Duality
of Human Existence* [Boston: Beacon, 1967], pp. 14–15.)

Agency and communion are in many respects less colorful but less
controversial versions of Freud's death and Eros, and Bakan's book
represents a sympathetic if imaginative assessment of what Freud
was up to in the metapsychological speculations of his later years.

One of Bakan's fundamental points is that "the very split of
agency from communion, which is a separation, arises from the
agency feature itself; and that it represses the communion from
which it has separated itself." My argument here is that both the
agentic and the communal (though the oppositions I introduce are
somewhat different) are involved in the splitting, or the separations
we make, and that separation (as opposed to integration) is but our
one-sided human way of expressing the two sides of what is involved. Thus, Bakan fails to emphasize that it is only through more
clever applications of the knife that we patch things up. Surgeons
have a bit of the butcher in them, but the purpose of even the most
radical surgery is to heal, to bind. This is true of Bakan's distinctions, of course.

The upshot of this is that Bakan takes his own distinctions too
seriously, even as he is deploring our agentic tendency to do so.
Thus his treatment suffers from Freud's tendency to associate or
equate Eros with all the good things, and to equate the agentic
with the egoistic with the evil. Indeed, Bakan goes considerably
farther than Freud, associating communion with "lack and removal
of repression." But this is counter to Bakan's own (Nietzschean)
notion that what is actually evil is the denial, or separation of the
agentic and the communal. And elsewhere he does suggest that the
agentic must be merely mitigated by communion, not destroyed or
rooted out.

11. My claim here is merely that these concerns are crucially human; no doubt there are other such concerns. To the extent that
this conclusion derives from and depends on distinction-making itself, as opposed to the particular distinctions and dualism which
characterize, seduce, and vex Western culture, it might have a

measure of universal validity. This of course would be in the limited sense that any objective observer, observing and reflecting upon what is said, done, and meant in any other culture, and reporting on his findings in English, would nevertheless find such concerns and dispositions fundamental. Obviously there are cultures which strike a different balance between the poles than we do, and in which the oppositions I have introduced are at work "behind" the oppositions which count in that culture, rather than being directly expressed by those oppositions. In the first case the task of the analyst might be the reverse of mine here—i.e., to ferret out evidence of the wish to distinguish, separate, assert, and realize oneself. As the next section indicates, these efforts might be found in limited spheres of his life, or in projections, displacements, or the like. In the second case the interpretive task, while more difficult, is in principle no more difficult than the judgments routinely involved in any cross-cultural interpretation.

12. Melvin Seeman has argued ("On the Meaning of Alienation," *American Sociological Review*, vol. 24, no. 6 (December 1959), pp. 783-91) that various treatments of alienation have actually included one or more of five distinct dimensions—powerlessness, meaningless, normlessness, isolation, and self-estrangement—and has suggested ways in which these might be operationalized. Anomie is treated as a subcategory of alienation, for no obvious theoretical reason, but because many analysts have done so. The problem with this procedure is that the various uses and conceptualizations of alienation and anomie are lifted from the theoretical contexts (and therefore underlying views of man, critical perspectives on society, and so forth) which gave them meaning. A theory of alienation or anomie must differ from a collection of the ways in which the concept has been used. Otherwise the result may be little more than taxonomized confusion, which is still confusion. In this case, Seeman's analysis reflects the very anomie it fails to distinguish from alienation. That is, his conception of anomie is anomic.

Steven Lukes has correctly emphasized that Marx's alienation and Durkheim's anomie arise from two competing views of human nature, two different intellectual universes (Ada Finifter, ed., "Alienation and Anomie," in *Alienation and the Social System* [New York: John Wiley & Sons, 1972]). While he errs in overemphasizing the incompatibility, in not exploring a possible synthesis, and perhaps in assuming too much internal coherence to their perspectives, he is right in implying that a viable synthesis, should one exist, would have to come to terms with apparently opposed views of human nature and conceptions of basic human afflictions. Neither Marx nor Durkheim managed to do so. Marx's mistake is to slight anomie and to throw the two maladies together before adequately distinguishing them, burying these contradictions rather than overcoming them. Durkheim (see chap. 7), appears to seriously shortchange alienation. However, in passages where he appears to be defending himself against charges of conservatism, he comes closer than Marx to distinguishing these concerns and suggesting how both might be taken seriously.

From somewhat different premises, Peter Berger has fruitfully utilized the opposition I am introducing here in a number of contexts. See for example *The Social Construction of Reality*, with Thomas Luckmann (Garden City, N.Y.: Doubleday, Anchor, 1966); *The Sacred Canopy* (Garden City, N.Y.: Doubleday, Anchor, 1969), especially chap. 1; and again, "Reification and the Sociological Critique of Consciousness," *New Left Review* 35 (January–February 1966): 56–75. The difficulty is that insofar as Berger admits to any metapsychological basis for his perspective—which has to do with the constant possibility of anomic terror, the search for meaning, and an unfortunate lack of instinctual guidance—his account of why and how some individuals are able to even want to overcome their usual perception of social facts as objective and immutable tends to suffer. As one observer has pointed out, Berger's only examples of "de-reification" are quite unpleasant, involving extreme anarchy, anomie, and chaos. Thus the choice that Berger seems to offer is either rampant bad faith and alienation or reification on the one hand, or chaos and acute anomie on the other. Berger's rather stark alternatives, resembling those of Kaufmann and Lukes, seem to partake of the liberal culture from which his argument, according to his own argument in *Social Construction of Reality*, has been socially constructed. In this respect perhaps Berger has been insufficiently sociological with his own theoretical realities.

13. See Kaufmann, *Without Guilt and Justice* (New York: Dell Publishing Co., 1973), pp. 140–72; and his introduction to Richard Schacht's *Alienation* (Garden City, N.Y.: Doubleday, Anchor, 1970).

14. One wonders here whether Kaufmann has failed to follow Nietzsche closely enough for once, both with reference to that aspect of Nietzsche's thought on which I am drawing and to the example of Nietzsche's life. While it might be argued that the latter suggests that extreme autonomy is possible for some, even with

very few social supports, what seems more to the point is that this was an extraordinary man, engaged in a heroic struggle with sides of himself diametrically opposed to the desire for autonomy—with drives which, he insisted time and again, deserved *some* representation in one's life and thought, if only to be made "good servants" of other drives. Moreover, he repeatedly identified himself with the community of "good Europeans." While partly the figment of a lonely man's imagination, this identification was nevertheless of great psychological importance, one gathers, both in finding a spiritual "home" and in fending off bad Europeans—thus helping him maintain his autonomous course. However, it is possible that part of my difference with Kaufmann derives from the fact that Kaufmann is primarily concerned (in *Without Guilt and Justice*) with articulating an autonomous ethic or code, and is less concerned with the human and cultural obstacles to its acceptance and realization.

15. Such suspicions fuel recurrent efforts to characterize the whole of existence in terms of a continuum of one basic life-force, e.g., will to power, or Eros. To call it all one thing is profoundly tempting, it seems, but then at some point our human interest in distinction-making intrudes. Instead of observing a not particularly loving form of love, for example, a qualitative difference appears to emerge, and we have hate, or sadism. (Of course we could view all human behavior as exhibiting various degrees of sadism, say, with love being a particularly deficient form of sadism, a perversion of it. But this would be perverse.) Nietzsche encounters similar problems in attempting to express all the manifestations of life in terms of degrees of will to power.

16. When someone suggests to us, for example, that we should cultivate a "consciousness which does not negate any more" (Norman O. Brown, *Life Against Death* [New York: Random House, Vintage, 1959], p. 308), the chances are good we are in for another round of the oracular and the confusing (as in Brown's *Love's Body* [New York: Random House, 1966]). To the extent that Brown keeps cultivating and avoids assuming he has achieved such a consciousness, *Life Against Death* offers a most stimulating, if somewhat feverish assessment and interpretation of Freud.

17. Sherwood Anderson, *Winesburg, Ohio* (New York: Viking, 1960), pp. 24–25. Nietzsche entertains a quite similar fantasy in *Will to Power*, p. 276. The similarity is probably coincidental, but not accidental—that is, in terms of what they were trying to convey. Both passages are mock-historical accounts of the characteristics

of unconscious fantasy, which, as Anton Ehrenzweig argues, "does not distinguish between opposites . . . and allows all firm boundaries to melt in a free chaotic mingling of forms." (Anton Ehrenzweig, *The Hidden Order of Art* [Berkeley: University of California Press, 1971], p. 3.) I am grateful to Professor Graham Little for calling my attention to Ehrenzweig's most stimulating and neglected book.

18. Max Weber, *The Protestant Ethic and the Spirit of Capitalism*, trans. Talcott Parsons (1904: New York, Scribners, 1958), p. 182. Also quoted in Philip Rieff, *The Triumph of the Therapeutic: Uses of Faith Since Freud* (New York: Harper & Row, 1968).

19. At stake here is the recognition of *the* unconscious ("System Ucs") as well as the material which, having been repressed, has the *quality* of being unconscious. Freud considered the discovery of the former, together with his delineation of its laws, as one of his most significant contributions. The less differentiated mode of Ucs makes it inaccessible to consciousness, though it can be "translated" into the conscious mode, and known by its effects. In this connection see Ehrenzweig, *Hidden Order of Art*, chap. 2 ("Two Kinds of Attention") and chap. 3 ("Unconscious Scanning").

20. Ehrenzweig entertains a similar conception of the unconscious as the locus of undifferentiated modes of thought. (By undifferentiation he refers to the less differentiated state of consciousness; by dedifferentiation he refers to the process by which we move toward that state.) I suggest, however, that both dedifferentiation (or integrating, unitizing, making equal) as well as differentiation are always involved in conscious thought, though it is helpful and important to recognize a continuum of relative degrees of the one and the other. It is a differentiated mode of thought, after all, which distinguishes differentiated from undifferentiated modes of thought. This suggests that the unconscious is always with us in our conscious modes, and that all attempts to sharply differentiate it, to specify its contents, are themselves prone to error.

Similarly, Bakan (*Duality of Human Existence*) suggests that Freud's fundamental message is that qualities which seem irremediably "other" really are not, a message which applies both inwardly (mind/body) and outwardly (subject/object). "The intellectual task which psychoanalysis sets itself is that of making what is unconscious, conscious. To the degree that it tends to fix upon that which it has made conscious, it is idolatrous. But to the extent that it stresses the existence of that which is still unconscious, it avoids being idolatrous" (p. 11).

It is with these pitfalls in mind that Nietzsche suggests that the "whole surface of consciousness—and consciousness *is* a surface—should be kept clear of all great imperatives."

21. This device is employed by Philip Slater in "The Social Bases of Personality," in *Sociology*, ed. Neil Smelser (New York: John Wiley & Sons, 1967), and I am indebted here to his discussion of how ambivalences are distributed and accommodated.

22. Ehrenzweig writes that

the creative thinker is capable of alternating between differentiated and undifferentiated modes of thinking, harnessing them together to give him service for solving very definite tasks. The uncreative psychotic succumbs to the tension between conscious (differentiated) and unconscious (undifferentiated) modes of mental functioning. As he cannot integrate their divergent functions, true chaos ensues. The unconscious functions overcome and fragment the conscious surface sensibilities and tear reason into shreds (*The Hidden Order of Art*, p. xiii).

His boundaries are both more rigid and more brittle, fluid: "he has failed to erect a 'contact barrier' which bars access to the unconscious and at the same time facilitates interchange between conscious and unconscious" (p. 277).

23. Nietzsche, *Will to Power*, p. 207. In general Nietzsche contrasts a kind of "psychic economy of the affects" with a "moral mode of thought" which seeks instead to "dry them up." Elsewhere he distinguishes between letting flow and letting go.

24. It should be emphasized that the kind of argument that stresses the primacy of reason in ethics and decision-making, the need for it in setting priorities, delaying gratification, and so on, while often offered by those who purport to subscribe to a radical sociological relativism concerning the nature of man, has implicit in it a view of human nature as deficient in instinctual guidance. (Also see Kant: "Nature seems to have delighted in the greatest parsimony; she seems to have barely provided man's animal equipment and limited it to the most urgent needs of a beginning existence, as if nature intended that man should owe all to himself." In "Idea for a Universal History," in *The Philosophy of Kant*, ed. Carl Friedrich [New York: Random House, 1949], p. 119.) That is, their basis is a view of human nature, however much they may stress (e.g., Berger and Luckmann, *Social Construction of Reality*) instinctual plasticity and "the social construction of reality."

This relative freedom from instinct seems critically related to our capacity to symbolize and abstract, and to our long period of dependency on parents or adults, during which time our dealings with nature are mediated through them. On the latter points, see Weston La Barre, *The Human Animal* (Chicago: University of Chicago Press, 1954), especially chap. 12.

25. Nietzsche offers numerous arguments in this vein, and at one point even claims to have discovered the way that "leads [back] to the Yes and the No." See also his *Twilight of the Idols*, p. 473: "The formula of my happiness: a Yes, a No, a straight line, a *goal*." There are some surprising affinities here with Taoism, and it is known that Nietzsche recognized them. See *The Way of Life According to Lao Tzu*, trans. Witter Brynner (New York: Capricorn, 1962), p. 31: "Therefore the sensible man/Prefers the inner to the outer eye: He has his yes—he has his no." See also p. 36.

Chapter 6

1. Philip Rieff, *Freud: The Mind of a Moralist* (Garden City, N.Y.: Doubleday, 1959), especially chap. 10, "The Emergence of Psychological Man." His *Triumph of the Therapeutic: The Uses of Faith Since Freud* (New York: Harper & Row, 1968) is in large measure an extension and elaboration of the ideas in that chapter.

2. Though Freud's medicine was more stoic and severe, his diagnosis of our ills at this historic juncture was in this respect much the same. Much of *Triumph of the Therapeutic* is devoted to discussion of three post-Freudian figures—Jung, Reich, and Lawrence—who could not, as Rieff sees it, pass Freud's test of manhood and thus regressed to making a religion of *something*, notably sex in the case of Reich and Lawrence.

3. These paragraphs are a rough paraphrase-interpretation of chaps. 1–4 and chap. 8 of *Triumph of the Therapeutic*. Philip Slater and Warren Bennis experiment with much the same vision in *The Temporary Society* (New York: Harper & Row, 1968). Slater, like Rieff, has his second thoughts: see *The Pursuit of Loneliness* (Boston: Beacon, 1970); and *Earthwalk* (Garden City, N.Y.: Doubleday, Anchor, 1974). Also relevant here is John Seeley's *The Americanization of the Unconscious* (New York: International Science Press, 1967), which stresses the manipulative potential of the therapeutic community and is generally less seduced by this prospect. For a more favorable view of some of the same developments, see Robert J. Lifton, "Protean Man," *Partisan Review*, Winter 1968. Walter Kaufmann's *Without Guilt and Justice* (New York: Dell Publishing Co., 1973), is predicated on the same radically individualistic,

Nietzschean vision as Rieff's analysis. In effect he offers Rieff's therapeutic culture and psychological man an autonomous code to live by (the "new integrity"), though psychological man would probably find it too demanding, and not nearly hedonistic enough.

4. "Twas Grace that taught me how to fear/And Grace my fear relieved" (from the hymn "Amazing Grace"). Psychological man would probably ask—why bother?—saving his energy by short-circuiting the whole process.

5. *Beyond Good and Evil,* trans. with commentary by Walter Kaufmann (1886; reprinted ed. New York: Random House, 1966), p. 43. There is an early Bob Dylan song which comments ironically on those wrathful and reverent attitudes characteristic of youth. The refrain goes: "Ah, but I was so much older then, I'm younger than that now."

6. Ibid., p. 69.

7. See Rieff's "Impossible Culture," *Encounter* 35 (September 1970): 33-45.

8. Rieff makes an exception of his implicit conception of human nature in much the same way that Berger and Luckmann do. See above, chapter 5, note 24; and chapter 4, note 17.

9. This imagery is used by Rieff ("Impossible Culture") in making much the same point.

10. Nietzsche, *Beyond Good and Evil,* pp. 16-17.

11. These of course are not Nietzschean concerns. Here Kaufmann is closer to Nietzsche's view: "If every opportunity that cannot be offered to all is refused and goes to waste, few opportunities can be accepted." (*Without Guilt and Justice,* p. 84) The concern with shareability is not necessarily a recipe for uniformity and mediocrity, given that it is the *pattern* of freedom and goals and activities which must be shareable. Nevertheless, the difference runs deep, as does the difference concerning whether social ethics must make a place for justice. While Kaufmann pays occasional lip service to what he calls consequentialism, there is scant room for it in his code, despite the fact that one's success in living by it must surely depend on the social setting, on what others are doing or trying to do.

12. See especially "The Cognitive Development Approach to Socialization," pt. 3, "An Example of Social Development Defined in Cognitive-Structural Terms—Moral Stages," pp. 369-89, in *Handbook of Socialization Theory and Research,* ed. David Goslin (Chicago: Rand McNally, 1969). For antecedents in the work of Piaget, see Jean Piaget, *The Moral Judgment of the Child,* trans. Majorie Gabain (New York: Free Press, 1965). See also Erik Erikson, *Insight*

and Responsibility (New York: Norton, 1964), chap. 6. For an informal discussion of Kohlberg's stage-theory, see his "The Child as Moral Philosopher," *Psychology Today*, September 1968, pp. 25–30. Kenneth Keniston discusses some of the applications and implications of Kohlberg's work in "Moral Development, Youthful Activism, and Modern Society," *Youth and Society*, September 1969, pp. 109–27. I am also indebted here to Derek Wright's remarks on Piaget and Kohlberg in *The Psychology of Moral Behavior* (Middlesex, Eng.: Penguin, 1971), pp. 152–73, particularly in summarizing the characteristics of Kohlberg's stages.

13. Kohlberg, "Example of Social Development Defined in Cognitive-Structural Terms—Moral Stages," p. 376; and Wright, pp. 167–73.

14. Keniston, "Moral Development, Youthful Activism, and Modern Society," summarizes these data.

15. Ibid., p. 125.

16. Kaufmann has suggested (in *Nietzsche: Philosopher, Psychologist, Antichrist* [New York: Random House, 1968]) that the major task facing social ethics is to synthesize Kantian and Nietzschean ethics. I am interested here in tentatively exploring the possible relationship between two approaches to social criticism and social ethics which are related to their perspectives. It would appear that Kaufmann's hostility to moral rationalism has prevented his own most original and valuable contribution to ethics (see *Without Guilt and Justice*) from contributing to such a synthesis.

17. Jean Paul Sartre, "Existentialism is a Humanism," in *Existentialism from Dostoevsky to Sartre*, trans. Walter Kaufmann (New York: World Publishing, 1956), p. 291. Reportedly Sartre has repudiated this address. Given the baldness of this attempt to close the gap between freedom and responsibility, the reasons are undoubtedly significant. Hazel Barnes has attempted to defend this leap in *An Existentialist Ethics* (New York: Knopf, 1967); see especially pp. 61–62. Her argument is unconvincing. In essence she asserts that "if the ethical choice is to resolve to justify one's life, my relations with others cannot be ignored." This proposition is eminently undebatable and most uninformative. Ignoring others is one thing, and no doubt *my* freedom demands that I do not. But not ignoring others is still a far cry from "willing the liberty of others at the same time as my own." As Walter Kaufmann writes: "it is not true, as has sometimes been claimed, that those who are free *must*, by some logical necessity, work for the freedom of their fellow man" (*Without Guilt or Justice*, p. 229).

18. Sartre, "Existentialism in Humanism," p. 307.

19. Erik Erikson, "The Golden Rule," in *The Study of Lives*, ed. Robert W. White (New York: Atherton, 1969), pp. 413–28. See also *Insight and Responsibility*, chap. 6.

20. Arnold Brecht, *Political Theory* (Princeton, N.J.: Princeton University Press, 1959), chap. 10, "Universal Postulates of Justice," pp. 387–403. Another of the postulates of interest is the apparently universal notion that people should not be punished for not doing what is impossible for them to do.

21. Wilfred Desan, in his lucid critique of Sartre, expresses this as follows: "The fact is that dictates do not lie in the intention of the philosopher, his to make or not to make; they lie in the structure of the human mind, which tears down with great energy the walls of the absolute, only to build up new ones with no less alacrity. It seems that man cannot not judge. It is his obsession to make an ethical statement in absolute form because in *any* statement he makes, he faces this temptation toward absolutizing" (*The Marxism of Jean Paul Sartre* [New York: Doubleday, 1965], p. 256). See also Derek Wright, *The Psychology of Moral Behavior*: "We can't discount the possibility that genetic pre-disposition facilitates the development of moral controls" (p. 17).

22. Christopher Stone has argued (*Should Trees Have Standing?* [Los Altos, Calif.: William Kaufmann, Inc., 1974]) that the legal history of the West reveals a slow but steady extension of our capacity for empathy, from family to kin to tribe to nation to other races—to women—and that we may now be ready to begin to accord legal status to other natural objects. From the point of view of Kohlberg's emphases, this extension of empathy can be viewed in terms of an extension of the horizons—to our natural as well as social environment, and over time—within which we seek to find principles of behavior which are sustainable, reasonable. Whether there is such a stage seven of moral reasoning is anybody's guess— the concept of universalizability in Kohlberg's stage six is apparently limited to the human (social) universe, and the time dimension seems to be missing as well.

23. Ellen Meiksins Wood, *Mind and Politics* (Berkeley: University of California Press, 1972), especially chap. 2.

24. Apparently the boundaries the schizophrenic draws around himself are both more rigid and more brittle, more limited *and* more extensive. On the one hand, what he seems to regard as his ego incorporates far more than what we consider normal, and it is susceptible to intrusion by what are generally regarded as

aspects of his external environment. On the other hand, actual events or feelings which are not a part of his conceptual scheme may not even be experienced, not until they are thought. Paradoxically, his conception of self is so large, so extensive, as to be almost nonexistent. Many manic personalities, as well as the millions with normal neuroses, appear to differ from schizophrenics in this respect only by the degree of these difficulties.

25. George Herbert Mead, *Mind, Self, and Society*, ed. Charles W. Morris (Chicago: University of Chicago Press, 1934).

26. Philip Rieff, intro. to George Horton Cooley's *Human Nature and the Social Order* (New York: Schocken, 1964).

27. Kohlberg, "Example of Social Development Defined in Cognitive-Structural Terms—Moral Stages."

28. See Keniston's view of data on student protestors, and Milgram-type experiments. The reference is to one of Kohlberg's moral dilemmas. Ibid., pp. 379–82.

29. Keniston, "Moral Development, Youthful Activism, and Modern Society," p. 117.

30. Ibid., p. 125.

31. Compare with Erikson, *Insight and Responsibility*, p. 233. As we have seen (above, chapter 3, note 28), at a similar juncture in his argument Macpherson decides that essential human attributes and activities will be *defined* as those which can be simultaneously expressed and pursued by all. This procedure is most eccentric, and is a prime source of the overestimation of the contribution of views of human nature to social criticism.

Introduction to Part 3

1. This is essentially the argument Robert Nisbet makes in *The Sociological Tradition* (New York: Basic Books, 1966); it should be noted that this is an interpretation which tends to shortchange Marx, among other less conservative sociologists. In this connection also see Leon Bramson, *The Political Context of Sociology* (Princeton, N.J.: Princeton University Press, 1961).

Some key analyses of these historical sociologists are the following: Max Weber, *The Protestant Ethic and the Spirit of Capitalism*, trans. Talcott Parsons (1904: New York: Scribners, 1958); various pieces in *From Max Weber*, ed. C. Wright Mills and Hans Gerth (New York: Oxford University Press, 1946), especially "Science as a Vocation"; Emile Durkheim, *Suicide* (1897; reprinted ed. New York: Free Press, 1952), and especially *Division of Labor in Society* (1893;

reprinted ed. New York: Free Press, 1964); Georg Simmel, *The Sociology of Georg Simmel*, trans. and ed. Kurt Wolff (New York: Free Press, 1950), especially "Individual and Society in Eighteenth and Nineteenth Century Views of Life," and "Metropolis and Mental Life"; Frederick Toennies, *Community and Society*, trans. Charles Loomis (East Lansing: Michigan State University Press, 1964).

A few examples of analyses and perspectives which draw on this tradition are the following: "early" Erich Fromm, *Escape from Freedom* (New York: Avon Books, 1941); Robert Nisbet, *Community and Power* (New York: Oxford University Press, 1953), and various essays in *Tradition and Revolt* (New York: Random House, 1970); anything by Talcott Parsons; much of the literature on identity, beginning with Erik Erikson: see "Identity and Uprootedness in Our Time," in *Varieties of Modern Social Theory*, ed. Hendrik Ruitenbeek (New York: Dutton, 1963); Kenneth Keniston's *The Uncommited* (New York: Dell Publishing Co., Delta, 1960), especially pt. 2: "Alienating Society"; Philip Rieff, *The Triumph of the Therapeutic: The Uses of Faith Since Freud* (New York: Harper & Row, 1968); Hannah Arendt, *Between Past and Future* (New York: Viking, 1968); Maurice Stein, *The Eclipse of Community* (Princeton, N.J.: Princeton University Press, 1960); Allan Wheelis, *The Quest for Identity* (New York: Norton, 1958); Sebastian de Grazia, *The Political Community* (Chicago: University of Chicago Press, 1948); Philip Slater, *The Pursuit of Loneliness* (Boston: Beacon, 1970); Dennis Wrong, "Identity: Problem and Catchword," *Dissent*, September–October 1968; Peter Berger, *The Sacred Canopy* (Garden City, N.Y.: Doubleday, Anchor, 1969); John Schaar, in much of his work; see his critique of Fromm, *Escape from Authority* (New York: Harper & Row, 1961), and "Legitimacy in the Modern State" in *Power and Community*, ed. Philip Green and Sanford Levinson (New York: Random House, Vintage, 1970); Ezra Mishan, "Making the Future Safe for Mankind," *The Public Interest*, 24 (Summer 1971): 33–62; Alvin Toffler, *Future Shock* (New York: Random House, 1970).

2. This theme has been stressed by Rieff and Gouldner, among others: see Alvin Gouldner, *The Coming Crisis of Western Sociology* (New York: Avon, 1970).

3. The transition to such a society has been characterized by various dichotomous ideal-types, sometimes treated as analytical categories and sometimes as actual historical descriptions. Of these the most familiar is Toennies's distinction between Gemeinschaft

and Gesellschaft. Talcott Parsons's pattern variables represent the latest and perhaps most comprehensive attempt to conceptualize these transitions. See Talcott Parsons and Edward Shils, eds., *Toward a General Theory of Action* (Cambridge, Mass.: Harvard University Press, 1951), chap. 1, "Categories of the Orientation and Organization of Action."

4. The same general variety of social psychology was already in evidence by the late nineteenth century, not only in the work of the historical sociologists but also in the literature on crowds, and later in Freud's speculations in *Group Psychology and the Analysis of the Ego*, trans. James Strachey (1921; New York: Bantam Books, 1965). Perhaps the most significant of such efforts to comprehend Nazism came about through the efforts of the group of leftist emigré scholars who had been associated with the Frankfurt Institüt. Two particularly significant products of this school were Erich Fromm's *Escape from Freedom* and Theodore Adorno et al., *The Authoritarian Personality* (New York: Norton, 1969).

5. For example, see John Schaar, *Escape from Authority* and "Legitimacy in the Modern State"; Victor Ferkiss, *Technological Man: The Myth and the Reality* (New York: New American Library, Mentor, 1969), and *The Future of Technological Civilization* (New York: Braziller, 1974); Philip Slater, *Pursuit of Loneliness* and *Earthwalk* (Garden City, N.Y.: Doubleday, Anchor, 1974); E. J. Mishan, "The Spillover Enemy," *Encounter*, December 1959, and *The Costs of Economic Growth* (New York: Praeger, 1967); Garrett Hardin, "The Tragedy of the Commons," *Science* 162 (December 1968): 1243–48, and *Exploring New Ethics for Survival* (New York: Viking, 1968); Ervin Lazslo, *A Strategy for the Future* (New York: Braziller, 1974); Ludwig von Bertalanffy, *General Systems Theory* (New York: Braziller, 1968); Gregory Bateson, *Steps to an Ecology of Mind* (New York: Random House, Ballantine, 1972); Thomas Schelling, "On the Ecology of Micromotives," *The Public Interest* 25 (Fall 1971); Donella H. Meadows et al., *The Limits to Growth* (New York: New American Library, Signet, 1972); anything by Lewis Mumford. Helpful synopses of literature in this general area can be found in the pamphlets of the Harvard Program on Technology and Society: especially nos. 3 ("Technology and Values"), 4 ("Technology and the Polity"), and 6 ("Technology and the Individual").

Chapter 7

1. See *Suicide* (1897; reprinted ed. New York: Free Press, 1952), see especially pp. 152–216, and 241–94.

2. The relevant section of *Division of Labor in Society* (1893; reprinted ed. New York: Free Press, 1964), is "The Anomic Division of Labor," pp. 353–73. It is important to note his later uneasiness on this matter, as reflected in *Suicide* and his preface to the second edition of *Division of Labor*. There he advocates the formation of guild-like occupational groups as the most important integrative associations intermediate between the family and the state. This aspect of his argument amounts to a prototype of the persuasion I have labeled sociological pluralism (see chapter 1).

3. See *Division of Labor*, pp. 365, 368, 371.

4. The most prominent figure here is Talcott Parsons; my remarks apply less to his short essays, which show a lively concern with social strain, than his "grand-theoretical" work, in which somehow everything seems to work out as it's supposed to. (See, for examples of the former, his *Essays in Sociological Theory* [Glencoe, Ill.: Free Press, 1951].) For rather blatant functionalist jingoism (which captures the individuating trend of social change far better than most social critics) see Winston White, *Beyond Conformity* (Glencoe, Ill.: Free Press, 1961).

5. See G. Sjoberg, "Contradictory Functional Requirements in Social Systems," *Journal of Conflict Resolution*, vol. 4, no. 199 (1960); and also Slater's discussion in "Social Bases of Personality," in *Sociology*, ed. Neil Smelser (New York: John Wiley & Sons, 1967), which called my attention to this article. This is an argument which is implicit in the neo-Freudian emphasis on cultural contradictions and inconsistencies, as well.

6. See Slater, "Social Bases of Personality," p. 571.

7. Durkheim, *Division of Labor*, pp. 402–03. This invites comparison with the famous idyllic passage in Marx's *German Ideology*. Also compare with Max Weber's remarks in "Science as a Vocation," in *From Max Weber*, ed. C. Wright Mills and Hans Gerth (New York: Oxford University Press, 1946), p. 137; and p. 180: "Limitation to specialized work, with a renunciation of the Faustian universality of man which it involves, is a condition of any valuable work in the modern world; hence deeds and renunciation inevitably condition each other today." This is reminiscent of Goethe's assertion that "any man's task is to do *something* extraordinarily well, as no other man in his immediate environment can." Simmel's view, on the other hand, differs considerably, and is closer to that being argued here: "the greatest advance in a one-sided pursuit can only too frequently mean dearth to the personality of the individual" (Georg Simmel, *The Sociology of Georg Simmel*, trans. and ed. Kurt Wolff [New York: Free Press, 1950], p. 422). Simmel remarks

elsewhere that the most fundamental question to our social outlook is whether we believe that human beings are fundamentally alike or fundamentally different. Such crude alternatives are always interesting psychoanalytically, as if we could not really get the answer straight.

8. Robert Merton, "Social Structure and Anomie," in *Social Theory and Social Structure* (Glencoe, Ill.: Free Press, 1949; rev. ed., 1968). The original article was published in 1938.

9. In addition to those references cited by Merton, see Talcott Parsons's characterization of the "most general value orientation in American culture" ("instrumental activism") in *Structure and Process in Modern Societies* (Glencoe, Ill.: Free Press, 1960), especially p. 172. Other classic sources lending general support to Merton's contentions are Alexis de Tocqueville's *Democracy in America*, trans. Henry Reeve, revised by Francis Bowen (1862; New York: Random House, Vintage, 1945); Harold Lasswell's *Politics: Who Gets What, When, and How* (New York: McGraw-Hill, 1936), chap. 2; Margaret Mead, *And Keep Your Powder Dry* (New York: Morrow, 1942); and Florence Kluckhohn and Fred Strodtbeck, *Variations in Value Orientations* (New York: Harper & Row, 1961). See also Robin Williams's *American Society* (New York: Knopf, 1951), which is among the most detailed characterizations. Williams describes a series of American value clusters, most of which are either elaborations of Merton's theme or are defined in (peculiarly American) ways which do not conflict significantly with the cultural emphases described by Merton.

10. Irrespective of Merton's intentions, one unfortunate result of this way of conceptualizing anomie is the tendency to associate anomie with deviance, thus disallowing the possibility of deviant societies productive of an anomie more widespread than deviance. Bay's treatment of anomie, derived from Merton, exhibits the same difficulties (see chapter 3). This, as several commentators have pointed out, represents a step backward from Durkheim's analysis. It presents problems for empirical analysis as well: for example, status anxiety explanations of mass or anomic movements—McCarthyism, for example—suffer from the weakness that many or most of us are anxious about our status. There is a temptation to use the deviance as evidence of the anxiety which was supposed to explain the deviance. Explanations of extremism by reference to the individual's marginality (see William Kornhauser, *The Politics of Mass Society* [New York: Free Press, 1959], or White, *Beyond Conformity*) are susceptible to the same circularity.

11. I am indebted to Philip Slater's "Social Bases of Personality" for calling my attention to this aspect of Durkheim's argument.

12. See Maslow's "Synergy in the Society and in the Individual," *Journal of Individual Psychology*, vol. 20, no. 156 (1964), and Slater's discussion in "Social Bases of Personality."

13. See John Schaar, "Equality of Opportunity, and Beyond," in *Nomos IX: Equality*, ed. J. R. Pennock and J. W. Chapman (New York: Atherton Press, 1967); and Michael Young's social-science-fiction fantasy, *The Rise of the Meritocracy* (New York: Random House, 1955). John Rawls (*A Theory of Justice* [Cambridge, Mass.: Harvard University Press, 1971]) places both anti-ascriptive and antimeritorian arguments in the framework of his theory of justice. (See chapter 10.)

14. Merton's critics have often focused on his neglect of subcultures, and the fact that success means different things to different people in different social circumstances. The cultural contradictions I refer to here are not subcultures, but contradictions within the dominant culture, and thus individual ambivalence within all those touched by it. The role of these cultural contradictions or inconsistencies, a theme very important to the neo-Freudians, is absent from Merton's original argument, and from the perspective of many sociologists.

Merton expresses his position in criticizing Karen Horney: "Despite her consistent concern with 'culture' . . . Horney does not explore differences in the impact of this culture upon farmer, worker, and businessman, upon lower-, middle-, and upper-class individuals, upon members of various ethnic and racial groups, etc. As a result, the role of 'inconsistences in culture' is not located in its differential impact upon diversely situated groups." These are valid criticisms, but by means of them he manages to obscure the fact that he has dropped the neo-Freudian theme of individual ambivalence, as it relates to inconsistencies in culture.

15. Bakan (*The Duality of Human Existence* [Boston: Beacon, 1967]) associates separations with the agentic, the agentic with the masculine, and masculinity with males—as a matter of biology. (La Barre, (*The Human Animal* [Chicago: University of Chicago Press, 1954]) is an anthropologist who seems to agree.) I am inclined to believe that he overestimates our ability to judge this matter without using culture-bound spectacles. Most of the empirical evidence he refers to—Erikson's observations of children playing with blocks, for example; or studies which indicate that women separate themselves less radically from their environment—

can be interpreted either biologically or culturally. Bakan argues that the very fact that women exhibit less of the agentic may itself suggest that women are less susceptible to socialization (at least in an agentic culture), differing biologically in being more grounded biologically. La Barre speculates in a similar vein. This interesting line of argument ignores that obvious fact that women in Western culture have been shielded, if that is the word, from the agentic mainstream of society, irrespective of their wishes in the matter. As well as being oppressed, they have often been granted the luxury of being the cultural carriers of communal attitudes and values.

16. These requirements, again, are much broader than intelligence, at least as measured by standard tests. Moreover, there is genuine uncertainty on the question of where premiums are now being placed, and whether the society is actually becoming more meritorian in any meaningful sense. In Christopher Jencks's study, *Inequality* (New York: Basic Books, 1972), luck, the residual category left over after the effect of home environment, schooling, and intelligence, accounts for some 80 percent of the variation. Though Daniel Bell (in "Meritocracy and Equality," *The Public Interest*, 29 [Fall 1972]: 26–69) has hailed Jencks's study as a major challenge to the contention that this is either a class or meritorian society, I am skeptical on both scores. It is possible that Jencks's model has simply discredited his model.

17. One of Parsons's "pattern variables" is universalism, and while the concept itself does not involve the confusion referred to here, Parsons is among those who seem to have misconstrued the concept. For example, this is reflected in his notion that there exist "evolutionary universals" which result in "generalized increases in adaptive capacity" for those societies which come to possess them. His analysis neglects the fact that increases in adaptive capacity are not "general," but are specific to individual and cultural purposes; and that universalism along one dimension can be discrimination or mere arbitrariness along other dimensions. (See "Evolutionary Universals in Society," *American Sociological Review*, June 1964; and again, White's *Beyond Conformity*.)

18. In addition to the references under note 9 of this chapter, see also David Potter, "American Individualism in the Twentieth Century," in *Individualism*, ed. Ronald Gross and Paul Osterman (New York: Dell Publishing Co., 1971); Erik Erikson, "Reflections on the American Identity," in *Childhood and Society* (New York: Norton, rev. ed. 1963); on the theme of American innocence, see Graham

Greene, *The Quiet American* (London: W. Heinemann, 1953); Norman Mailer, *Miami and the Seige of Chicago* (New York: World Publishing Co., 1968), or *Of a Fire on the Moon* (London: Weidenfeld and Nicolson, 1970), or practically anything else by him, with the understanding that he constitutes the better part of the data on which he claims to be reporting; similarly for Tom Wolfe: see for example *The Kandy-Colored-Tangerine-Flake-Streamlined Baby* (New York: Simon & Schuster, Pocket Books, 1968); Saul Bellow, *Herzog* (New York: Viking Press, 1964), and *Humboldt's Gift* (New York: Viking Press, 1975); and for the vast area between Greenwich Village and Berkeley: Larry McMurtry, *In a Narrow Grave: Essays on Texas* (Austin: Encino Press, 1968), and the most delightful *Norwood*, by Charles Portis (New York: Random House, Ballantine, 1966).

19. Erikson, *Insight and Responsibility* (New York: Norton, 1964), p. 285.

20. Potter, "American Individualism in the Twentieth Century."

21. Simmel, *Sociology of Georg Simmel*, pp. 58–84. Also see Tocqueville, *Democracy in America*, 2: 104.

22. Simmel, *Sociology of Georg Simmel*, p. 72.

23. Ibid., p. 82.

24. Ibid., p. 83; see also p. 79.

25. Tocqueville, *Democracy in America*, 2: 239.

26. Ibid., 2: 240.

27. Compare with Slater, *The Pursuit of Loneliness* (Boston: Beacon, 1970), p. 5.

28. *Will to Power*, trans. Walter Kaufmann, ed. R. J. Hollingdale and Walter Kaufmann (New York: Random House, 1967), p. 328. Ludwig von Bertalanffy (*General Systems Theory*) argues that the progress of science involves a progressive de-anthropomorphization of our knowledge, a movement away from the restraints of our psychological equipment and our biological ambient.

29. Tocqueville spoke in several passages of how American extremes seem to feed off one another. The following is from chap. 12, vol. 2, *Democracy in America* ("Why Some Americans Manifest a Sort of Fanatical Spiritualism"):

If their social condition, their present circumstances, and their laws did not confine the Americans so closely to the pursuit of worldly welfare, it is probably that they would display more reserve and more experience whenever their attention is turned to things immaterial, and that they would check themselves without difficulty. But they feel imprisoned within bounds, which they will apparently never be allowed to pass. As soon as they have passed those bounds, their minds do not know where to fix themselves and often rush unrestrained beyond the range of common sense.

30. Williams, *American Society*. On American religiosity, also see John Seeley's *Americanization of the Unconscious* (New York: International Science Press, 1967):

Americans, who have disestablished religion, tend in a profound sense to make a religion of everything. . . . If devotion to an Idea, if ardor in its affectionate development, if the rendering of the idea immanent in the body of thought of the time, and if the pervasive embodiment of the idea in behavior, are, as I believe, the hallmarks of a religious attitude toward it, then ideas are religiously treated in America. It is true that one religion readily succeeds another, but this is rather from the devotion to the general religious quest than from disloyalty to the particular religion abandoned (p. 6).

31. Some group therapies have exhibited tendencies and practices which border on fascist, and the pressure in some circles to prove how liberated you are has assumed thoroughly repressive dimensions. In the connection see Eva Hoffman, "EST—the Magic of Brutality," *Dissent*, Spring 1977, pp. 208–12. Ms. Hoffman sees the psychological brutality of EST in the service of the lesson: "Get your act together and toe the line"; not the "Let it all hang out" message of earlier encounter groups. The distance between the two messages, as I suggest in the text, is not so great as it may appear.

32. Nietzsche, *Beyond Good and Evil*, trans. with commentary by Walter Kaufmann (1886; reprinted ed. New York: Random House, 1966), p. 69.

33. Both Simmel and Nietzsche have pointed to the relationship of fear to the inability to wonder and be fascinated. See Simmel's "Metropolis and Mental Life," *Sociology of Georg Simmel*, pp. 409–24.

34. Mead, Parsons, and Keniston and many others have pointed to the significance of the disparity between "family, feeling, and fun" (as Keniston puts it) and the affective neutrality, universalism, etc., of the larger business and bureaucratic world which youth must eventually enter. (See for example Parsons's "Youth in the Context of American Society," in Erik Erikson, ed., *The Challenge of Youth* [Garden City, N.Y.: Doubleday, 1965]; and Keniston,

The Uncommitted [New York: Dell Publishing Co., Delta, 1960], chap. 10.) The apparent dispute with those who, like Slater, stress the compatibility of the small isolated nuclear family, with its intense emotional ties between mother and children, is mainly apparent. Such families would appear to be both well suited and poorly suited to the larger society. The importance of Oedipal motivation in social climbing, the role of mother's vicarious thrills in raising doctors and prima donnas, the significance of receiving affection and discipline from the same source in the repression and channeling of aggression—these and other elements of affinity or compatibility have been rightly stressed. Of course this is potent, explosive stuff, using powerful emotional ties as a means of teaching someone to make it in a world of tie-breaking, separations and segmentalized, instrumental, fleeting relationships; a world of dry abstractions, cognitive demands, repression of emotion and delay of gratification. Thus the products of some of these best, most compatible families have played a large role in the student revolt and the new culture of the 1960s. In a society to some extent predicated on dissatisfaction with itself (a point rarely given adequate attention by liberal and leftist critics alike), it is helpful to have the kind of family that produces malcontents. So long as the process does not get out of hand, they fit right in.

35. The fantasy underlying this exaggerated aversion for things as they are apparently concerns some ultimate, perfect thing (as in Simon and Garfunkel's "Big Bright Green Pleasure Machine") which, in the word of a Bob Dylan song, will do what's never been done, win what's never been won for him. With luck his wife, or some future imagined wife, might be such a possession, costing relatively little to maintain. If he is really lucky she might measure up to his mother, or some mythical idealized mother. (Among others, Philip Slater has effectively stressed the Oedipal nature of our motivating fantasies; see especially *Earthwalk* [Garden City, N.Y.: Doubleday, Anchor, 1974], chap. 4.) Bob Dylan has expressed this theme in "It's Alright, Ma, I'm Only Bleeding," from an album titled, interestingly, "Bringing It All Back Home"; "Advertising signs they con/You into thinking you're the one/who can win what's never been won/who can do what's never been done/ Meanwhile life outside goes on/All around you." The refrain ends on this note: ". . . but it's alright, Ma, if I can't please them." Apparently they can't please him, either, and Ma seems to have something to do with his dissatisfaction ("I got nothing, Ma, to live up to."). Perfect, perfectly inaccessible Ma-phantoms and

Ma-ideals often serve to keep us loose and nimble, keep us running, working, buying. And under certain conditions, protesting.

Chapter 8

1. Whether free market distributional criteria should prevail, and whether factors actually receive their marginal contribution in pretax income, are matters of considerable controversy. (See Lester Thurow, "Toward a Definition of Economic Justice," *The Public Interest* 31 [Spring 1973] : 56–80.) But it is probably fair to say that much of liberal economics is built around the assumptions that factors are and should be paid their marginal value-product. It is arguable that marginal principles merely specify how economists prefer that redistribution should proceed, should we desire it, but it is easy to underestimate the number of economists who tacitly accept it as a principle of equity as well. Moreover, within and outside economics, marginal productivity is embedded in a pervasive cultural matrix which, in Irving Kristol's words, "prescribes a connection between personal merit—as represented by such bourgeois virtues as honesty, sobriety, diligence, and thrift—and worldly success." (in "Capitalism, Socialism, and Nihilism," *The Public Interest* 21 [Fall 1970] : 16–43). He contrasts this with a positive conception of justice under capitalism ("whatever is, is just"), which he attributes to Hume and Mandeville. He assumes that this will not suffice for the average American ("only a philosopher could be satisified with an *ex post facto* theory of justice"). I share that assumption, though not, I hope, the limited imagination which assumes that any point of view neither capitalist nor socialist must be nihilist.

2. Strictly speaking, this requires the additional assumptions of perfect competition and the absence of economies of scale, neither of which obtain in real economies. The criticisms offered here gain in force when these conditions are not met. In this connection see C. B. Macpherson's argument in *The Real World of Democracy* (Oxford: Clarendon Press, 1966), chap. 5; also his *Democratic Theory: Essays in Retrieval* (Oxford: Clarendon Press, 1971), especially chap. 1 and chap. 2.

3. For Marx the labor theory of value led to the conclusion that labor tends to exchange for the amount required to produce it: i.e., to keep it alive and well enough to work. This contributed to a conveniently pessimistic prognosis of the long-run fate of the working class under capitalism, and it stripped the analysis of exploitation of the personal element—since it supposedly proceeds

irrespective of how greedy or well-meaning the individual capitalist might be.

4. Cosmic luck should be distinguished from Jencks's luck (the residual category which accounted for 80 percent of the inequality in his study; his other variables were home environment, schooling, and intelligence: see *Inequality* [New York: Basic Books, 1972]). His is luck only relative to the model he uses; in particular, I.Q. is probably both too narrow and too imprecise to get at what it takes to advance. He may have demonstrated that this society is neither a class society nor a meritocracy, but only as his model implicitly defines the two. (See chapter 7, note 16.)

5. This bit of intellectual history is recounted in Joan Robinson's *Economic Philosophy* (Garden City, N.Y.: Doubleday, 1964), and I have found her account most helpful in preparing my remarks. See also Gunnar Myrdal, *The Political Element in the Development of Economic Theory* (Cambridge, Mass.: Harvard University Press, 1954); and Macpherson, *Democratic Theory*, especially chap. 9, "Post-Liberal Democracy?".

6. Alfred Marshall, *Principles of Economics* (London: MacMillan & Co., 1925), p. 19; quoted in Robinson, *Economic Philosophy*, p. 5.

7. F. Y. Edgeworth, *Mathematical Psychics* (London, 1888), p. 8; quoted in Robinson, *Economic Philosophy*, p. 69.

8. Robinson (*Economic Philosophy*, p. 139), attributes this to a Professor Harberler. Surely his remark, if serious, represents some kind of solipsistic low point in Western social thought.

9. Of course there are other forms the assault on equality can take. See the issue of *Social Policy* (May–June 1972) devoted to "The New Assault on Equality," especially the articles "The American Resignation: The New Assault on Equality," by S. M. Miller and Ronnie Ratner; and "The Fallacy of Richard Herrnstein's I.Q." by Noam Chomsky. The question of why this research is being carried on at all is certainly a valid and interesting one, as it is for any research. But it strikes me that these critics often miss the opportunity of stressing that any criterion of merit will inevitably have a discriminatory aspect to it. And they leave themselves, and racial minorities, vulnerable should the Jensen-Schockley findings prove true and significant. The question that should be kept in the forefront of this debate is: so what? What have such findings to do with a truly democratic understanding of equality? Why do these differences make a difference? And in the last analysis: what kind of society do we want, given that nature is no longer our guide?

10. This is the empirical question which Rawls's difference principle brings to the fore. It is interesting that so much commentary on Rawls has assumed that his is a radically egalitarian argument, as if no one really believed in the trickle down effects of present inequalities, nor the disincentive effects of reducing them. See for example Daniel Bell, "Meritocracy and Inequality," *The Public Interest* 29 (Fall 1972).

11. Bertram Gross has made this point, citing several instances (by economists) of this confusion of mean with median. He points out that average income in 1971 (4th quarter) for a family of four would be approximately $17,000. See "A Closer Look at Income Distribution," *Social Policy*, May–June 1972, p. 61.

In general, what redistribution might accomplish can be easily underestimated, and the cost to the relatively affluent overestimated. According to Willard Johnson, to bring all households in America up to the official poverty line in 1971 by transfers from the richest 5 percent would have reduced the pretax money incomes of the top 5 percent by only 8.2 percent, and reduced their share of the nation's total income from 21.6 percent to 19.8 percent. See "Should the Poor Buy No Growth?, *The No-Growth Society, Daedalus*, Fall 1973, pp. 165–89; especially pp. 180–81.

12. See George F. Break, "The Effects of Taxation on Work Incentives," in *Private Wants and Public Needs*, ed. Edmund Phelps (New York: Norton, 1962), pp. 55–65.

13. Paul Samuelson, "Public Responsibility for Growth and Stability," in *The Goal of Economic Growth*, ed. Edmund Phelps (New York: Norton, 1969), pp. 70–75.

14. See Ben B. Seligman, *Permanent Poverty* (Chicago: Quadrangle Books, 1968), and Alan B. Batchelder, *The Economics of Poverty* (New York: John Wiley & Sons, 1971). Theodore Schultz argues that the significant declines in poverty have been due to increases in income from labor, due to increased demand for highly skilled workers, but that the elderly, women, blacks, agricultural workers and workers in the South have been generally excluded from these labor markets. ("Public Approaches to Minimize Poverty," in *Poverty Amid Affluence*, ed. L. Fishman [New Haven and London: Yale University Press, 1966]) See also the references cited in "Should the Poor Buy No Growth?". Johnson points out that "by 1968, the able-bodied poor who were capable of doing so had already worked their way out of poverty. But work, in itself, is not sufficient to remove a family from poverty. In 1970 the

heads of nearly three million poor families were employed, but this did not protect them from poverty" (p. 169).

15. See "Should the Poor Buy No Growth?", and "Public Approaches to Minimize Poverty."

16. By and large poverty has been reduced, if we follow the somewhat dubious practice of setting a supposed cultural standard, and then not permitting it to rise over time. Income distribution—relative shares—is another matter. For the bottom end, see Herbert Gans, "The New Egalitarianism," *Saturday Review*, June 1972; for the top, see Robert Lampman, *The Share of Top Wealth-Holders in National Wealth: 1922-1956* (Princeton, N.J.: Princeton University Press, 1962); especially p. 23.

17. See Richard A. Easterlin, "Does Money Buy Happiness?" *The Public Interest* 30 (Winter 1973): 3-10. His data indicate that individual happiness increases with income, while there is little or no connection between national income and happiness: the hedonic paradox, or treadmill, some have called it. I would further suggest that the conscious pursuit of happiness may have become more of a responsibility with increased incomes; in some circles there is no worse failure than the failure to achieve happiness, and the failure is not readily admitted, particularly to pollsters.

18. E. J. Mishan, "The Spillover Enemy," *Encounter*, December 1959, pp. 3-14.

19. Thomas Schelling ("On the Ecology of Micromotives," *The Public Interest* 25 [Fall 1971]), discusses a "new Malthusianism" in the higher-income countries, in which, unlike the nineteenth century, "food supply does not play a unique role, nor even consumer goods generally, but shares attention with the disposal of wastes, the management of space and traffic, noise and the loss of privacy." By "congestion" I refer to roughly the same phenomenon. Admittedly the term is awkward, especially in that its narrow connotation, as Schelling points out, is "too much of a (presumably) good thing," while I intend it to cover such phenomena as pollution ("too much of something not good in any amount"), the possibility of various ecological disasters, and other aspects of congestion-induced scarcity (the energy crisis, the depletion of nonrenewable resources, etc.).

While congestion or the new Malthusianism are helpful umbrella concepts, they should not be used to obscure distinctions among those who argue that further growth is desirable yet impossible, or undesirable though possible, or both undesirable and impossible; and between those who seek to deal with externalities in terms of a reallocation of resources and a price system which better reflects actual social costs and benefits, and those who argue or imply that growth should simply be halted. (Further distinctions are explored by Mancur Olson, Hans H. Landsberg, and Joseph L. Fisher in their epilogue to *The No-Growth Society, Daedalus,* Fall 1973, pp. 229–41. Their categories include "eco-freaks," "socio-freaks," "psycho-freaks" (not clearly distinguished), "safety-freaks," plus the un-examined category of "growth-freaks."

E. J. Mishan, who often speaks in an aristocratic accent, generally finds growth more undesirable than impossible; the Club of Rome, in its initial study, tends to find growth impossible in the long run (due to nonrenewable resources and pollution); E. F. Schumacher (*Small is Beautiful: Economics as if People Mattered* [New York: Harper & Row, 1973]) and many others mix the two kinds of critiques. Wilfred Beckerman (*Two Cheers for the Affluent Society* [New York: St. Martin's, 1973]) is among those who argue that growth must be redirected to deal with externalities; see especially his critique of Mishan and the Club of Rome's world model. That model is effectively dissected in a series of article in *Futures* (February and April 1973).

20. Several efforts to assess how we are doing in a way more comprehensive and meaningful than the national income accounts deserve mention here. The first is associated with the social indicators movement: HEW's *Toward a Social Report,* edited by Mancur Olson. Its value lies primarily in pointing out how much we do not know, and how divided we are on the question of what it is we want or need to know. Its oversights are gross, even allowing for the constraints of the political setting in which it was prepared. An extended discussion of the inadequacies of health care delivery manages to avoid mentioning the AMA; to my knowledge, *nowhere* in this 1968 assessment of the state of American society is the Vietnam War mentioned. The naiveté of some of those involved is well symbolized by Olson's notion (expressed in a talk given at the 1968 HUD Summer Conference on the Future of the Cities, at Berkeley, California) that the only real impediment to developing a single national measure of the Gross Social Product is that our data and indicators are currently inadequate.

A more modest effort by Tobin and Nordhaus ("Is Growth Obsolete?", W. Nordhaus and James Tobin, *Economic Growth* [New York: National Bureau of Economic Research, 1972]) purchases some precision at the price of limiting the scope of the question. They attempt to separate Measurable Economic Welfare (MEW)

from the national income statistics by adding in the costs and benefits of those items not traded in the market (services of housewives,
etc.) and by subtracting those consumption items which are "regrettable necessities" (commuting costs, for example). While the
concept of regrettable necessity is regrettably controversial, and
while both adjustments are shot through with guesstimates, theirs
is a significant pioneering effort. They find, in the period from 1929
to 1965, that MEW was higher than NNP roughly by a factor of
three. The growth rate in MEW was less than the growth rate in
NNP, but only because the value of leisure time and nonmarket
activities in 1929 was so high relative to 1929 NNP.

Those who have most consistently immersed themselves in quantifiable data have generally taken a more favorable view of how
the society is changing, though this a gross generalization, to be
sure. This may mean that social critics are simply scornful of data,
and not really interested in what is going on out there—in some
cases this is undoubtedly the case. Or it could mean that it is primarily the quantifiable things which are improving.

21. See the somewhat different use of the same example made
by Garrett Hardin in "The Tragedy of the Commons," *Science*
162 (December 1968): 1243–48. Hardin seems to overestimate
the contribution of overpopulation, as such, to the problem of
externalities, though otherwise the two arguments are similar.

22. That profit-generated externalities are not the whole story,
that growth and technology play important independent roles, are
suggested by the considerable evidence of environmental despoilation and pollution in the USSR and Eastern Europe. See the references cited in Beckerman, *Two Cheers for the Affluent Society*.

23. See Leon R. Kass, "Making Babies: The New Biology and the
'Old' Morality," *The Public Interest* 26 (Winter 1972): 18–57.
Also see Victor Ferkiss, *Technological Man: The Myth and the
Reality* (New York: New American Library, Mentor, 1969), es-
pecially pp. 98-100.

24. In this connection, see Jacques Ellul, *The Technological Society*, trans. John Wilkinson, introduction by Robert Merton (New
York: Knopf, 1964); and John Schaar, "Legitimacy in the Modern
State," in *Power and Community*, ed. Philip Green and Sanford
Levinson (New York: Random House, Vintage, 1970). Victor Ferkiss
(*Technological Man*) effectively criticizes the more deterministic
views of the impact of technology, of which Ellul is representative. Marcuse has written in this deterministic vein as well: "Not
only the application of technology but technology itself is domina-

tion (of nature and men)—methodical, scientific, calculated, calculating control. Specific purposes and interests of domination
are not foisted upon technology 'subsequently' and from the outside; they enter the very construction of the technical apparatus"
(*Negations* [Boston: Beacon, 1968], p. 233). See chapter 3.

25. "Roughly the same"; the question is from what perspective,
and the answer has to do with the relevant scarcities and congested
situations. A general food shortage would mean that the relevant
fact about Jack Sprat and wife is that they are both voracious
eaters, not that their tastes in food differ. The way the picture
changes when we change the dimensions along which we view it
has important implications for the image of this country as pluralistic. See chapter 4, note 9.

26. Schelling, "On the Ecology of Micromotives," p. 96.

27. Mishan, "The Spillover Enemy," p. 11.

28. P. H. Partridge, "Politics, Philosophy, and Ideology," in
Political Philosophy, ed. Anthony Quinton (Oxford: Oxford University Press, 1967), p. 39.

29. See Beckerman, *Two Cheers for the Affluent Society*, chap. 5.

30. Distribution and redistribution receive very little attention in
The Limits to Growth, for example, and in most of the ecologically-
minded treatments of social ills and social ethics: two other examples are Slater's *Earthwalk* (Garden City, N.Y.: Doubleday, Anchor,
1974), and Garrett Hardin's *Exploring New Ethics for Survival*
(New York: Viking, 1968). The concern with survival has a way of
stealing attention from other problems, but there are additional
sources of the conservative and quietistic aspects of ecologically-
minded social theory. Hardin suggests that, in light of the causal
interrelatedness of everything, the basic rule of ecology is that you
can never do just one thing. This calls to mind Galbraith's definition of a conservative: someone who believes that one thing leads
to another. It also calls to mind criticisms of the functionalist view
of society: with everything closely interrelated, the alternatives
appear to be either no change whatsoever, or total revolution.

31. John Maynard Keynes, "The Economic Prospects of Our
Grandchildren," in *Essays in Persuasion* (New York: Norton, 1963),
p. 369.

32. See Slater, *The Pursuit of Loneliness* (Boston: Beacon, 1970),
and *Earthwalk*; Yankelovitch and Barrett, *Ego and Instinct* (New
York: Random House, 1970); and Schaar, "Legitimacy in the Modern State." Pirsig (*Zen and the Art of Motorcycle Maintenance*
[Toronto: Bantam, 1974]) along with legions of other pop-psychol-

ogists, makes the assumption that if we only get ourselves together, psychologically and epistemologically, then we will apparently deal simultaneously and effectively with everything from personal relationships to pollution. (Also see chapters 3 and 4.) The democratic critics, I have suggested, often make similarly rosy assumptions concerning the desirable effects of increased democratization (see chapters 1 and 2).

33. Freud, *Civilization and Its Discontents*, trans. and ed. James Strachey (1930; reprinted ed. New York: Norton, 1961), p. 61. "It is always possible to bind together a considerable number of people in love, so long as there are other people left over to receive the manifestations of their aggressiveness."

34. See Irving Kristol's essay "About Equality," *Commentary*, vol. 54, no. 5 (November 1972). Kristol sees equality as the battle cry of the new college-educated professional classes in their struggle to wrest power from the business community. Scheler and Nietzsche have pointed out that behind the obsessive concern with equality there is often a strong interest in a new order of inequalities. Kristol, along with Nietzsche and Scheler, appears to believe he has devastated the argument for less inequality once he discovers that its advocates have motives which are less than pure.

35. Robert Lane, *Political Ideology* (New York: Free Press, 1962), p. 226.

36. Ibid., p. 227.

37. See Lewis Lipsitz, "Forgotten Roots," in *Frontiers of Democratic Theory*, ed. Henry Kariel (New York: Random House, 1970), pp. 394–403. Also David Easton and Robert D. Hess, "The Child's Political World," *Midwest Journal of Political Science* 6 (August 1962), especially pp. 238–39. Surely this confusion of God with father with president is not limited to nine-year olds. Will Herberg and Robert Bellah, among others, have pointed to the peculiar secular religion which for so many constitutes Americanism.

John Seeley's *Americanization of the Unconscious* (New York: International Science Press, 1967), suggests the connection of anomie to that secular religion, and to a dangerous proclivity for hero-worship:

It might be said that Americans who take no one seriously—almost never a European, and rarely one of their own—are hero-makers and hero-worshippers. The statement understates the case. An air of Messianic expectation pervades the culture—as one would expect in a society where the conventional belief is in fundamental equality. The secular version is the much-worn log cabin to White Houses, but this masks rather than reveals the much deeper conviction that some much more general and profounder savior from something more pervasive than the moment's political problems will any moment appear and be recognized (p. 5).

38. Schelling, "On the Ecology of Micromotives"; Slater, *Pursuit of Loneliness* and *Earthwalk*.

39. I should point out that while Schelling builds much of his argument about the traffic light and similar examples, Slater's reference, however revealing, is brief and casual.

40. Perhaps it is the hallmark of an increasingly psychologized culture that the distinction between private motives and the psychic state of the individual, and the social results of private behavior gets blurred; the ghost of Adam Smith may now reside in pop psychology as well as liberal economics. If only we get ourselves together, the community will flourish. Our first responsibility to others is to be responsive to ourselves . . . and so on.

41. See Beckerman, *Two Cheers for the Affluent Society*, chap. 2, for a more extensive consideration of the various interests and motives underlying the critique of economic growth. The following thought-experiment is helpful in sorting out what really troubles us about technology and growth: suppose the gloom-and-doomsters are completely mistaken, and that we could in fact continue to get away with this frantic activity, this world-winning, this not knowing our place in the great scheme of things, this Promethean lack of humility. As my way of framing the question implies, there may be, among other, more valid factors involved, a kind of fundamentalist asceticism. Or perhaps a form of populist, or fundamentalist-populist *ressentiment* toward the beneficiaries of growth.

Chapter 9

1. For a parallel analysis of the use of market concepts in modern liberal democratic theory, see Macpherson, *Democratic Theory: Essays in Retrieval* (Oxford, Clarendon Press, 1966), especially chap. 10 "Market Concepts in Political Theory," which he summarizes as follows: "Political theorists have paid too much attention to the superficial analogy between the market and the political process at the operative level, and not enough attention to the market concept at the deeper level of postulates about the nature of society and the nature of human freedom" (p. 194).

2. Macpherson appears to claim that modern liberal democratic

theory is explicitly based on a Benthamite claim to maximize utilities, and that this represents a step back beyond John Stuart Mill ". . . to the indifferent weighing of the utilities of individuals, with their existing habits, tastes, and preferences taken as given, as the ultimate data." (*Democratic Theory*, p. 177.) I think this is as much interpretation as text, though I agree with his latter point. As he points out, in important respects neoclassical economics represents a step "back even beyond the original classical economists," who after all criticized rentier morality, the uses to which labor was put by the existing social order, unproductive labor, idle aristocrats, and existing political arrangements. But the individual utilities on which neoclassical economists and the neoutilitarians build their system "are given by the preferences and tastes of individuals as they are" (p. 177). On this point also see Thomas Sowell, *Classical Economics Reconsidered* (Princeton, N.J.: Princeton University Press, 1974), especially chap. 1.

3. See Kaufmann's remarks on "the fallacies in the liberal faith" (*Without Guilt and Justice* [New York: Dell Publishing Co., 1973], p. 93.)

4. Dahl and Lindblom, *Politics, Economics, and Welfare* (New York: Harper & Row, 1953), p. 28.

5. Ibid.

6. See Dahl's *A Preface to Democratic Theory* (Chicago: University of Chicago Press, 1956), chap. 3, and the appendix to chap. 3. See also Plamenatz, *Democracy and Illusion* (London: Longmans, 1973).

7. The careful research of the mysterious Mark Epernay once revealed, to his utter consternation, that Charles De Gaulle was actually incredibly selfless, to the point of lacking an ego altogether. Epernay's ingenious testing instrument consisted of observing the individual subject over a period of time in order to compute the average length of time elapsing between occasions on which the individual thought of himself. Tested the first time, DeGaulle scored seven minutes—very high. Unbelievably high. Further research was called for, and on closer study Epernay discovered that in all the time intervening between thoughts of himself, De Gaulle had been thinking of France. Still closer study revealed that De Gaulle had been making no distinction between himself and France. That is, psychological egoism is one thing, and the social content and consequences of our thoughts and actions, however self-regarding, are quite another. (Mark Epernay (John Kenneth Galbraith), *The McLandress Dimension* [New York: New American Library, 1968].)

8. In fairness to economists and economically-minded political theorists, I should again indicate that the same kind of criticism applies to many sociologists and sociologically-minded political theorists, who tend to confuse consensus, or shared attitudes, character traits, and the like, with the question of shareability.

9. Plamenatz voices similar skepticism, *Democracy and Illusion*, pp. 183–84. Referring to Dahl's interpretation of Arrow's theorem, he suggests that "his point . . . is that, even if every citizen did have such an order (of preferences), there could still arise situations in which no course of action could be said to be either the most popular or the least unpopular, in which no decision could be taken on strictly democratic grounds. It is this that Kenneth Arrow, according to Dahl, has proved. But he has proved it only if we accept some such account of democracy as Dahl offers." He goes on to point out that if acting democratically required that the representative invite his constituents

> to choose between different courses of action and then take the course they prefer to any other, it might quite often happen that he could not act democratically. But since his acting democratically requires only that they should have elected him to act on their behalf, that they should be free to criticize his actions and to make their wishes known to him, and that his right to act on their behalf beyond a certain period should depend on their again electing him to do so, he can act democratically no matter how often there is no decision which his constituents want him to take in preference to any other (p. 184).

For further discussion as to the significance of Arrow's impossibility theorem, see Dahl's *Preface to Democratic Theory*, pp. 42–43; Robert Paul Wolff, *In Defense of Anarchism* (New York: Harper & Row, 1970), pp. 58–67, in which it is treated indiscriminately as yet another telling indictment of majoritarian democracy; and Riker and Ordeshook's *An Introduction to Positive Political Theory* (Englewood Cliffs, N.J.: Prentice-Hall, 1973), chaps. 2 and 4, in which research bearing on the empirical significance of Arrow's theorem is discussed and summarized.

10. A similar point applies to Black's assumption of the "single-peakedness" of individual preferences, which also makes possible a consistent social ordering by majority rule. (Single-peakedness requires that if "U_1, U_2, . . . , U_n are utility indicators for the individual orderings R_1, R_2, . . . R_n, then the alternative social states can be represented by a one-dimensional variable in such a way that

each of the graphs of U_1, U_2, . . . , U_n has a single peak." [Arrow, *Social Choice and Individual Values* (New Haven: Yale University Press, 1951), p. 75.]) That a consistent social ordering is possible under these conditions "sheds new light," Arrow contends, "on what is meant by similarity of social attitudes." (p. 80) The similarity seems to consist not so much in the rank-orderings of alternatives, but rather in the basic classificatory dimension along which alternatives are conceived: a cultural uniformity, Riker and Ordeshook suggest, as to the standard of judgment. Yet the significance of this kind of uniformity is unclear, *precisely* to the extent that we entertain an egoistic, instrumentalist conception of democratic institutions. For if a more complicated pattern of individual preferences happened to mean that those who had been on the short end (when preferences were single-peaked) would now manage to win a few for a change, no doubt they would see this as an improvement, no matter how inconsistent the new social ordering might be. Indeed, taking their cue from some of the axiomatic theorists we have discussed, and from the egoism they posit, those citizens might confuse winning more often with increased democratization. But if there were no change in their status as a standing minority (given the new, more complicated pattern of preferences), it is not clear why they would feel any more oppressed, or see the decision-making process or the decisions themselves as any less democratic. If winning is everything, how one loses is a matter of indifference.

11. This point concerning consensus also applies to the question of transitivity of collective preferences, as Arrow makes clear in his chapter on "similarity as the basis for social welfare judgments" (chap. 7). Though he is primarily concerned with similarity insofar as it contributes to transitivity (as opposed to its contribution to correct, or workable, wise, or humane judgments), it is noteworthy that this economist does not dismiss idealist interpretations of the "true" consensus, nor a sociological reliance on the given consensus, out of hand. Perhaps this is because he feels that democratic theory has sustained a mortal wound, and the dagger is in his hands. Quoting with approval Knight's position ("We contend not only that such ideals are real to individuals, but that they are part of our culture and sufficiently uniform and objective to form a useful standard of comparison for a given country at a given time."), he points out that "this formulation is especially valuable for pointing out that the consensus on moral imperatives need not be grounded in a metaphysical absolute but may be based on the relative socioethical norms of a particular culture" (p. 83). However, he is uneasy with

Knight's formulation, which "depends on ethical relativism, and leads to the danger of glorification of the status quo" (p. 85).

The trajectory of Arrow's ideas here is most instructive, describing a path that a number of thoughtful liberals have walked. Described briefly, the path leads from reflections on the chaos implicit in their individualistic conception of democracy to a most uneasy reliance on whatever the consensus might be, however unstable or productive of chaos or injustice it might be. Or, more elaborately: the neo-Benthamite fantasy that somehow with the right set of institutions, everyone might win, first degenerates into a concern with supposedly impartial, somehow acceptable laws, rules, decision-making rules (as with Arrow's concern to aggregate preferences fairly, consistently). The maximizing, instrumentalist claims are quietly dropped at this point. And then when this solution also proves impossible, the analysis turns to the last and not very attractive resort, the reliance on the consensus, to try to save those rules and institutions, if not their maximizing claims.

Concerning the liberal's reliance on and fascination with rules, Roberto Unger writes that "the ideas that there is no natural community of common ends and that group life is a creature of will help explain the importance of rules and their coercive enforcement" (*Knowledge and Politics* [New York: Free Press, 1975], p. 75). Concerning the claims that laws (or decision-making rules) can be instrumental to individual purposes, he observes that "the war of men against one another precludes the constant and general agreement about ends that would be necessary for instrumental rules to serve effectively as a basis for the ordering of social relations" (p. 69). Finally, concerning the liberal's unhappy reliance on consensus, he argues that "every sharing of values is bound to be both precarious and morally indifferent. It is precarious because the individual will is the true and only seat of value, forever changing direction as the dangers and opportunities of the struggle for comfort and glory shift. The sharing of values is also without ethical significance" (p. 68). "As long as the sharing of ends is conceived simply as a convergence of individual preferences, with no change of other postulates of liberal thought, it does not truly qualify the principle that values are individual and subjective. . . . thus each convergence of preferences remains a precarious alliance of interests" (p. 78).

12. In the Benthamite calculus which apparently animates and guides their analyses, all wants are of equal merit, for poetry or pushpins. Moreover, each person is to "count for one." Ironically,

it is partly because of these ostensibly egalitarian assumptions that, once we allow effective demand to determine whose wants and what kinds of wants are met, the effect is to reflect current inequalities, not to correct them—and even to promote further inequality.

13. Of course neither Dahl nor Wolff explicitly address individuals in this way. Dahl, for example, proceeds by explaining what kinds of criteria, arguments, and institutions *he* finds acceptable. Nevertheless, reframing their arguments this way is not only a helpful expositional device, it is also integral to the case I am making, in that it helps reveal the sociological and psychosociological particulars on which their abstract arguments actually depend. To characterize their arguments as abstract does not contradict the fact that Dahl personalizes his analysis, for he does so in only a limited sense. We learn nothing of his personal preferences, and he implies that accepting his argument for democracy is largely a matter of accepting his logic, whatever your interests and those of the rest of the polity. In this crucial sense Dahl's argument is *most* abstract and universalistic—as if all sentient beings capable of reason would be bound by reason to accept the argument and the institutions it implies.

14. Wolff, *In Defense of Anarchism*, p. 21.

15. Wolff, *The Poverty of Liberalism* (Boston, Beacon, 1968), especially "On Tolerance" and "On Power." See above, chapter 1.

16. *In Defense of Anarchism*, p. vii.

17. Ibid., p. 59.

18. Ibid.

19. Ibid., p. 72.

20. Ibid., p. 76.

21. Ibid., p. 78. Given his initial insistence that autonomy and authority are always and everywhere utterly opposed, that liberty retreats as authority advances, it seems clear that the only possible solutions open to Wolff were either a magic solution, or no solution at all.

22. Plamenatz, *Democracy and Illusion*, p. 161.

23. John Rawls, *A Theory of Justice* (Cambridge, Mass.: Harvard University Press, 1971).

24. Kaufmann, *Without Guilt or Justice*, p. 93.

25. Bay's human rights approach to circumscribing majoritarianism and constitutionalism (see chapter 3) can be viewed as a less philosophical but in some ways more ambitious attempt to articulate a nonutilitarian conception of democracy. The similarities are instructive, beginning with the overall nature of their projects and

extending to their use of lexical rank-orderings of principles. Rawls's first principle (the "priority of liberty") states that basic liberties should be extended to all. His second principle, the difference principle, follows the first in a lexical ordering, thus precluding the trading of economic advantage for basic liberties. (See Rawls's *Theory of Justice*, pp. 60–63.) Bay's lexical ordering of various possible freedoms is an expanded version of Rawls's first principle, one in which freedoms are extended in a sequence chosen ultimately by the majority, and in which those least well off who have yet to receive a given freedom must be granted it before another freedom is extended. The most revealing similarity concerns the kind of compromises both must make in order to make their solutions convincing. Just as Bay must finally jettison his use of humanistic psychology, falling back on the use of political majorities and reliance on consensus in order to establish a lexical rank-order of priorities among various possible human freedoms and rights, Rawls must abandon his more abstract game-theoretical considerations for a series of sociological assumptions concerning the attitudes, values, and priorities of those people who stand behind his veil of ignorance. One notable difference is that Bay eventually faces up squarely to his necessity of relying, after all, on majoritarianism and consensus (albeit limited by his stipulation that these freedoms must be shareable and lexically ordered), while Rawls never directly admits his reliance on such sociological assumptions. Perhaps this boldness is one source of another notable difference, the much greater attention Rawls's book has received.

26. *Understanding Rawls: A Reconstruction and Critique of "A Theory of Justice"* (Princeton, N.J.: Princeton University Press, 1976).

27. Kaufmann (*Without Guilt and Justice*, pp. 89–92) sees Rawls's theory of justice as the latest "resort to moral rationalism," escapist in the sense of avoiding a direct discussion of competing goals and visions of society, and intellectually dishonest in so stacking the cards that the desired solution, actually decided upon at the outset, comes back to him with the enhanced authority provided by supposedly sovereign reason. Admittedly there are other possible virtues and concerns—the concern with self-realization, or excellence, or alienation, or anomie, for example—which are by no means reducible to or fully compatible with merely splitting the given pie fairly. Certainly the sleight of hand by which Rawls builds his conclusions into his assumptions, into the original position ("we

want to define the original position so that we can get the desired solution" [p. 141], quoted in Kaufmann, p. 92) is disconcerting, and bears a strong resemblance to the neoutilitarian escapism I have criticized. But surely Kaufmann overstates his point, because Rawls's work is a *relatively* explicit and substantial attempt to specify and defend some basic aspects of the good society. The fact that some of his conclusions are commonplaces of the liberal left, and that some of them are built into his assumptions, should not blind us to the refreshing audaciousness of his effort to *demonstrate* their validity. Moreover, in addition to inspiring further escapist tinkering by moral rationalists and utilitarians alike, it has also spawned precisely the kind of debate over contending social goals and visions that Kaufmann accuses Rawls and the advocates of justice of ignoring and obscuring. For example, much of Kaufmann's *Without Guilt and Justice* consists of a sustained polemic against Rawls's *Theory of Justice*. Kaufmann's criticism of Rawls is part of his multifaceted Nietzschean polemic against the preoccupation with justice, a preoccupation that he finds "misguided and unfruitful": "it is . . . impossible to proportion rewards, whether financial or not, to the relevant differences among people. . . . even if the distribution could be proportionate, it would not follow that it ought to be imposed," given that there are other, competing virtues in his code. Underlying such efforts, he contends, is the wish to avoid such complexities and moral ambiguities ("decidophobia"), as well as still less savory motives such as envy and vindictiveness. But this, too, is overkill. Perhaps a just society could dispense with such efforts as Rawls's, but a society in which systematic and structured inequalities coexist with an official ideology which has always had strong egalitarian emphases—and a society apparently missing or fast losing a viable shareable conception of what is just—must surely do so at its peril, and at the peril of the virtues Kaufmann himself espouses. In this respect Kaufmann appears to exhibit some of the decidophobia he decries. As he points out in criticizing Kant, consequentialism is a necessary part of any responsible social ethic.

Chapter 10

1. Daniel Bell, *The End of Ideology* (Glencoe, Ill.: Free Press, 1961).

2. See especially Bell's "The Corporation and Society in the 1970s," *The Public Interest* 24 (Summer 1971): 5–32; and also, "Meritocracy and Equality," *The Public Interest* 29 (Fall 1972).

Index

Accepted. *See* Included

Accommodation, 102, 103

Adaptability, 248n*11*, 268n*17*

Adaptations, 29, 172

Adelphi method, 239n*10*

Affection, 57, 59, 178, 180

Affects: employment of, 102; kinds of, 103; strength of, 101

Affluence, 51; mass, 105–06

After the Revolution (Dahl), 204–14

Agency and communion, 251–52n*10*

Agentic, the, 267–68n*15*

Aggression, 67–68, 81, 82; in therapeutic culture, 106

Alienation, 1, 3, 5, 66, 87–103, 191, 218, 221, 246n*63*; acute, 145, 184; in American society, 50–51, 142–43, 147–48, 152, 154; and basic human needs, 56–60; distinct from reification, 245n*59*; economic, 71; intellectual, 71; in leftist literature of freedom, 76, 78; Marxist view of, 47–49, 95, 96, 235n*5*, 253–54n*12*; as protection against anomie, 49–50, 87; relationship with anomie, 6, 85, 121, 122, 222, 253n*12*; religious, 71; treatment of, 253n*12*; and view of man, 50–51

Allport, Gordon, 238n*3*

Ambivalence: accommodation of, 99–103; central problem for psychological man, 105; of freedom, 167; primal, 89–99; and therapeutic culture, 106–07; toward politicians, 197. *See also* Human ambivalence

American citizen, average, 18, 26, 33, 66, 198–99, 272n*1*

Americanism, 279n*37*

American life, quality of, 23

American society, 204; and alienation, 50–51; anomie in, 125–26, 127–55; critique of, 31; cultural contradictions in, 139–52; distribution of power in, 227n*3*; egalitarianism in, 165, 221; extremes in, 269–70n*29*; in leftist literature of freedom, 1–3, 78; needs in, 151–52, 155; out of control, 121–22, 125; religiosity in, 270n*30*; therapeutic culture in, 105. *See also* Excluded; Ideals

Anarchistic fallacy, 22

Anarchy, 121, 227n*3*; bourgeois, 147

Anomie, 3, 5, 76, 87–103, 104, 123, 253–54n*12*; acute, 145, 254n*12*; alienation as protection against, 49–50; in American society, 125–26, 127–55; denial of, 103; and deviance, 247n*6*, 266n*10*; and distributive justice, 156–66, 195; Etzioni on, 59; and the excluded, 180–87; fear of, 218; pathology of utilitarian culture, 215; reinterpretation of, 4–5, 152–53, 191; relationship with alienation, 6, 85, 121, 122, 222, 253n*12*; and secular religion, 279–80n*37*; in sociologically-minded pluralism, 13–14; subjective, 87; transitional, 124

Anthropology, philosophical, 47

Arendt, Hannah, 92, 105

Arrow, Kenneth, 43, 44, 283n*10*, 283–84n*11*; impossibility theorem, 194, 202, 207, 282n*9*

Artists, society of, 245n*60*

Authenticity, 245–46n*63*, 246n*65*

Authoritarian personality, 70

Authority, 15, 54, 105, 122, 123, 147, 192; concept of, 125, 236n*1*; democratic, 20, 25, 26, 28, 42, 43, 204–14, 216, 217; in family, 69; inseparable from liberty, 108; in leftist literature of freedom, 78; need for, 142; submission to, 96; youthful craving for, 107

Schelling, Thomas, 27, 82, 172, 174, 185, 186, 275n*19*
Schizophrenia, 98, 261–62n*24*
Schultz, Theodore, 274n*14*
Schumacher, E. F., 276n*19*
Schumpeter, Joseph, 34, 147
Schweitzer, Albert, 82
Science: motivations in, 144; progress in, 269n*28*
Security, 90, 91, 94, 95, 101, 103, 142, 143, 144, 147, 150, 151, 180, 185, 187, 218, 222
Seeley, John, 279–80n*37*
Seeman, Melvin, 253n*12*
Segregation, 97, 98
Self, 55, 114
Self-actualization, 86
Self-alienation, 95
Self-conceptions, 101, 102
Self-consciousness, 103, 114
Self-control, 69, 70
Self-determination, 244n*50*
Self-distinguishing, 142, 143, 144, 151, 219, 222–23
Self-estrangement, 253n*12*
Self-image, 14, 130
Self-interest, 33, 34–36, 42, 82; as basis for social order, 16; divergence of, 35; enlightened, 165; radically enlightened, 105, 106; ration, 1, 21–22, 215, 216
Selfishness, 199, 201
Self-knowledge, 114
Self-overcoming, 4, 89, 94–95, 103, 117
Self-realization, 94, 95, 96, 142, 143, 144
Self-regarding, 42, 199, 201, 202
Self-reliance, 140; in American society, 143
Separation, 90, 91, 94, 97, 98, 103, 252n*10*, 267–68n*15*
Sex, 84; polymorphous, 67, 68
Sexuality, liberated, 244n*52*
Shareability, 4, 82, 88, 104–17, 124, 125, 192, 201, 217, 221, 248n*9*, 259n*11*, 282n*8*; of freedoms, 63, 241n*28*; of goals, 134, 153, 154, 155; of rights and freedoms, 61–62
Sharing, 56

Shils, Edward, 14, 228n*3*
Shklar, Judith, 51
Significant others, 114
Simmel, Georg, 123, 140, 151, 183, 186, 265–66n*7*, 270n*33*
Singleness, individualism of, 140
Single-peakedness, 282–83n*10*
Skinner, B. F., 76
Slater, Philip, 100–01, 106, 128, 129, 130, 138–39, 144, 151, 180, 185–86; on American society, 142, 145; on family, 271n*34*; on goals, 134
Smith, Adam, 157, 179, 280n*40*; *The Wealth of Nations*, 132
Smith, M. Brewster, 63
Social complexity, 99
Social contract, 215, 233–34n*24*
Social criticism, 4, 47, 58, 64, 79–80, 96, 103, 110, 115, 121–26, 262n*31*; limitations of, 104; modes of, relying on human ambivalence, 109, 111, 116; psychology and, 237n*3*. *See also* Critics
Social duty, 81
Social ethic, 64, 104, 111, 259n*11*, 260n*16*, 287n*27*; and ambivalence, 116; moral reasoning and, 115–16
Social interaction, 186–87
Socialism, 54; biological basis for, 65–70; and freedom, 79
Socialist solidarity, 244n*50*
Sociality, 48, 114, 115, 122
Socialization, 57, 64, 65, 124, 147, 151, 154; costs of, 59; human nature and, 84–85; women and, 268n*15*
Social order, 95, 123, 228n*3*, 282–83n*10*; and enlightened self-interest, 16
Social Product, gross, 276n*20*
Social psychology, 264n*4*
Social roles, 95
Social structure: stratified, 133, 134, 135–36, 138, 140, 152–53; variance in, 57
Society, 81, 149; active, 56–60; attitude toward, in leftist literature of freedom, 77–78, 79–81; as by-product of economy, 177; coemergent with self and mind,